THE GREYFRIARS HOLIDAY ANNUAL

1935

HOWARD BAKER
LONDON

THE GREYFRIARS HOLIDAY ANNUAL 1935

ISBN: 0 7030 0206 6

Published by Howard Baker Press Ltd. (The Greyfriars Press)
27a Arterberry Road, Wimbledon, London, SW20, England
Printed in Great Britain by
A. Wheaton & Co. Ltd. of Exeter

Frank Richards versus Greyfriars!

By HARRY WHARTON

Challenged by many Greyfriars characters as to the manner in which they are depicted in his stories, Frank Richards, at Harry Wharton's invitation, takes up the challenge—to the discomfiture of those concerned!

I'D heard so many complaints from Greyfriars men about the manner in which they were depicted in Frank Richards' stories that I thought it a good idea to invite Mr. Richards to Greyfriars especially to deal with them. I didn't expect for a moment, however, that he'd accept the invitation, so it came as a real surprise when Trotter, the page, poked his head round the door of No. 1 Study one half-holiday and announced that Mr. Richards himself was in the waiting-room.

You can bet your life I scooted down the stairs like a flash of greased lightning. Frank Richards, whom I have met, of course, on other occasions, greeted me with his customary friendly grip.

"Well, Wharton, what's the trouble?" he asked, as soon as we had exchanged conventional greetings.

I explained that some of the fellows had been raising objections to the characters they had been given in the "Magnet" and "Holiday Annual" yarns. Mr. Richards smiled as he listened.

"Do you consider yourself that I've treated any of them unjustly?" he asked.

"Not a bit!" was my prompt reply. "Personally, Mr. Richards, I think you size up their characters in an amazingly accurate fashion."

"Then who are the objectors?"

"Principally, the fellows you describe as either outsiders or fatheads. Loder, for instance——"

"Well, what about Loder?" asked Mr. Richards, a trifle grimly.

Gerald Loder smoked cigarettes and played penny nap the other evening when the Head was only two doors away from him.

" He strongly resents being depicted as a smoky outsider. He thinks he ought to be the hero of the Sixth ! "

Frank Richards simply roared at that quaint idea.

" Well, that's the choicest bit I've heard for a long time ! " he declared, as he wiped the tears of mirth from his eyes. " You'll be telling me next that Bunter fancies his luck as the hero of the Remove ! "

" He does ! "

" Ha, ha, ha ! "

" Fact ! " I grinned. " And there are plenty of chaps with other bees in their bonnets. Coker denies that he's the dumb-bell you make him out to be. Potter and Greene deny that they give Coker soft sawder because of the material advantages they get out of his friendship. Temple thinks it's the limit for you to depict him as a conceited ass. Mr. Prout regards himself as a genial and entertaining old sport, quite unlike the pompous and pedantic old person called Mr. Prout in your stories."

" This is really too bad," Mr. Richards said, with a sad shake of his head. " I had no idea I was arousing such hostility among the originals of my characters. Are there any more to add to your list ? "

" Several in the Remove," I answered. " Bolsover completely repudiates the suggestion that he's a bully, and Fish considers he's simply a smart American business man with lots of bright ideas—and not a mean, grasping bounder, as you make out. Oh, and Tom Dutton is furious because you call him deaf—his own idea is that he's just a little hard of hearing. That's about all I can remember just now."

" And quite enough, too, for one sitting ! " gasped the author. " Look here, Wharton, do you think you can get all the fellows you've mentioned to meet me ? "

" They'll jump at the chance ! " I told him. " In fact, while we're about it, what's wrong with assembling the whole school to meet you ? The Head will certainly allow us the use of the Hall when he hears who's here."

" I'll see him myself and fix it up, then," Mr. Richards said. " I think I can justify myself to the school at large and perhaps—who knows ?—I may be able to convince even the fellows who're kicking that they're wrong and I'm right ! "

As a result of this little confab., Mr. Frank Richards was within half an hour facing in Big Hall the cordial though curious eyes of nearly all the school.

After Wingate of the Sixth had made a neat little speech of welcome, Mr. Richards stepped to the front of the platform and thanked us for the hospitable reception he had received.

Then he touched on the subject of the grievances of fellows who felt they were being libelled in the stories. Finally, he reeled off the names I had previously mentioned to him and invited the owners to step up on to the platform.

The invitation was accepted with alacrity, even Mr. Prout joining the crowd. Frank Richards turned to this gentleman first.

" Mr. Prout," he said, in his most soothing voice, " may I assure you that I have the highest regard for your character and that I do my best to show that regard for you at all times in my stories ? "

Mr. Prout swelled almost visibly.

" Your intentions, my dear sir, are, I doubt not, of the best ! " he boomed. " Nevertheless, it is, to my mind, altogether regrettable that you should convey an impression that any suspicion of pomposity or pedantry attaches to me. Grmph ! "

" Ha, ha, ha ! "

It was a spontaneous yell from the school. Prout's method of denying that he was pompous and pedantic merely made it quite clear to everybody that he was ; he was convicted out of his own mouth in the very attempt to state his innocence.

Before Prouty had recovered from his astonishment at our mirth, Mr. Richards was turning to Loder.

" Loder, I understand your grumble to be that I don't make you the hero of the Sixth. Can you tell me of any incident where you showed up in an heroic light ? "

" I can ! " yelled Bob Cherry from the middle of the crowded hall. " He smoked cigarettes and played penny nap the other evening when the Head was only two doors away from him in Wingate's study."

" Ha, ha, ha ! "

" You—you cheeky young hound !" hissed Loder.

He looked as though he would have given lots for the chance of wading through the crowd and wielding his ashplant over Bob's back ; but that was hardly possible, of course, in the presence of the distinguished visitor.

" That was certainly heroism of a kind," remarked Frank Richards, with a smile. " Unfortunately, it's not quite the kind of heroism I mean. Well, Coker ? "

" I want to tell you something," growled Coker, who had aggressively forced his way to the front of the crowd. " You make out I'm a dense kind of fathead. Well, I'll prove I'm not by showing you I can read your inmost thoughts. I've jolly well found out why you say I'm dense—by my own unaided brain power, too ! "

" And why is it ? "

" Because you're jolly well jealous of me ! " was Coker's triumphant answer. " Now say I'm dense again, and see how many will believe you

Mr. Prout: " It is regrettable that you, Mr. Richards, should convey the impression that any suspicion of pomposity or pedantry attaches to me. Grmph ! "

now my powers of deduction have shown you up in your true light ! "

" Ha, ha, ha ! "

" Really, Coker, your logic is irrefutable ! " gasped Mr. Richards. "But now here are Potter and Greene. I believe you resent my suggestions that your friendliness to Coker is not altogether unconnected with his ample supplies of pocket-money ? "

" It's a base suggestion ! " said Potter.

" Absolutely ! " said Greene.

" Then supposing I told you that

Fisher T. Fish bounded out of the Hall like a greyhound on being told that Mr. Richards had dropped sixpence outside—not waiting to hear that he had also picked it up again !

Coker's Aunt Judy had just lost all her money——"

" *What !* " yelled Potter and Greene simultaneously, their admiration for Coker giving way suddenly to looks of concern for themselves.

" Oh, it was only a suggestion ! " said Mr. Richards quickly. " But, judging by your faces, it might make just a little difference, mightn't it ? "

And the assembled school simply rocked with mirth.

By this time it was obvious to everyone with a grain of savvy that Mr. Richards was neatly tricking all the objectors into displaying the very characteristics which they denied belonged to them. Mr. Richards found it easy to hoodwink the remainder of the fellows on the platform on similar lines. Temple was soon displayed as just the kind of conceited ass he thought he wasn't. Bolsover, after protesting that he wasn't a bully, wanted to slaughter a Second Form fag on being told the kid had made a " long nose " at him. And Fisher T. Fish bounded out of the Hall like a racing greyhound on being told that Mr. Richards had dropped sixpence outside—not even waiting to hear Mr. Richards add that he had also picked it up again !

Finally, the author dealt with Tom Dutton.

" I believe you object to my telling my readers that you can't hear ? " he yelled.

Tom Dutton looked surprised.

" Blessed if I can tell you ! " he said. " How should I know what's happened to your aunt's beer ? If you think I took it, you're wrong ! I don't touch the stuff myself ! "

And we just yelled !

Frank Richards had justified himself without any difficulty ; there was no possible doubt left on that point.

. . . . .

" Gentlemen, chaps and fellows," said Frank Richards breezily, when the laughter had died down, " I've done my best to prove that I have not been unjust in my analysis of the gentlemen who have protested against the way I describe them in my stories. I think I have succeeded."

" Hear, hear ! "

"If I allowed it to rest at that, however," went on the author, with a friendly smile at the crowd on the platform, "I shouldn't feel satisfied with my trip to Greyfriars. What I do want to say before I go is that none of them need feel perturbed because their little failings are held up to the light. It takes all sorts to make a world."

"Hear, hear!"

"Greyfriars would be a dull old place if you all did the same thing and behaved in the same way, you know. And if it gives my friends here any satisfaction to know it, most of the colour and variety I get into my yarns comes from their little individual habits and weaknesses.

"Now that I have put it in that way I hope they'll all be able to shake me by the hand and look on me for the future, not as a carping critic, but as a sympathetic friend."

Frank Richards' words went home. There wasn't one of the objectors who wasn't glad to shake him by the hand after that, and when he left Greyfriars later in the day the loudest cheers of all came from the men who had thought Frank Richards was unjust to them!

But I'm afraid the impression Mr. Richards' words made did not last very long. A few days after he had gone, the old complaints started again, and I heard that Billy Bunter had been seen writing to Frank Richards protesting against being called "fat, greedy and obtuse," that Fisher T. Fish had been grousing about being described as a Shylock, and even Mr. Prout was up in arms at being referred to as pompous and pedantic. People never seem to like hearing the truth about themselves!

THE END

Wiles of a War Pilot!

THE Great War pilot who invented a brand new flying manœuvre was lucky; he was like a cricketer with a deadly break in his bowling, and stood a good chance of bagging several "wickets" before his scheme was rumbled.

One of the first manœuvres invented was hiding in the sun—that is, keeping your 'plane between the sun and the enemy, so that the other fellow was blinded by the glare and couldn't spot you. Then you waited your chance to dive down on the enemy 'plane like a bolt from the blue, trusting to a well-aimed burst of bullets to put him out of action before he had a chance to return your fire. The coloured plate facing page one shows a British pilot in a Sopwith Camel scout machine carrying out this neat little manœuvre on a German two-seater. Both pilot and gunman in the German machine are "caught napping," being quite unaware of the death-spitting fury diving on them.

A more spectacular stunt was to aim your 'plane straight at an enemy machine as if you were going to collide in a terrific head-on crash. Both 'planes would rush together with their guns ablaze, the pilots trusting to the engine in front of them to stop the bullets. It was a test of nerves—each pilot waiting for the other to turn aside to avoid the inevitable collision.

Sometimes, in the fury of combat, neither would give way, and the 'planes would crash and hurtle to earth locked together. But if one did turn aside, the other pilot had a perfect, if brief, target—a chance to rake the enemy machine from nose to tail!

The St. Jim's Band

By *MONTY LOWTHER*
(*of the Shell*)

WE each have planned in our military band
To kick up a terrible din,
With a ghastly groan from the saxophone
And a shriek from the violin.
The time's all wrong, but we still go strong,
Though we don't care much for the tune,
With a rum-tum-tum
On the big bass drum,
And a growl from the deep bassoon.

The cornet played by Herries
(What a tone !)
Keeps company with Merry's
Saxophone,
While Gussy on the cymbals
Can't displace
The roar of Baggy Trimble's
Double-bass.

But they all play grand in the military band,
Though they can't tell ray from doh,
With Bernard Glyn and his old violin
And Dig with his G banjo.
If Blake starts sharp on his automatic harp
He can win by half a bar,
With a tootle-toot
On the frivolous flute
And a twang on the soft guitar.

It's left to me to thump it
On the keys,
While Figgins does the trumpet
Melodies,
And Kerr must practise daily
On his own
To give his ukelele
Such a tone.

But we take our stand in the military band ;
It's a sight you never could forget
To see Manners blow his little piccolo
And Gore on his long clarinet.
They shout " encore ! " with a devastating roar
As we march on the scene,
With a ran-tan-tan
On the old tin can,
And a clang on the tambourine.

Hurrah ! Pom-pom !
Hurrah ! Pom-pom !
Make way, for here we come !
With a toodle-oodle-oo
On a fife or two
And a bang on the big bass drum !

BAGGY TRIMBLE'S BRAINWAVE

By
MARTIN CLIFFORD

A humorous story of popular Tom Merry & Co. of St. Jim's, starring Baggy Trimble, the fat and fatuous Fourth-Former

THE FIRST CHAPTER

BAGGY IN A FIX

"NOTHING!"

There was a world of disgust in Baggy Trimble's voice as he finished scanning the letter-rack in the outer hall at St. Jim's.

There was nothing in the pigeon-holes for Baggy. There very rarely was—at least, not a letter containing a remittance.

Big remittances never came Baggy Trimble's way.

Still, Baggy was a hopeful youth. Twice a day, six days a week, Baggy visited the letter-rack as regularly as clockwork, and almost as regularly was he disappointed.

Baggy's life, accordingly, was one continual round of disappointments.

"Nothing!" he repeated dismally. "Not even a blessed postcard! Other fellows have whacking great remittances from paters and maters and uncles and aunts, but nobody ever sends me any. It jolly well isn't fair. Why—hallo!"

Baggy broke off as his roving eyes fell upon a little pile of parcels on the rack reserved for the masters. All of them were addressed to Mr. Railton, Housemaster of the School House.

"Jolly queer!" mused Baggy, shaking his head. "Now, why should old Railton get a pile of parcels and letters at once like this?"

He proceeded to investigate. Baggy possessed a large bump of inquisitiveness. He jerked down one of the parcels and examined it. The string happened to have worked loose at one end. By slipping open the brown paper, Baggy was able to see inside.

He was rewarded with a glimpse of a silver photo-frame. In this was the portrait of a pretty girl whose face held a likeness to Mr. Railton's own features. Further poking by Baggy's fat fingers brought to light a slip of cardboard on which was inscribed the following:

"To dear Victor, with all good wishes for a happy birthday. From his affectionate sister, Clara."

The mystery of the numerous parcels and letters was solved. It was Mr. Railton's birthday.

It had never occurred to Baggy that even Housemasters are human, and have birthdays like ordinary mortals.

But he had little time to reflect upon this truth, for just then a footstep sounded behind the fat junior. It startled Baggy so much that he dropped the photo-frame, and there was an ominous crash of breaking glass.

"Oh, crumbs!" gasped Baggy; and he gasped in greater alarm as he recognised the newcomer as Mr. Linton, the Shell master.

Mr. Linton might have passed on, but the guilty confusion on Baggy's fat face was too obvious to mistake. While Baggy stood gasping, Mr. Linton picked up the smashed photo-frame, and it took him just three seconds to discover to whom it belonged.

"Why, what is this, Trimble?" he demanded sternly. "Boy, how dare you interfere with other people's property? Bless my soul, you—you have dared to open a parcel addressed to Mr. Railton! Upon my word, boy——"

"Nunno, sir! Not at all, sir!" Baggy's fat wits were well accustomed to manufacturing "whoppers" on the spot, and they did not fail him now. "Nunno, sir! You—you see, sir, Mr. Railton sent me to get his p-post from the rack. You—you made me jump and drop it, sir."

Baggy hoped this explanation would satisfy Mr. Linton, and he was not disappointed. Mr. Linton's frown disappeared.

"Ah! That alters the case, of course, Trimble," he said, smiling. "In the circumstances, you can hardly be blamed. You had better explain to Mr. Railton just how the accident happened, my boy."

"Oh, yes, sir," said Baggy.

He was grinning now, but Mr. Linton's next words wiped the grin from his face, so to speak.

"At the moment, Mr. Railton is over in the New House, I believe," he added. "But I myself will explain the matter when I see him, Trimble."

With that Mr. Linton passed on.

Baggy Trimble groaned—a deep, hollow groan. Matters were a thousand times worse now. Mr. Railton would immediately deny that he had sent Baggy for his post, and then—well, the fat would be in the fire with a vengeance.

Dismally, Baggy wrapped up the broken remains of the photo-frame and replaced the parcel in the rack. He had no intention of taking it along to Mr. Railton, and he rolled away.

In the School House doorway, he met Levison of the Fourth. Levison noticed Baggy's dejected look at once.

"Hallo, fatty, what's the matter?" he demanded. "You look absolutely ghastly, old bean!"

In his desperate plight, Baggy was ready to grasp at any straw.

"I—I say, Levison, I'm in an awful hole!" he groaned. "You might try to help a fellow out. You're rather a tricky chap, I know."

"What?"

"I—I mean, you're awfully cute—clever, you know," amended Baggy hastily. "I say, I'm booked for an awful licking if something isn't done."

And he related his unfortunate position to Levison, in the despairing hope that Levison might perhaps help him out. But Levison wasn't very sympathetic.

"Serves you jolly well right, you prying, sneaking little beast!" he said candidly. "Still, if you really want me to help you out——"

"Yes, rather! If you can think of something, Levison, old fellow——"

"I can't think of anything," said Levison grimly. "But I can help you out, Trimble—like this!"

Levison grabbed Baggy by the coat-collar, twirled him round, and helped him out of the House by planting a vigorous kick behind Baggy's fat person.

Baggy sailed through the open doorway, landed with a heavy bump on the top step, and rolled down to the bottom with a series of heavy bumps and fiendish howls.

Evidently that was all the "helping out" Ernest Levison intended doing for Baggy Trimble!

"I can help you out," said Levison grimly—"like this!" He grabbed Trimble by the coat-collar, twirled him round, and helped him out of the House by planting a vigorous kick behind Baggy's fat person.

THE SECOND CHAPTER

A BRAINWAVE

BAGGY scrambled up at last, groaning. He dusted himself down, nursed his aches and pains for a few moments, and then began to consider the matter. It was serious; there was no doubt about that. Baggy thought so, and he knew perfectly well that Mr. Railton would also look upon it as serious.

Baggy Trimble was booked for a record licking unless something were done.

He rolled away through the gates, his face doleful, but his fat wits working overtime upon the problem. Hardly had Baggy reached the lane outside, when he came upon something that brought his thoughts to a momentary full stop.

It was a small parcel, rolled in brown tissue-paper, lying in the road, and it had rather the appearance of a bar of chocolate. Baggy hoped it was, anyway. He picked it up. The paper was clean, and it was evident the parcel had recently been dropped by someone. As Baggy's thoughts always revolved round grub, he imagined it felt like a bar of chocolate, and he was quite disappointed when he opened the package and found it was a pipe. It was a beautiful new pipe, and it was in a handsome leather case, inscribed in gold lettering on the inside of which was the name of a Rylcombe tobacconist.

"Must have cost a quid, easily," reflected Baggy, his disappointment giving place quickly to glee. "M-my hat! I'll take it to the village, blowed if I don't! If I can't raise ten bob on it, I'll—phew!"

Almost on the heels of the first thought came another, a better one; in fact, a real brainwave!

Why not give the pipe as a birthday present to Railton? Great idea! The Housemaster smoked a pipe, and, dash it all, any pipe-smoker would be delighted with such a ripping present! Even a beast like Railton couldn't possibly be so ungrateful as to lick a fellow who had presented him with such a handsome and magnificent birthday present!

"M-mum-my hat! I'll do it, blowed if I don't!" breathed Baggy, his eyes glimmering. "I'll do that interfering beast, Linton, down, after all! I'll be well in with Railton after this!"

The thought was a pleasant one. With the pipe safe in his pocket, Baggy rolled indoors cheerily. In the Hall he met Tom Merry, Monty Lowther and Manners, and they stared as he gave them rather a vaunting glance.

"Hallo, what's the joke, Baggy-bus?" demanded Monty Lowther. "Don't say you've at last met someone with a worse-looking chivvy than your own!"

"Now I've met you fellows—yes!" grinned Baggy. "He, he, he! Think you're clever and funny, don't you, Lowther? I say, you fellows, care to see my birthday present to Railton?"

"Eh? Is it Railton's birthday?" asked Tom Merry.

"Yes, old chap. Look at this! What d'you think of it, eh?"

And Baggy hauled out the pipe-case, opened it and revealed his "birthday present." It was a chance to swank that Trimble simply couldn't resist.

"Rather decent, what?" he observed, a trifle loftily. "Cost me a quid!"

"You mean you've burgled Stimson's shop?" gasped Monty Lowther, eyeing the handsome pipe blankly. "Where the dickens could you get a quid from, Trimble?"

"Where on earth have you got this from, Trimble?" demanded Tom Merry.

"Aren't I telling you I bought it for a quid?" said Baggy warmly. "A quid my pater sent me this morning! I'm handing this to Railton now. He, he, he! I'll be well in with Railton after this, and no mistake!"

"You fat idiot!"

"No good you fellows feeling jealous," said Baggy. "Still, if you'd care to be in with me on this I've no objection. Lemme see; four into a quid would be five-bob apiece, wouldn't it? If you chaps would like to hand me fifteen bob I'll tell Railton you're in it with me, That's fair enough."

"Why, you—you——"

"Jolly cheap way of getting well in with Railton, if you ask me," said Trimble. "Think what it'll mean. After accepting a jolly decent present like this from us, he'll never be so ungrateful as to lick any of us again. And he won't like to refuse favours like exeats and things, either. I tell you, we'll be in clover with that beast Railton when—— Here, what—why—ow! Yarooooop!"

Bump!

Trimble sat down hard on the floor, hardly knowing how he got there.

Nor did he know which of the three grabbed the pipe-case from his fat fist and rammed it down between his collar and the back of his fat neck.

He sat up dizzily and saw Tom Merry & Co. walking away.

"Beasts!" he gasped. "Ow, ow, ow! The awful beasts! Fancy turning down a splendid offer like that! Ow! Beasts!"

But it was only too painfully clear that the Terrible Three had turned his offer down, generous as it was. Apparently Tom Merry & Co. did not want to be "well in" with Railton on those terms.

For a few moments Baggy struggled desperately, and by turning himself into a human pocket-knife, he managed to regain the pipe. Then he staggered to his feet, dusted himself down, and proceeded to the Housemaster's study. Forcing a cheery smile on his fat, grubby face, Baggy knocked at Mr. Railton's door.

THE THIRD CHAPTER

PAINFUL FOR BAGGY!

Mr. Railton was in. Apparently someone had brought along the post, for the parcels and letters were on the table. Baggy trembled as he noted that the Housemaster had just opened the parcel containing the smashed photo-frame, and was frowning over it.

Obviously Mr. Railton was annoyed about it, for he gave Trimble anything but a pleasant greeting.

"Well, Trimble," he snapped, "what is it?"

"I hope you won't think me pre-presumptuous, sir," said Baggy nervously, "but I've ventured to bring you a birthday present. Many happy returns of the day, Mr. Railton."

With that Baggy brought out the parcel, opened the case and revealed the glimmering new pipe.

Mr. Railton almost fell down.

"Bless my soul!" he gasped. "How—how did you know it was my birthday, Trimble, my boy?"

"Oh, I'm not likely to overlook the birthday of a master I admire so much, sir," said Baggy. "Other fellows might forget or ignore it, but not me, sir. I admire your splendid qualities too much, you know. I—I hope you'll accept it in the spirit in which it is given, sir."

"Dear me," gasped the astonished Mr. Railton. "Your—your kindness overwhelms me, Trimble. You—you've brought this to me as a birthday present, my boy?"

"Certainly, sir."

"But, really," said Mr. Railton, examining the pipe. "It is an expensive present for a junior to give, Trimble. Really——"

"A mere nothing, sir," said Baggy airily. "The pater happened to send along a pound, and I hope I'm not too mean to lavish it on a present for a master I admire like I do you, sir."

"Bless my soul! Really, Trimble——" Mr. Railton was at a loss to know what to do. But he was too good-natured to hurt Baggy's feelings—if that was possible—by refusing. So, after a moment's reflection, he nodded and smiled. "Very well, my boy, I will certainly do as you wish—accept it in the spirit it is given. Thank you very much, Trimble. It is really an exceptionally nice pipe. One moment, my boy; you must have a slice of birthday cake."

Trimble's eyes had already fallen upon the big birthday cake lying opened on the table; possibly Mr. Railton had noted his rather hungry glance. At all events, he picked up a knife and started to cut a slice—to Trimble's immense delight.

But Trimble's delight didn't last long—nor was his hunger to be satisfied. For just as Mr. Railton was about to hand the slice over, a tap came on the door and Mr. Linton walked in.

"Oh, lor'!" groaned Trimble.

His sudden fear was amply justified. Mr. Linton got down to brass tacks at once.

"Ah! I see Trimble has explained about the smashed photo-frame, Mr. Railton," he began, his glance going from the photo-frame to Baggy. "It was purely an accident, as Trimble will have told you, and I assure you that if anyone was to blame, it was myself, Mr. Railton."

"I fail to understand you, Mr. Linton," said the Housemaster. "What can Trimble know about this—this photo-frame?"

"Dear me! Then—— However, I will explain," said Mr. Linton.

And he did. Trimble didn't enjoy listening to the explanation, nor did he like the growing look of wrath on Mr. Railton's face.

"Upon my word!" exclaimed the Housemaster at last. "But I did not send Trimble for the post, Mr. Linton. The boy most certainly had no right whatever to interfere with the parcels. Trimble!"

"Oh, dear! Y-e-es, sir!"

Baggy's fat knees knocked together. But once again came an interruption—this time in the form of Dr. Richard Holmes, the Head of St. Jim's. The Head entered the Housemaster's study, and, after looking at Mr. Linton and Trimble, turned to Mr. Railton,

"Ah! I am glad to find you in, Railton," he exclaimed genially. "No, no, pray do not go, my dear Linton. I will not keep Mr. Railton a moment. I have merely looked in to perform a small, but to me a very pleasant ceremony. Allow me to congratulate you upon your birthday, my dear Railton."

He shook hands warmly with Mr. Railton. There had always been a deep bond of regard between the Head and his youthful Housemaster.

"I only remembered it half an hour ago," resumed the Head, smiling. "I immediately walked to the village, and I have brought you a small token of my regard for one who is, to me, not only a valued colleague but a friend."

Having made his preliminary speech, the Head started to go through his pockets—apparently in search of the "small token." He felt in one pocket after another, growing rather red as he proceeded. A rather uncomfortable silence followed. He went through his pockets, and then did so again—in vain.

He was in quite a flustered state when he gave it up at last.

"Dear me!" he frowned. "Really, how very annoying! I am afraid, my dear Railton, that I have lost the small present I had bought for you. It must have fallen from my pocket during my walk from the village. It was merely a pipe, and—good gracious! There it is!"

The Head's eyes had suddenly fallen upon the pipe lying in its velvet-lined case on the table.

"Oh!" groaned Baggy Trimble involuntarily. "Oh lor'!"

Quite suddenly he understood. But Railton didn't understand—yet!

"I—I do not quite understand, Dr. Holmes," he gasped. "This pipe has just been presented to me by this boy Trimble!"

The Head jumped.

"Indeed!" he exclaimed, bending a grim glance upon the shivering Baggy. "Then obviously the boy must have found it in the lane. It is undoubtedly the pipe I selected from Stimson's in the village."

The Head looked at Baggy—they all looked at Baggy. That scheming junior felt like a cornered rat.

"Trimble!" rumbled Mr. Railton. "Did you find this pipe in Rylcombe Lane this afternoon?"

Trimble groaned.

"Nunno, sir!" he gasped. "Nothing of the k-kik-kind, sir! M-m-my Uncle Joe sent me a pound, and I bought it out of that as a pup-present for Mr. Railton."

"Trimble!" said Mr. Railton sternly. "You distinctly stated to me that you bought the pipe out of a pound sent by your father."

"Dud-did I, sir? Oh, yes, sir! You—you see, they both sent me a pound—the pater and my Uncle Joe. And I spent ten shillings out of each pip-pound on the pip-pipe. That's it, sir! It was really seventeen-and-sixpence, and I b-bought it in Wayland, sir."

"Then," said the Head, in grinding accents, "how do you explain the fact that the name Stimson is gold-lettered on the case, Trimble?"

That was rather a poser, but Baggy was equal to it.

"It was like this, sir," he gasped. "The pip-pipe I bought in Wayland was a curved one, and—and as I thought it might not suit Mr. Railton's f-face, I got it changed at Stimson's for a straight one. That—that's just how it happened, sir! K-k-can I go now I've explained the matter, sir?"

"No, you may not go, Trimble!" thundered Mr. Railton. "It is quite clear to me now that this pipe is the one Dr. Holmes lost while returning to St. Jim's. Upon my word! Such audacity—such impudence——"

"Oh, dear!" gasped Baggy, quite losing his head then. "It—it's quite a mistake, sir! Not at all, sir! I didn't find the pip-pipe in the lane at all, sir. You see, having bought it in Lexham, I—"

"What?"

"I—I mean in Wayland, sir!" gasped Baggy hastily. "I assure you, sir, that it never even entered my head to pretend I'd bought it and to present it to Mr. Railton so he wouldn't lick me for smashing his photo-frame. S-such a wicked idea never even occurred to me, s-sir. You—you see, it was like this, sir——"

"Silence!" thundered Mr. Railton. "Enough, Trimble! Do not add further absurd falsehoods to your gross deceit, boy! The matter is now quite clear, Dr. Holmes. This afternoon Mr. Linton caught Trimble interfering with a parcel belonging to me

"You will accompany me at once to my study, sir!" said the Head in a terrific voice. "Come!" Trimble went. With the Head's fingers clutching his ear like a vice, he had no option in the matter.

in the post-rack. Trimble told an untruth then, stating that I had sent him for the parcel. I had done nothing of the kind. Apparently Trimble anticipated punishment from me, and having found that pipe in the lane, he brought it to me as a birthday present from himself, hoping thereby to save himself from punishment by his deceitful action."

"Bless my soul!" gasped the Head. "Such unscrupulous deceit, such abominable duplicity, I have never known from a boy! Upon my word! Trimble!"

"Ow! Oh, dear! I sus-say, sir, shall I go and sus-search for your pip-pipe in the lane now, sir?"

Trimble fairly trembled as he asked the ludicrous question in a last vain hope to save his skin. Even to the fat and fatuous Fourth-Former it must have been obvious that he was "for it" with a vengeance.

He realised now that his last plight was far worse than his first. Baggy's brainwave had led him into serious trouble instead of getting him out of it.

If he cherished any hope of escaping punishment, however, it was dispelled by the Head's answer.

"You will do nothing of the kind, Trimble!" he said in a terrific voice. "You will accompany me at once to my study, sir. Come!"

Trimble went—with the Head's fingers clutching his ear like a vice he had no choice in the matter. A few minutes later howls of anguish were echoing far and wide in the School House at St. Jim's. Tom Merry & Co. heard the sounds from afar, and when they heard all about the affair later, they felt thankful that they had not shared in the results of Baggy's brainwave to get "well in" with Railton on his birthday.

THE END

ST. JIM'S JINGLES

BAGLEY TRIMBLE

(the Paul Pry of the Fourth)

MOST cheery schoolboys at St. Jim's
  Are active, blithe, and nimble;
They lack the plump and lazy limbs
  Of Master Bagley Trimble.
Some chaps are sturdy, some are spare,
  And just a few are scraggy;
But only Wynn can you compare
  With the inflated Baggy!

He is the Falstaff of his Form,
  And his colossal figure
Would take a music-hall by storm,
  And make its patrons snigger.
He turns the scale at fourteen stone
  (Although he's oft denied it);
His bed begins to creak and groan
  When Baggy gets inside it!

A worm, a toady, and a sneak,
  Is Baggy's reputation;
He's always running to a "beak"
  With secret information.
He "listens-in" at every door,
  And likes it more than wireless;
He gleans news items by the score—
  His energy is tireless!

The appetite that he can boast
  Would rival that of Bunter;
He tackles tarts and buns and toast,
  And he's a keen tuck-hunter.
The helpings he consumes in Hall
  Fill us with consternation;
And yet he says, to one and all,
  "I'm sinking with starvation!"

He fancies he is brave and bold,
  A valiant son of Britain;
Yet, if the honest truth be told,
  He's timid as a kitten.
If Baggy ever saw a spook,
  A phantom fierce and frightening,
He wouldn't take a second look—
  He'd streak away like lightning!

The decent fellows in the school
  Detest him and despise him;
They never scruple, as a rule,
  To capture and chastise him.
A cad, a glutton, and a sneak,
  They cannot suffer gladly;
He gets a bumping twice a week,
  And needs that bumping badly!

Golden Goals!

By WALTER EDWARDS

THE FIRST CHAPTER

THE WILL TO WIN

"I GAVE instructions that I was not to be disturbed, Terry!"

There was a note of mild protest in Professor Craig's voice as he looked up from his writing, and his manner suggested that he was not altogether at ease. "I will see you after dinner," he added, tossing a half-smoked cigarette into the fireplace.

A small fortune is the offer made to Terry Craig and his enemy, "Fruity" Carstairs, for the one who can score the most goals in a game. Yet despite the fortune at stake, Terry plays for the success of the team; "Fruity" for himself. Who wins?

The youngster in the doorway said nothing as he ran his clear eyes round the bare walls of his father's study. The book-lined walls of the comfortable "den" had fascinated him for as many years as he could remember, but now the rows of shelves were empty. He was quick to notice too, that the valuable little etching by Corton was missing from its honoured position over the fireplace. The atmosphere of the study was no longer mellow and friendly; it had no more character than an empty barn.

"What I've got to say cannot wait, dad," said Terry Craig quietly. He closed the door, walked across the shabby carpet and faced his father. "We're going to hammer this thing out—at once!" he announced.

Sighing softly, the grey-haired professor pushed his papers aside and sat back in his armchair.

"Exactly what do you mean by that, my boy?" he asked, with a peculiar smile. "If it's a matter of money——"

A hard kind of laugh broke from Terry Craig.

"Yes, it's a matter of money, dad," he said, "for I see it all now. I know what kind of a blind, selfish rotter I've been for the last few years. I know what sort of a cad——"

"Come, come, my dear boy!" broke in Professor Craig, half-rising from his chair. "What has come over you—what are you talking about?"

"You know exactly what I'm talking about, dad!" The youngster's voice was low and tense as he took a firm hold upon himself. " I'm not blind, and I'm not altogether a fool, yet it has taken me nearly a week to find out that we are as hard up as people can be."

" Come, come ! " protested the professor, a tinge of warm colour creeping into his thin cheeks. " Matters aren't nearly as bad as that, Terry ! Times may have been a little difficult during the past year or so——"

" A *little difficult !* " echoed Terry, with a mirthless laugh. " You've had to sell the books you loved more than most things in the world, you've had to part with the etching, you've given up cigars——"

" My—er—throat, my boy," put in the professor. " I—er—found that I was smoking too much——"

" It's no good trying to fib to me, dad ! " cried Terry, flushed and moist-eyed. " You've made all these sacrifices in order that I might stay on at Stonebridge, and you know it. It wasn't fair to mother, dad ; it wasn't fair to yourself, and it wasn't altogether fair to me. Not that I don't appreciate all that you've done. A fellow never had a more generous and unselfish father and mother ! But you must know how I feel about it. I could have left school two or three years ago——"

" That is where we fail to see eye to eye, my boy," declared the professor, in quiet tones. " You are young, with your life before you, and you will doubtless have your share of worry and trouble all in good time. So we decided that you should stay on at Stonebridge, and I must say that you have justified the decision ! "

" Just because I was captain of Rayner's House and skippered the school soccer eleven ? "

" You are a fine all-round athlete," said the professor, a great rowing-man in his day, "and it is a grand thing to start the battle of life with the will to win and a sound body ! Our sacrifice, as you are pleased to call it, has been no hardship—no true sacrifice ever is—and you will oblige your mother and myself by saying no more about it ! "

" Well, perhaps I won't say much about it," returned Terry, " but I shall never forget it till my dying day." He squared his shoulders and gazed round the bare apartment. " I'm going to have those shelves filled again," he announced ; " I'm going to have another etching over the fireplace, and I'm going to see that you have a supply of your favourite Havana cigars every month. And if there's anything that mother wants —well, she's only got to say the word ! I'm going to repay you for the years you scraped and saved to keep me at Stonebridge. First of all, though," he added, some of the boyish enthusiasm dying out of his voice, " I've got to find a job of work ! But that shouldn't be difficult ! "

" The Head's report should carry weight, my boy," said the professor, " and your athletic record cannot do you any harm ! But it's going to be a hard fight——"

" That's the sort of fight that suits me down to the ground, dad," laughed Terry. " Don't worry about me ! I can get in touch with plenty of Old Boys who are making good in business, and I ought to be able to squeeze in somewhere or other ! All I want is a start, dad ! "

" That's the spirit, my boy," smiled Professor Craig ; " but it would have been much easier for you had I not lost most of my capital in the North Borneo Mines crash a couple of years ago ! Still, we must make the best of things, Terry ! Don't forget what I said about a healthy body and the will to win ! "

" You bet I won't, dad ! " laughed the youngster, gripping his father's outstretched hand. " The fight's on ! "

THE SECOND CHAPTER

A JOB AT LAST

WEEKS dragged by, and slowly but surely it dawned upon Terry Craig that no employer was likely to get killed in the rush to secure his services. The few business men who gave him a minute or so of their valuable time did not seem to be particularly interested in either his sound body or his will to win ; what they wanted to know was what else he had to offer for a weekly wage ? Which was a very considerable snag, of course, for Terry knew nothing of shorthand or book-keeping, and even ordinary office routine was a mystery to him. No one asked him about his athletic prowess, and the fact thát he had skippered Stonebridge soccer eleven did not even enter into the scheme of things.

Terry Craig was having a rough passage, but he kept pegging away.

He sought out a number of Old Boys who had gone into the City, but none seemed able to find a post for the inexperienced youngster who had scored the winning goal in that great game between Stonebridge and Rambourne. There appeared to be no openings—for the time being, at any rate. The Old Boys made a note of Terry's address, saying they would drop him a line should anything suitable turn up.

" Good - morning, Fruity ! " said Terry, striding forward with outstretched hand. Mr. Stephen Carstairs lifted a flabby countenance and stared fixedly at his smiling visitor.

But nothing did turn up.

Then, in sheer desperation, the youngster decided to swallow his pride and call upon " Fruity " Carstairs.

" Fruity," nephew of Sir John Critchell, the famous shipping magnate, was a couple of years older than Terry, and there had been bad feeling between the two since Terry's earliest days at Stonebridge, when two years made a lot of difference. Fruity, on his part, had taken an immediate dislike to the new kid with the quiet manner and steady eyes, and he had lost no time in "taking it out" of the new boy. Later, in the years that followed, Terry had put up with a lot from the big fellow, and then had come the memorable bare-knuckle fight, when Terry had given the beefy, red-headed bully the licking of his life in Cutler's Copse; and from that moment Terry Craig was bullied no more. But Fruity Carstairs could neither forgive nor forget, and he never lost an opportunity of making things unpleasant for his enemy.

Then, to cap it all, Terry had been given the centre-forward position in the most important fixture of the year, the game against Rambourne. Terry having been given his place in the school team, Fruity had to watch the game from the touchline, and the fact that the new centre-forward scored a brilliant goal that made the game safe for Stonebridge was positively the last straw, so far as Fruity was concerned.

Terry continued to play for the first eleven, and a few months later Stonebridge saw the last of Fruity Carstairs.

Terry stayed on for another eighteen months, and during that time some of the seniors heard from Fruity.

The big fellow made it abundantly clear that he was doing great things in shipping circles, that he was the pillar of the Critchell Line, although rumour had it that he was under-secretary to his uncle, Sir John Critchell.

But that was just like Fruity.

There was a thoughtful expression in Terry Craig's brown eyes as, following his decision, he made his way towards the shipping offices in Leadenhall Street. Personally, he felt no shade of animosity against Fruity; rather did he wish to have a talk and laugh over old times. And he hoped that Fruity, now a successful business man, would feel much the same way about things.

"After all, we're not schoolboys any more," mused Terry, passing up the broad stone steps of Critchell House. "Anyway, here goes!"

A notice-board informed him that the Critchell Line occupied the whole of the first floor, and on reaching the landing Terry found himself confronted by a door marked "Inquiries." Opening the door, he walked across to the polished counter and announced that he wished to see Mr. Stephen Carstairs on most important business.

"Fill up one o' these forms!" ordered a young clerk, with a superior air. He was a youth of about Terry's own age, and he seemed to resent the latter's breezy manner. "Mr. Carstairs is busy to-day," he added meaningly.

"That's all right," returned Terry easily. "He'll see me!"

The clerk was absent for the greater part of ten minutes, and when he returned there was a curious expression upon his pale face.

"Mr. Carstairs will see you in a minute or two," he announced.

"Thanks," nodded Terry, well pleased with the way things were going.

Five minutes ticked away, ten minutes, fifteen, and Terry was still sitting on a hard form beside the counter. He looked up at the moon-faced clock upon the wall; tried to catch the clerk's eye, but without success. At last, at the end of twenty-five minutes, he pressed the brass bell.

"Do you think Mr. Carstairs has forgotten all about me?" he asked of the clerk. "I've been admiring the scenery for nearly half an hour, so do you mind telling him that I'm still alive?"

There followed another period of waiting, but at length the clerk said that Mr. Carstairs had two minutes to spare.

Terry was conscious of a sudden quickening of the pulses as he was shown into an oak-panelled, comfortably furnished room. The imposing furniture was of carved oak, and a restful green carpet covered the floor. Seated at a massive roll-topped desk was a bulky individual who appeared to be clad in immaculate morning dress—tail coat, striped trousers, white spats, and a gardenia. From the neck up, all Terry could see was the top of a sleek red head, for the owner of the head was busily engaged in putting his flourishing signature to a pile of letters.

The visitor gave a slight cough as the clerk tip-toed out of the room and closed the door. Then, nothing happening:

"Good-morning, Fruity!" said Terry, striding forward with outstretched hand.

Mr. Stephen Sinclair Carstairs lifted a flabby, freckled countenance and stared fixedly at the smiling visitor through a gold-rimmed monocle. Fruity had never been a thing of beauty even to his particular cronies at Stonebridge, but now he was less lovely than ever, for he had put on a lot of weight since leaving school.

"Did I understand you to say—ah—*Fruity?*" he demanded at last.

"Yes, old man," returned Terry.

Fruity tried to look dignified, but the experiment was not altogether a success.

"I—ah—don't quite follow you," he said frigidly, reaching for the slip of paper on which Terry had written his name and other particulars. "You are Crag?"

"Craig!" corrected Terry, wondering if the whole business was a leg-pull. "We were at Stonebridge together, you know. That's how the 'Fruity' slipped out! I thought you might remember Terry Craig!"

A ripe flush overspread the flabby face of Fruity Carstairs; his small eyes narrowed as he sat back in his padded armchair.

"Ah, yes, I do remember you—er—vaguely," he said, his shrewd gaze taking in every detail of Terry's attire. The youngster was not actually shabby, but there was just that little something about him which suggested that the world was not treating him as well as it could have done. "What can I do for you, Craig?" asked Fruity, almost pleasantly; but a nasty gleam crept into his light blue eyes.

The great moment had come, and Terry, for once in his life, felt a shade of embarrassment. He knew what he wanted to say, but somehow the words wouldn't come. The idea of asking a favour of Fruity Carstairs went right against the grain, but the thought of his fruitless search for a job urged him to go through with it.

"I must remind you that I am a busy man, Craig," put in Carstairs.

"Quite, Fruity, quite," nodded Terry, preparing to take the plunge. "As a matter of fact, things have been a bit upside down with me since I left Stonebridge, and I've been wondering if you could put me on to a job of some sort. Anything will do, you know, just to start with. I'm willing to start at the bottom——"

"I'm sure that's very reasonable of you," said Fruity, "but we demand a certain amount of efficiency, even in our junior office-boys!"

It was Terry's turn to flush, but he managed to control the hot retort that leapt to his lips.

"I'm pretty quick at figures, and

so on," he said, " and I'd soon get the hang of things. Honestly, Fruity, things are pretty serious, for I don't want to sponge on the old people at home ! "

" I see," murmured Fruity, with a slow nod of his sleek red head. " You'd rather come crawling round me for a job, even though you're not worth five shillings a month of anybody's money ! What do you think this is, Craig, an institute for down-and-outs ? You've been too big for your boots ever since you fluked your way into Stonebridge's first eleven, and I knew dashed well that you'd come a cropper before long ! I've had a big score to settle with you for some time, and I guess this about squares matters. Now get out of my office and stay out, unless you want me to ring for the porter and have you removed ! "

Terry Craig's face was unusually pale as he looked into the other fellow's mocking eyes, and it was only with the greatest difficulty that he fought down a desire to send his hard fist crashing into the flabby features. He knew that by making a scene he would not help matters, yet it went clean against the grain to take these insults lying down.

" I suppose I was a fool to come to you, Fruity," he said very quietly. " I ought to have known that you are the sort of vindictive, unsportsmanlike rotter who would kick a fellow when he's down ! "

Again Fruity flushed, and Terry was surprised to see his thick lips stretch into a broad grin.

" Perhaps there's something in that accusation, Craig," he said, " so I feel inclined to change my mind about turning you down ! Look here, I'll give you a junior clerk's job at a pound a week ! What about it ? " Then, as Terry hesitated : " It isn't a princely salary, but I'll bet it's more than you're worth ! "

" I'm not disputing that, Fruity," smiled Terry, making up his mind. " A pound a week is better than nothing——"

" That's so," said Fruity briskly, " and you know the present state of the unskilled labour market." He wrote rapidly and handed a slip of paper to Terry. " Take this to Mr. Screen, the chief clerk, and tell him that you are to start in the morning ! "

" I say, this is awfully decent of you, Fruity," began Terry impulsively. " I can understand about you feeling a bit sore about that——"

" That's all right," cut in the other, with a wave of his fleshy hand. " And —ah, Craig ! "

Terry, on his way to the door, paused and looked over his shoulder.

" What's that, Fruity ? "

" You will address me as ' sir ' in future, Craig ! " said Fruity.

" Very good—sir ! "

And Terry went out and softly closed the door.

THE THIRD CHAPTER

TERRY, THE GOAL-GETTER

TERRY saw very little of Fruity Carstairs during the week that followed, but it was soon made clear to the new junior clerk that Fruity was a person of some importance. For one thing, he had a certain amount of " pull " and prestige as Sir John Critchell's nephew ; for another, he was captain of the firm's football eleven. The mere mention of football made Terry sit up and take notice, as he phrased it, and after a day or so he started to make a few tactful inquiries about the strength of the side, and so on.

But the other clerks did not seem at all willing to discuss the matter with the new fellow, and it was soon brought home to Terry that he was getting the cold shoulder from every-

As the ball dropped towards the goal-mouth, several players jumped for it together; but it was the head of Terry that reached the leather and deflected it past the goalkeeper.

body. Furthermore, it was not long before he had very good reasons for knowing that Screen, the lantern-jawed chief clerk, had taken an almost vicious dislike to him. Time and again Screen reported him to Fruity Carstairs, and Fruity, an expensive cigar jutting from the corner of his mouth, seemed to take a sinister delight in giving the new man a dressing down in the presence of the smirking chief clerk.

But Terry Craig squared his shoulders and stuck it; that pound a week gave him independence of a sort. It was a tight squeeze, but he managed to live on that sum, and all the while he was looking round for another job. It was a stiff, up-hill fight, but the sort of fight that appealed to him. The one thing he missed was his football, and at last he managed to get an interview with Fruity Carstairs.

Fruity kept the youngster waiting outside the door for over half an hour, and there was a mocking gleam in the big fellow's light blue eyes when at last Terry was admitted into his presence.

"I am doing you a great favour, Craig," said Fruity, "for it is not my habit to grant interviews to my office-boys! What do you wish to see me about?"

"The firm has a football team——" began Terry.

"Well, what about it?" demanded Fruity, with an unpleasant smirk.

"I was wondering if I could get a trial game with them," answered Terry.

"Which is like your confounded cheek, Craig!" declared Fruity. "You may have been a dickens of a whale in a school eleven, but we play an entirely different class of football! We've only lost three games during the whole season, and we stand a good chance of beating the West London Bank in the City Cup final on Saturday week! As to giving you a trial game, you seem to forget that you hold a lowly position in the firm! Our players, men with responsible positions in Critchell's, have no wish to hob-nob with office-boys, and the sooner you forget that you are no longer the Big Noise at Stonebridge the better I shall like it! I am sorry that you thought fit to waste my time!"

The short interview took place on Friday evening, and on the following morning Sir John Critchell walked into Fruity's office, and nodded pleasantly to his nephew.

"By the way, Stephen," he said, "how's that new youngster shaping?"

There was genuine interest in the tone, and Fruity Carstairs shot a swift, shrewd glance at Sir John's rugged countenance.

"Craig's nothing to write home about, uncle," he said, with a supercilious smile. "He came whining to me with a hard-luck story, and I fell—as usual!"

"I like the look of the lad," declared Sir John, "for he's got the cut of an athlete! He carries himself well, and I'm willing to wager that he plays a useful game of football! Has he turned out for a trial game yet?"

Fruity gave a short snigger.

"That's a good one," he said. "I was at Stonebridge with him, and many a tanning he's had for refusing to turn out for sports! He funked soccer and cricket, and he used to fall sick at the mere mention of a cross-country run! He was the biggest washout in the school, and he got the cold shoulder from almost everybody! Then you ask me if he's turned up for a trial game! You are miles out in your estimate of Terry Craig, Uncle Lawson!"

"So it seems, my boy," murmured the shipping magnate, with a frown of disappointment and displeasure. "Yet I'm not usually far out in weighing up a youngster! I was hoping he might strengthen our side against West London Bank on Saturday, for we've got to lift the City Cup!"

"Don't worry about that, uncle," grinned Fruity Carstairs; "we'll be all over 'em! And you needn't think any more about Terry Craig, who'd run a mile from a footer match!"

Sir John's lips were set and stern as he nodded his fine head.

"I find it difficult to believe that, even now, Stephen," he said. "Young Craig doesn't look like a funk to me!"

"Well, there it is, uncle," returned Fruity, with a shrug of his beefy shoulders. "As a matter of fact, I very much doubt whether he knows that we've got a private footer pitch!"

But Fruity was wrong for once.

Leaving Leadenhall Street at one o'clock, Saturday being a "half day," Terry set off at a brisk pace for Kennington, where Critchell's had their footer pitch. His idea was to see for himself how the team shaped, and deep down within him was a hope that he might get a game, the firm having no fixture for that afternoon.

The ground adjoined some public playing fields, and Terry's eyes lit up as he paused on the edge of the dusty square and watched a crowd of working lads who were "picking up" sides for a scratch game between themselves. Piles of coats took the place of regulation goalposts, and only four or five players sported jerseys; but enthusiasm was there in plenty. At least half a dozen games were in progress—noisy, rough, kick-and-rush stuff, for the most part—but the right spirit was there all the time.

His toes itching, Terry watched the animated scene for some time; then, a ball coming his way, he judged his kick with nice precision and sent the leather hurtling to the far side of the pitch.

And that kick settled matters.

Striding across the dusty square, he approached the band of young men who were "picking up" sides.

"Is there any chance of a game?" he asked, addressing a lanky, red-eared youth in skimpy shorts and a bright yellow jersey.

Lanky and the others regarded the neatly dressed stranger with suspicious, half-resentful eyes. Terry was not the usual type of youngster who kicked a ball about on Kennington Marshes, and Lanky jumped to the conclusion that there must be a catch in it somewhere.

"Do you reely want a game?" he demanded, a threat in his tone and manner. "Or is this your idea of a little joke?"

"Of course I'd like a game," declared Terry, with a smile. "There's nothing I want more at the moment! How about it?"

"Sure, mate," nodded Lanky. "I'm a man short, so you can play on my side! Wot's yer position?"

"I usually play somewhere in the forward line," answered Terry, "but it's all the same to me!"

"Inside-right suit yer!"

"Down to the ground!"

"That's the stuff!" grinned Lanky. "Wot about taking off yer 'quaker oat'?"

Terry was already slipping out of his coat, and by the time he lined up he had much in common with the other players. With his shirt-sleeves tucked up above the elbow, and his collar, tie and waistcoat removed, he looked eager and ready for anything; and no sooner did the whistle shrill than he snapped up a pass from Lanky and went away down the field with a turn of speed that brought a wild yell from the sprinkling of spectators that had gathered on the edge of the field.

"Up, up!"

"Go through with it!"

Tackled by a stocky, red-headed little whirlwind, Terry pushed the ball out to "Smudge" Griffin, on the wing, and "Smudge," having made rings round a big-limbed labourer, streaked away to the corner flag and put over a centre that dropped within a yard or so of the goal-mouth.

"'Eads up!"

"In with it, Smiffy!"

A shout of excitement went up from the onlookers as several players leapt for the ball, and it was the dark head of Terry Craig that reached the leather and deflected it past the clutching hands of the wild-eyed goalkeeper.

"Goal!"

Trotting across the pitch, "Smudge" Griffin shook hands in professional style, and it was to a rousing yell of encouragement that the ball was set in motion once more. Terry appeared to be a marked man from that moment, for he could scarcely move a yard without finding two or three "shadows" upon his heels. And he was soon to learn that these Saturday afternoon footballers knew more than a little about spoiling tactics.

The other side began to press hard, and the heated scrimmage that took place in front of the goal-mouth was anything but a peace conference. Rough and ready methods were employed, heavy charges were given and taken as a matter of course, and it was not until the goalie had at least a dozen players piled on top of him that the referee—a bow-legged little man in a bowler hat—thought it about time to blow the whistle.

" Goal kick ! " he announced briefly —and that was that.

The ball went out to the right wing, and " Smudge " Griffin beat the left-half for possession, and pushed over a pretty pass to Terry. Tackled by a scowling young coal-heaver, Terry tapped the leather to Lanky, and Lanky returned it almost at once.

Giving a swift glance round as he pounced upon the pass, Terry went away on his own in a way reminiscent of his Stonebridge days. Covering the ground with a curious, swerving movement, he beat man after man with what appeared to be perfect ease, and a shrill yell of excitement broke out when he finished up by tricking both backs and scoring a second goal with a hot shot that skimmed through the dust with a terrific speed which gave the custodian not a chance.

" G-o-a-l ! "

" Well done, stranger ! "

" Hi, young fellow ! "

It was a stentorian voice that rang out above the din and reached Terry's ears, and on swinging round he saw a tall, well-built man beckoning him from the edge of the playing pitch. The stranger was a man of about fifty, quietly dressed, with an air of authority about him.

" Were you calling me, sir ? " asked Terry, racing across the pitch.

" Yes," nodded the stranger, his keen gaze upon the youngster's flushed face. " Your name is Craig, is it not ? "

" Yes, sir," answered Terry, in surprise. " But——"

" I am Sir John Critchell," cut in the famous shipping magnate brusquely. " Report at my private office at ten o'clock on Monday morning ! "

Then, with a brief nod, he swung round upon his heel and strode away.

THE FOURTH CHAPTER

THE CUP FINAL !

THE week-end was anything but a pleasant interlude for Terry Craig, for he felt sure that Monday morning would find him looking for another job. Sir John Critchell meant to fire him ; there could be no doubt about that. Not that he had done any harm in playing a scratch game with Lanky, " Smudge " Griffin, and the others ; at least, not so far as he could see. They were all good chaps —a bit on the rough-and-ready side, perhaps—and he wasn't ashamed of being found playing football with them. What was more, he meant to point that fact out to Sir John. The firm didn't own him—for a pound a week !

It was in this frame of mind that he made his way to the great man's private office on Monday morning. A smooth-voiced secretary said that Sir John would see him at once.

Seated at a table near the window, with his broad shoulders hunched and his lean jaw jutting, the shipping magnate looked a formidable figure as he fixed his steely eyes upon the youngster who did not hesitate to meet his steady gaze.

" Sit down, Craig ! "

Somewhat puzzled, Terry obeyed the quiet command, and a moment later the door opened and Fruity Carstairs strolled into the room. Fruity's freckled brow creased into a puzzled frown as he caught sight of Terry ; there was a questioning light in his washed-out blue eyes as he looked from his enemy to the granite-faced man at the table.

" Craig in trouble again, uncle ? " he asked, with an oily smirk. " He ——"

" Sit down, Stephen ! " ordered Sir John.

Fruity was a very puzzled young man as he obeyed the curt command.

"Hi, young fellow!" Terry was being congratulated for scoring a second goal when the stentorian yell reached him, and on looking round he saw a well-built man beckoning to him from the edge of the playing pitch.

Sir John ran on:

"I have been in touch with Stonebridge over the week-end, Craig," he said, "and I learn that you skippered the first eleven during your last season at the school. Also, I understand that you left with a very excellent athletic record."

Slowly the rich colour had ebbed out of Fruity's flabby countenance, and he was about to blurt out something when his uncle lifted a restraining hand.

"I asked my nephew about you a day or so ago, Craig," continued the shipping magnate, "and it seems that he must have got you mixed up with another fellow."

"Yes, that is so, Uncle Lawson!" broke in Fruity. "I had another chap in mind all the time. Strange the tricks a fellow's memory gets up to—what?"

"Yes, very strange," agreed Sir John Critchell, his hard gaze upon the big fellow's moist countenance, "So I may take it that Terry Craig was not a funk and a wash-out and all the rest of it when he was at Stonebridge? I might even go so far as to suggest that he was the best forward the old school has had for years?"

Fruity shifted uneasily and rolled his thick neck inside his collar.

"He was certainly pretty good," he growled, at length, "but nothing to write home about!" Then: "Hang it all," he exploded, "has the mealy-mouthed rotter been whining to you because I wouldn't give him a trial——" He broke off, realising that he had given himself away. "I mean, uncle, he came pestering me when I was up to my eyes in work, and I told him I'd attend to him later."

"Do I understand that he asked

for a trial game and that you turned him down ? "

The millionaire's voice was harsh as he put the question.

" Well—er—no, not exactly, sir," returned Fruity, his ears going red, " but I guessed—that is, I mean, if he'd only said the word——"

" He didn't say the word, eh ?" cut in Sir John, with a shrewd smile. " That surprises me, for he had to go elsewhere for a kick-about on Saturday afternoon. And he played a fine game in fine company. I liked the look of your pals, Craig ; sportsmen to the core." Then, turning to the wide-eyed Fruity : " Seeing that Craig didn't say the word, Stephen, I'm going to say it for him. He is going to turn out for Critchell's against the West London Bank on Saturday next."

" What ? " It was a shrill bleat that broke from Fruity Carstairs. " B-but you can't do that, uncle ! It's out of the question ! I mean, he hasn't been with the firm for more than five minutes——"

" He has been with the firm for over a week, which means that he is eligible to play for us," declared Sir John Critchell. " I say that Craig is going to turn out, so there is no more to be said ! I am determined that Critchell's shall lift the City Cup this season——"

" That's all very well, uncle," broke in Fruity, " but what's the use of importing new blood on the eve of the final ? Craig will mess up everything, put the whole forward line out of gear ! As I've said before, he plays a fair game on his day, but Saturday may find him clean off colour, a complete wash-out ! "

" Do you mind chancing that, sir?"

Terry was smiling as he put the quiet question to Sir John Critchell.

" You can rest assured that I'm going to chance it," declared the shipping magnate, " and you two fellows are going to get the chance of a lifetime ! Listen ! To the one of you who scores the greater number of goals on Saturday I am going to give a hundred-pound note, a block of shares, and a promise of speedy promotion. I am a millionaire, so I can afford to indulge in a harmless whim now and again—and this is one of them ! It isn't very difficult to see that you two don't hit it off, so I'm giving you a chance to prove who's the better man. Also, I want to make sure of the City Cup ! "

Terry Craig scarcely knew whether he was on his head or his heels when, three minutes later, he left Sir John's private office ; and on the following Saturday, as he changed in the dressing-room, he still found it difficult to believe that so much was at stake. A hundred-pound note, a block of shares, and speedy promotion ! And all he had to do was to score a few goals ! He and Fruity were to fill the inside forward positions, so each would have an equal chance of finding the net.

Well, that arrangement suited Terry down to the ground, and he was smiling with quiet confidence as he and the other players followed Fruity on to the field.

The Bank team looked a hefty lot in comparison to their opponents, and the game was no more than three minutes old when it became abundantly clear that they were out for an early lead. Throwing their full weight into the attack, they went down the field with a beautiful passing movement, swinging the ball from wing to wing, and a mighty roar went up from their supporters when their outside-left slammed in a tricky cross-shot—and found the net !

" Don't worry, boys ! We've got the great Terry Craig with us !"

A mantle of warm colour overspread

Terry's cheeks as the taunting remark reached his ears, but he did not give Fruity Carstairs the satisfaction of making him look round. And if Fruity thought he was going to put Terry off his game he was making a big mistake. So much Terry told himself as, to a thunder of hoarse cheers, the players trotted up the field and lined up for the restart.

Kettle, the Critchell centre-forward, touched the ball to Fruity Carstairs, on his left, and Fruity barged ahead, sent the opposing man staggering, and went away, covering the ground at a good rate for a fellow of his build. Beating the Bank centre-half, he carried on until a towering back bore down upon him, and then, unquestionably, was the time for him to get rid of the leather. Both Kettle and Terry were unmarked at that particular moment, and the former clapped his hands to attract Fruity's attention.

"Pass, man!" yelled the Critchell supporters. "Get rid of it, Carstairs!"

But Fruity was deaf to the wild shouts, and he merely grinned when the back robbed him and sent the ball hurtling up the field.

A powerful return kick from a Critchell defender dropped the leather within Terry Craig's radius, and there was a characteristic gleam in the youngster's dark eyes as he pounced on the pass and went off with that peculiar swerving movement so well known at Stonebridge. Once properly in his stride, there was no stopping Terry, and the shot that found the net was a red-hot snorter that flashed beneath the bar with the speed of an express train.

Man after man "Fruity" dribbled with the ball. Then taking his kick on the run, he beat the goalie with a shot that flashed into the net.

"GOAL!"

"Well done, Craig!"

"Good kid!"

Fruity's flabby countenance showed no signs of pleasure as the players lined up, and no sooner did the whistle shrill than he plunged into the enemy ranks, relieved the inside man of the ball, and went away on an individual run that brought round after round of applause from the crowd. Man after man he beat with seeming ease, and he even managed to slip between the two giant backs who bore down upon him.

Then, taking his kick on the run, he beat the goalie with a rising shot that beat the goalie all the way and flashed into the net.

"GOAL!"

"Good old Fruity!"

"Up, up, Critchell's!"

No more goals were scored that half, and the second session was drawing to a close before the Bank found the net from a corner-kick. Most of the play took place in mid-field, and for long periods on end the custodians had nothing to do. Both Terry and Fruity Carstairs were marked men, and all their attempts to break away ended in failure. The Bank skipper seemed to be content to play on the defensive, with a special eye for Critchell's inside forwards, so Terry and Fruity weren't allowed to move a yard unless accompanied by hard-eyed, grim-faced young men who stoutly refused to be shaken off.

Then came the last desperate bid.

With only a matter of seconds to go, Terry gave his guardians the slip, darted across to the wing, and snatched up a short pass from the wing man; then, setting off at a hot pace that left his "shadows" standing, he swerved in towards the goal area, to find that a burly back and the centre-half were almost on top of him.

"Shoot!"

"Take a shot! Chance it, kid!"

Terry had a sporting chance of finding the net as the Bank men rushed down upon him, and he was about to try his luck when he glanced to his left and saw that Fruity Carstairs was unmarked, with what looked like an open goal in front of him. This was a sure goal, and Terry hesitated; but only for a fraction of a second. In that short space of time all manner of tantalising thoughts raced through his mind; he thought of what the goal would mean to Fruity Carstairs—a hundred-pound note, a block of shares, a promise of speedy promotion; he thought of what Fruity's goal would mean to him—an end to his wonderful day-dreams, in which he filled his father's bookshelves, replaced the etching over the fireplace, and ordered the professor's monthly supply of favourite Havanas.

Terry was sorely tempted in that fleeting fraction of time, but that was all.

Drawing the defence, he beat first one man, then another, and the giant back was almost on top of him when he pushed the ball out to Fruity Carstairs.

"SHOOT!"

"In with it!"

"A-h-h-h-h-h!"

A long-drawn-out groan broke from the disappointed crowd as Fruity took a mighty kick and sent the leather soaring high over the crossbar, and the next moment the final whistle shrilled its message that denoted the end of full time. As the score was 2–2, extra time had to be played, and it was near the end of this period that Kettle managed to score the winning goal for Critchell's.

Both Terry and Fruity had a big hand in this goal. Receiving the ball from the centre-half, Fruity made ground. But near the penalty area his path was blocked by defenders, and Fruity slipped the ball to Terry. Terry ran a few yards, drew the Bank defence out of position, and then passed to Kettle. The opposing goalkeeper never stood a chance of reaching the centre-forward's flashing drive.

A few moments later the final whistle sounded.

Fruity, swinging round upon his heel, a strange expression upon his freckled face, set off for the dressing-room; and close upon his heels followed Terry Craig.

They had the dressing-room to themselves as they faced each other, and Fruity looked pale and uncomfortable as Terry shot out a muscular hand.

"Thanks, old man," said the youngster. "That was sporting of you!"

The big fellow flushed, but did not meet Terry's steady gaze.

"Why thank me?" he growled, with a return of his old aggressive manner. "I don't know what you're talking about!"

"You can't get away with that, Fruity," smiled Terry. "You didn't try to get the goal that would have meant so much to you; you deliberately skied the leather over the crossbar!"

"Well, and what if I did?" demanded Fruity. "Why make a song about it? Look here, Craig!" His tone and manner changed as he looked straight into Terry's brown eyes. "It seems to me that we've never understood each other till this afternoon, and I don't mind telling you that I got a bit of a shock when you chucked away your chance of bagging the hundred-pound note and the rest of it; and you, on your part, must have got a big surprise when I did the only decent and sportsmanlike thing and shoved the ball over the bar! That clears the air, I guess, and later on we'll go along to Uncle Lawson and tell him we've decided to split the prize—fifty-fifty! Shake!"

THE END

ST. JIM'S JINGLES

G. A. GRUNDY

(the fool of the Shell)

"BREATHES there a boy with soul so dead
  Who fails to worship Grundy?"
(Thus the sarcastic Lowther said
  Whilst having tea on Monday.)
For Grundy thinks he's quite a King,
  A giant, a Colossus;
And he'd be pleased as anything
  If only he could boss us!

This burly member of the Shell
  Was first at Redclyffe College;
A place where he did nothing well,
  And gained but little knowledge.
He smote a prefect hip and thigh,
  And caused a fearful flurry;
And this explains the reason why
  He "packed up" in a hurry!

He's wooden-headed, dull, and dense,
  And in his "upper story"
Sawdust you'd find instead of sense;
  And yet he struts in glory,
And gives himself majestic airs,
  And thinks himself fine and famous;
Yet everybody else declares
  That he's an ignoramus!

To watch old Grundy playing games
  Is quite an education;
Within his breast ambition flames,
  And fierce determination.
Barging and charging like a bull,
  And making fearful bellows
Of "On the ball!" and "Play up, School!"
  He scatters all his fellows!

Pity poor Wilkins! Pity Gunn!
  They have to share his study;
And when the match is fought and won,
  And Grundy's tired and muddy,
They have to say, in duty bound:
  "Grundy, your form is topping!
No finer player could be found
  From Wayland unto Wapping!"

St. Jim's would be a sadder place
  If Grundy wasn't in it;
He brings a smile to every face
  A dozen times a minute!
He's as bombastic as can be;
  We're half inclined to scrag him;
But, as his name is "G. A. G.,"
  Perhaps we'd better "Gag" him!

The ruins of the old Greyfriars monastery still stand to-day, and they have been the scene of many thrilling incidents in Mr. Frank Richards' popular school stories. Above, THE HOLIDAY ANNUAL artist gives us his impressions of everyday scenes in the monastery four hundred years ago.

THE FOOTPRINT IN THE SAND!

By FRANK RICHARDS

To Harry Wharton & Co. a visit to the old smugglers' cave at Pegg seems a pleasant enough way of spending a half-holiday. But little do the chums of Greyfriars realise the amazing discovery they are destined to make!

THE FIRST CHAPTER

A RAG IN THE SECOND!

MR. QUELCH frowned.

The Remove smiled.

What was happening was exasperating, or entertaining, according to the point of view. On this matter, as on many others, the views of the Greyfriars Remove and their Form-master were wide as the poles asunder.

From the Second Form-room, across the corridor, came strange and unaccustomed sounds. The Remove were in class; and the Second Form were—or should have been—in class also. Judging by the terrific uproar that proceeded from the Second Form-room, classes were " off " there—very much off!

The sound of a tin-whistle blended—more or less—with the notes of a mouth-organ. Repeated bangs indicated that some festive fag was beating on a desk-lid with a ruler, perhaps keeping time to the music. Scuffling of feet and gasping and yelling seemed to hint that a fight was also in progress—perhaps more than one fight. From what could be heard of them, the fags of the Second Form were having a high old time.

Mr. Quelch's frown intensified.

No doubt the din penetrated into other Form-rooms. But the door of the Remove-room was almost opposite that of the Second, so the Remove got most of the benefit.

It interrupted lessons.

The Remove did not mind that—few of them were really keen and eager on Latin prose. But Mr. Quelch seemed to mind very much.

"Bless my soul!" ejaculated Mr. Quelch at last. "This is really growing intolerable."

Bump! Crash! Bang! Yell! came across the corridor.

"Wharton!" rapped out Mr. Quelch.

"Yes, sir?"

"Step across into the Second Form-room, and tell Walker of the Sixth that I insist upon his keeping order there!"

"Certainly, sir!"

"Tell him," boomed Mr. Quelch, "that if order is not kept, I shall place the matter before the Head."

"Very well, sir."

Harry Wharton crossed to the door of the Remove-room, and opened it. With the door open, the din rang in with additional volume. It really was almost deafening.

"Shut the door, Wharton!"

Mr. Quelch fairly barked.

Harry Wharton stepped quickly into the corridor, and closed the door after him.

He smiled as he strolled across the passage.

Walker of the Sixth was in charge of the Second Form that morning; but he did not seem to be making much of a success of it. The master of the Second had lately left Greyfriars, and the new master appointed to take his place had been prevented, at the last moment, from arriving by an attack of influenza. A temporary master had been hurriedly engaged by the Head, but he was not yet at Greyfriars. For a few days, therefore, the Second Form had been without a master, and were "taken" by a Sixth Form prefect instead. It appeared to be the view of the Second that a Form without a Form-master was like unto the Israelites of old, when there was no King in Israel, and every man did what was right in his own eyes.

Wharton threw open the door of the Second Form-room.

Quite a startling scene met his gaze.

Gatty of the Second was extracting sweet music from a tin-whistle. Myers was blowing the mouth-organ. Sammy Bunter was beating time with a ruler. Dicky Nugent was engaged in deadly combat with another fag. Five or six fellows were stamping their feet, with the laudable object of making as much row as possible. Another enterprising youth was lifting the heavy lid of the Form-master's desk, and letting it fall again, with a series of terrific bangs.

The Second Form seemed to be enjoying themselves.

Of Walker of the Sixth nothing was to be seen. Walker was a good deal of a slacker, and evidently he had not yet arrived to take his class. While the cat was away the mice were playing.

"Here, you young hooligans——" called out Wharton.

"What?"

"Remove cad!"

"Clear off!"

"Where's Walker?" demanded Wharton.

"Walking, probably," said Gatty, ceasing the torture of the tin-whistle for a moment. "You'd better walk, too. We don't allow Remove cads in our Form-room."

"You've got to stop this row!"

"Rats!"

"Go home!"

"Chuck it!"

"Why, you cheeky Remove duffer!" Dicky Nugent disengaged himself from his adversary. "What the thump do you mean by butting into our Form-room? Beat it while you're safe!"

Harry Wharton laughed.

"You young ass! You can be heard all over Greyfriars!" he said. "Walker ought to be here——"

"Oh, he's slacking somewhere!" said Nugent minor. "He's later and later every time. Not that we'd let Walker boss us. Who's Walker?"

"I've got a message for him from Mr. Quelch," said the captain of the Remove. "This row has got to stop!"

"Tell Quelchy to go and eat coke!" retorted Dicky Nugent independently. "He's not our Form-master!"

"Look here——"

"Chuck that Remove cad out!" roared Gatty. "What's he doing in our Form-room?"

"Outside!" yelled the Second.

A mob of belligerent fags gathered round the captain of the Remove. Harry Wharton did not back out of the Form-room, as would have been only prudent with the Second Form in this wild and woolly state. It was miles beneath the dignity of a Remove man to retreat before any number of fags.

"Look here, you young asses——"

"Can it!"

"Outside!"

"Hurrah! Chuck him out!" yelled Nugent minor.

There was a rush.

"Hands off!" roared Wharton. "I tell you, I'll—— Oh, my hat!"

Three or four fags were knocked right and left, but numbers told. The captain of the Remove was swept out into the passage, sprawling, with six or seven breathless fags sprawling over him.

"Ha, ha, ha!"

"Give him socks!"

"Tap his napper!"

"Whoooop!" roared the captain of the Remove, as his head was tapped—not gently—on the hard, unsympathetic floor.

"Ha, ha, ha!"

"Give him another!"

Bang!

"Ow! Oh, my hat! You young villains—yaroooop!"

"Ha, ha, ha!"

"Now come in again, you Remove sweep!" yelled Dicky Nugent; and the fags retreated into their Form-room and banged the door.

Harry Wharton staggered to his feet. He was dusty and breathless, and he rubbed his head ruefully. He was strongly tempted to rush into the Second Form-room, hitting out right and left. But he restrained that natural impulse and returned to his own Form-room to report.

THE SECOND CHAPTER

THE HEAVY HAND!

"SCANDALOUS!"

Mr. Quelch fairly hooted.

The news that Wharton was unable to deliver his message, owing to the absence of Walker of the Sixth from the post of duty, seemed to have an exciting effect on the Remove master.

Wharton said nothing of the rousing reception the fags had given him personally, but he had to say that Walker was not there, for as soon as he re-entered the Remove-room, Mr. Quelch demanded whether he had delivered his message. Uproar was still proceeding from the happy quarters of the Second.

" Scandalous ! " hooted Mr. Quelch. " I shall leave you in charge here for a few minutes, Wharton. You will keep order here while I am gone."

" Oh, certainly, sir ! "

Mr. Quelch looked at his class.

" You will proceed with your Latin papers," he said. " If there is any disorder in this room while I am absent, the whole Form will be detained this afternoon."

That was enough for the Removites. Fellows who were already thinking of allowing themselves a little relaxation while their Form-master's back was turned gave up the idea on the spot. That afternoon was a half-holiday, and there was no doubt that Mr. Quelch would keep his word. Every fellow in the Remove decided to keep the most meticulous order.

Mr. Quelch picked up his cane and left the Remove-room.

The Remove fellows grinned at one another as soon as he was gone. They relaxed so far as to grin. That, at least, was safe.

There was a sudden silence. It indicated that the Remove master had entered the Second Form-room.

And the Remove fellows grinned and went on with their Latin papers. They had no doubt that their Form-master would soon have the uproarious fags well in hand. Mr. Quelch had taken his cane with him. Properly speaking, the Remove master was not entitled to use his cane in any Form-room but the one where he reigned supreme. The Removites guessed that Mr. Quelch was about to do that to which he was not entitled.

And they were right.

Mr. Quelch opened the door of the Second Form-room, and as he did so there was a howl.

" That Remove rotter again ! "

" Chuck him out ! "

There was a rush of the fags towards the door. Then, as Mr. Quelch strode in, the Second Form saw who it was.

They stopped suddenly.

Silence fell on the Second Form-room. The fags backed away from the awful apparition of the Remove master, cane in hand, with frowning brow, and eyes that glinted. The glance of the fabled basilisk could not have had a more dismaying effect on the heroes of the Second.

" What does this mean ? " thundered Mr. Quelch.

" Oh ! "

" Hem ! "

" How dare you make this disturbance ! "

" Um ! "

" Why are you not at your lessons ? "

" We—we—we're waiting for Walker, sir," stammered Dicky Nugent. " We—we were just wondering what had become of him."

Snort from Mr. Quelch.

" Our—our Form-master has left, sir," said Nugent minor, as if Mr. Quelch did not know that already, " and—and the new master, sir, can't come as he's got the 'flu, and—and Mr. Sutcliffe doesn't get here till this afternoon, and—and—and——"

" I am aware of that, Nugent minor."

" Um ! "

" Take your places at once ! "

The Second Form were already taking their places. They sneaked to their desks softly, but with suppressed wrath. After all, Quelchy was not their Form-master. What the thump did he mean by butting into their Form-room ? It was like his cheek, in the opinion of the Second. They did not, however, tell Mr. Quelch that it was like his cheek.

Bump ! Crash ! Bang ! The din that the fags made was terrific, as they thoroughly enjoyed themselves in the Form-room. Temporarily without a master, the Second Form were making full use of their freedom !

" I shall take charge of this class until Walker arrives," rumbled the Remove master.

" Oh dear ! " ejaculated Sammy Bunter involuntarily, in his dismay.

" Bunter minor ! "

" Oh ! Yes, sir ? "

" What did you say ? "

" N-n-nothing, sir ! " gasped Sammy.

" What is the lesson ? " snapped Mr. Quelch, having pulverised Sammy Bunter with a glance.

" Hem ! "

" Answer me, Nugent minor ! "

Dicky Nugent breathed hard. He was a great favourite in the Second Form. He was popularly supposed to have nerve enough to float a battleship. His nerve failed him, however, under the Remove master's basilisk eyes.

" Geography, sir," he faltered.

There had never been so orderly a class at Greyfriars as that which now had the benefit of geographical instruction from Mr. Quelch. The Second Form hung on Mr. Quelch's words as if they were pearls of wisdom falling from the Remove master's lips. They watched him anxiously, eager to anticipate his wishes.

Walker of the Sixth, strolling along the corridor with his novel in his pocket, was surprised and pleased to hear no sound of disorder in the Form-room of which he was supposed to have taken charge. He had left it rather late—he realised that. He had rather feared that the young sweeps would be kicking up a row playing leap-frog, or something of the kind. Instead of which order reigned—there was scarcely a sound from the Form-room as James Walker arrived at the door.

He pushed it open and entered.

" Well, you young rascals——"

Walker broke off suddenly at the sight of Mr. Quelch.

The Remove master laid down his book. He gave James Walker one glance—one was enough. It almost shrivelled up Walker of the Sixth.

" I will now hand this class over to you, Walker, if you have time to attend to it ! " said Mr. Quelch icily.

" Oh, yes, sir ! Certainly, sir ! I—I—the fact is, I——" stammered Walker, greatly flurried.

Mr. Quelch, ruthlessly regardless, walked out of the Second Form-room, leaving Walker stuttering.

" Oh, gad ! " gasped Walker.

" I—I say, Walker, it's a shame ! " said Gatty. " Mr. Quelch oughtn't to have butted in here."

" I suppose you were kicking up a row ? " said Walker.

" I—I—I think somebody dropped a book," said Gatty cautiously. George Gatty was really understating the case.

" You young sweeps ! " said Walker. " This may mean a jaw from the Head. You make another sound, and your lives won't be worth living ! "

And James Walker sat down at the master's desk with his novel, leaving the Second to imbibe knowledge from their geography books if they liked, and as much as they liked. That was Walker's way of taking a class when the eye of authority was not on him. The Second Form liked it better than Mr. Quelch's way.

THE THIRD CHAPTER

CASH REQUIRED !

" ROT ! "

That was the opinion of Legge of the Second Form.

In the Second Form at Greyfriars they stated their opinions without any beating about the bush. In that juvenile Form Chesterfieldian politeness was at a heavy discount.

Dicky Nugent glared at Legge. Dicky Nugent regarded himself as cock of the walk in the Second. George Gatty also regarded himself as cock of the walk in the Form. This difference of views sometimes led to internecine strife. On the present occasion, however, the chiefs of the Second were in accord, and it was Legge—a mere nobody—who had ventured to characterise Nugent minor's remark as " rot."

" Did you say rot, young Legge ? " inquired Nugent minor, pushing back his cuffs with an air of preparation.

" Yes, I jolly well did ! " retorted Legge.

" Where will you have it ? " further inquired Nugent minor.

" Wherever you can put it ! " retorted Legge independently.

And then there was a pause in the discussion that was being held in the Second Form-room after dinner, while Nugent minor and " young Legge " rolled on the floor in a terrific struggle, collecting and scattering dust, gasping and spluttering, and breathing blood-curdling threats.

Nugent minor emerged victorious from the combat, wiping a crimson nose, what time Legge struggled for his second wind under the desks.

"And now——" said Dicky Nugent breathlessly.

"I think it's a jolly good idea," said Gatty. "A bit out of the common."

"Think Sutcliffe will be pleased?" asked Myers.

"Pleased?" retorted Dicky Nugent. "I should jolly well think so. Delighted!"

"He might think it a cheek," said Sammy Bunter.

"He might if he were a silly idiot like you, Bunter mi; but we've no reason to suppose that he's a silly idiot like you."

"Look here, young Nugent——"

"Shut up, Bunter mi," said Gatty. "Nobody wants to hear your opinion. You're as silly an ass as your major in the Remove, and that's saying a lot."

"I jolly well think——"

"Shut up!" roared Gatty.

"All you've got to do, Bunter mi, is to make your contribution like other men," said Nugent minor. "We don't want your opinion."

Snort from Sammy Bunter. He would rather have given his opinion than his cash at any time. He had a serious objection to giving his cash.

"How much each?" asked Myers.

"Well," said Dicky Nugent thoughtfully, "it's six bob for a taxi from Courtfield. Say a bob tip for the chauffeur——"

"I don't believe in tipping," said Sammy Bunter.

"You wouldn't," agreed Dicky Nugent. "But I've told you we don't want your opinion, Bunter mi. Threepence each all round ought to wangle it. Where are you going, young Bunter?"

Young Bunter did not delay to state where he was going; he went. The Form-room door slammed after him in a hurry.

"Mingy toad!" said Gatty. "We can do without his measly threepence. You fellows shell out."

Legge emerged from under the desks.

"Rot!" he said.

"What?" roared Nugent minor.

"Rot!"

And Legge of the Second hurriedly departed from the Form-room. And, oddly enough, quite a number of the fags who had attended the meeting called by Dicky Nugent followed him hastily. Most of them had agreed that the "stunt" propounded by Dicky was great. But when the time came for the collection they seemed to have pressing business elsewhere.

"Well, my hat!" said Gatty, as he found himself left in the Form-room with only Myers and Nugent minor. "My only hat! What have the men cleared off like that for?"

Dicky Nugent sniffed.

"Look here, we can manage it," he said. "And we'll get a ride in the car—see?"

"Will Sutcliffe like three kids in the car with him?" asked Myers doubtfully.

"What rot! Why shouldn't he? Anyhow, if he doesn't like it he can lump it; it's our car."

"That's so."

"But that will be two bob each for us if the taxi is six bob," said Gatty. "Too jolly expensive, Nugent mi."

"I've got two bob," said Dicky.

"I've got threepence."

"Same here, and a ha'penny over," said Myers.

Dicky Nugent grunted. He had thought of a great wheeze; he was the fellow for wheezes. Most of the Second had thought it a great wheeze, too, and had been prepared to give it their moral support. Unfortunately, moral support would not pay the taximan. Financial support was required for that, and financial support seemed to be lacking.

"Well, I can squeeze a loan out of my major in the Remove," said Dicky, after some thought. "The mater told him specially to look after me this term. He does a lot of elder-brotherly bizney. He can't expect to do it on the cheap."

"That's so," agreed Gatty. "It's against a man to have a brother in an upper Form. He ought to make up for it somehow."

"I believe those Remove bounders are going out this afternoon," said Myers. "I heard Cherry saying something about going to the smugglers' cave at Pegg."

"Buck up, then, Dicky," said Gatty. "If you don't get it out of your major, the game's up."

Dicky Nugent nodded, and hurried out of the Form-room. Three-and-sixpence was required to make Nugent minor's scheme a success; that was really not a large sum for Frank Nugent, of the Remove, to expend upon a fascinating young brother.

. . . . . .

"Hallo, hallo, hallo! Is your giddy minor coming, Franky?"

"Not that I know of."

"There he is, anyhow."

Frank Nugent looked back. The chums of the Remove had left the school gates, and were tramping cheerily down the lane towards Friardale, when Bob Cherry glanced back at the stile and spotted Dicky Nugent.

Dicky was coming after the Famous Five at breathless speed.

The Famous Five had to cross the stile to take the short cut across the fields to the cliffs. Nugent stopped.

"Waiting for him?" asked Johnny Bull.

"Yes," said Nugent, rather curtly.

Johnny's tone implied that fags of the Second were hardly worth waiting for.

"Oh, all right," said Johnny, amicably. "I'll sit down for a bit." And he straddled the top bar of the stile.

"The waitfulness is the proper caper," said Hurree Jamset Ram Singh gracefully. "If the esteemed and ridiculous Dicky desires to accompany us explorefully in the caves, the addition of his honourable society will be the boonful blessing."

"Hear, hear!" grinned Bob Cherry.

And the Famous Five waited for the fag to come up. Frank Nugent was a dutiful and affectionate major. His chums did not, perhaps, quite see what there was in Dicky Nugent to inspire attachment. But they bore patiently with Frank on that subject.

"I suppose there's no harm if Dicky comes along," said Nugent.

"None at all," agreed Wharton, with great politeness.

Remove men really did not yearn for the company of Second Form fags, as a rule. But the Co. were prepared to make an exception in favour of Frank's minor—cheerfully, if not enthusiastically.

Dicky came panting up.

"Come on, kid," said Frank.

"Eh! What? Where?" asked Dicky breathlessly.

"We're going to explore the caves at Pegg——"

"Kid's game," said Nugent minor.

"What?"

"Catch me!" said Dicky derisively.

Johnny Bull winked at Bob Cherry, who turned away his head to hide his smiles. Harry Wharton coughed, and Hurree Jamset Ram Singh remained as grave as a bronze image.

" You cheeky little sweep ! " exclaimed Nugent, nettled. " What the thump do you come bolting after us for, then, and making us waste time ? Buzz off ! "

" Oh, don't get waxy, old bean ! " said Nugent minor. " I've got something on more jolly important than mucking about in silly old caves ! "

" Go and get on with it, then ! " snapped Frank ; and he turned to the stile.

" Hold on a minute, fathead ! I want three-and-six ! "

" Rats ! "

" Don't be a waxy idiot, Frank ! " urged Nugent minor. " It's jolly important. We've got two-and-six, and we want three-and-six to make up six bob—see ? "

" What's it for ? " grunted Nugent.

" I don't mind telling you, old chap," said Dicky. " It's a great stunt ! Look here, you lend me three-and-six, and I'll do the letter home this week. Honest Injun ! "

" Ha, ha, ha ! "

" You know our Form-master's gone—your Form-master came messing about in our Form-room this

" Chuck that Remove cad out ! " roared Gatty. " What's he doing in our Form-room ? " A mob of belligerent fags quickly gathered round Harry Wharton. " Look here, you young asses——" began Wharton. " Can it ! " yelled the Second. " Outside ! "

morning," said Dicky—"and the new master can't come yet, and a man named Sutcliffe is filling the job pro tem. Well, this man Sutcliffe is arriving by the three-thirty at Courtfield—I've found that out. He's a beast, of course——"

"How do you know he's a beast?"

"Oh, don't be a goat! Ain't all Form-masters beasts? But we're going to get on the right side of him to begin with," said Dicky. "We're going to the station to meet him. We're standing him a car to the school!" added the fag, in an offhand way.

"Oh, my hat!" said Bob Cherry.

"Some stunt, what?" said Nugent minor complacently. "The idea is, we want to welcome our new Form-master, and show him what nice chaps we are—respectful to our kind teachers, and all that—story-book stuff, you know. It was my idea."

"Sounds as if it might have been!" remarked Bob.

"Oh, don't you be funny!" said Nugent minor. "It's a ripping wheeze, and Gatty thinks so, too. Of course, we get the drive in the car, and that's worth the money, so we don't really lose anything. We meet Mr. Sutcliffe on the platform at Courtfield—we speak to him nicely, and tell him that we've got a car outside to take him to the school. Even a beast will be bound to be pleased at getting kind attentions like that from his Form. It will put him in a good temper, and it ought to get us off prep to-night at the very least."

"Ha, ha, ha!"

"Well, you can cackle," said Dicky, "but I jolly well think it's a great wheeze. You'd never have thought of it in a month of Sundays."

"They only think of these great things in the Second Form," said Bob Cherry solemnly.

"You see, Quelchy is certain to speak to him—tip him that we're a rowdy mob, and all that," said Dicky. "He carried on like a Hun in our Form-room this morning. I came jolly near buzzing my geography book at his napper, I can tell you. Only I—I didn't."

"You needn't mention that you didn't," said Harry Wharton gravely. "We can guess that."

"Ha, ha, ha!"

"Oh, rats!" said Dicky crossly. "You see the idea, Franky. If he hears that we're a rowdy gang, he won't take any notice, after being met at the station and talked to nicely and respectfully, and brought to the school in a car. But, of course, we shall have to pay for the car. If he had to shell out it would spoil the effect."

"The spoilfulness would be terrific."

"You're a young ass!" said Frank, laughing. "It's a risky game pulling a master's leg."

"It isn't exactly pulling his leg, you know. We want to make a good impression on the beast," explained Dicky. "We want to bottle up Quelchy in advance, too. Anyhow, we get the ride—see? 'Tain't throwing money away, like buying a master a birthday present, f'rinstance."

"Ha, ha, ha!"

"Well, here's the tin, and I wish you luck!" said Nugent. "I've got only half-a-crown. One of you fellows lend me a bob."

"The lendfulness will be the esteemed pleasure."

"Thanks!" said Dicky, pocketing the half-crown and the shilling. "I'll settle this, of course, Franky, along with the other little lots, some time."

" This year, next year, sometime, never ! " chanted Bob Cherry softly.

" Ha, ha, ha ! "

" Sorry I can't come with you," said Dicky patronisingly. " You want somebody to look after you if you're going into the smugglers' cave. It's haunted, you know. I can see you bolting when you hear the groans."

Dicky Nugent dodged a lunge of Bob Cherry's boot, and started back to Greyfriars at a run.

The Famous Five clambered over the stile, and pursued their way with smiling faces. Whether Mr. Sutcliffe, the temporary master of the Second Form at Greyfriars, would be pleased and gratified at finding a gang of fags waiting for him with a taxicab was, to their minds, a doubtful question. Still, Dicky Nugent was greatly pleased with his scheme, and as he so sapiently observed, the fags would get the ride in the car at any rate. Even if Mr. Sutcliffe wasn't pleased, a joy-ride on a half-holiday was grateful and comforting.

THE FOURTH CHAPTER

THE MAN ON THE CLIFF !

" CAREFUL, here ! "

" You bet ! "

" The carefulness is terrific."

Care was needed on the path the chums of the Remove were taking down from the great chalk cliffs to the caves. From the summit of the mighty Shoulder the beach looked a pebbly strip, the fishermen's boats like dots. It was a long way down to the caves on the sea level, and the way was perilous. Rifts and faults in the great mass of chalk formed a kind of rough staircase, and the steps were steep and irregular, and wet with the spray that dashed up when the sea was rough, as it very often was below the Shoulder.

But the five juniors were lithe and active, and they tramped down the rocky way, here and there holding on with their hands when it was necessary, their faces glowing with the rough exercise and the keen wind from the North Sea.

Half-way down there was a plateau of chalk, from which there was a magnificent view of the sea, with ships far out in the distance. There the Greyfriars juniors stopped to rest a little.

" Jolly here, isn't it ? " said Bob Cherry, breathing hard and deep.

" Top-hole, old bean ! "

" I don't think your minor would have been equal to this if he had condescended to come, Franky."

" We could have gone round on the level, by way of Pegg," said Nugent.

" Hem ! So we could ! " said Bob, closing one eye at Wharton. " It's a longer way round, and rather uninteresting ; but your minor's company would have made up for that."

" Fathead ! " said Frank.

" Hallo, hallo, hallo ! There's somebody else on the giddy cliff-path as well as our noble selves ! " ejaculated Bob.

The clink of a falling stone came from below. Someone was coming up the natural stairway from the beach, and had almost reached the plateau where the schoolboys were resting.

They could not see him yet ; the rough windings and projections of the chalk hid the newcomer from sight, so far.

A hat came in sight at last, rising into view up the steep, and it was followed by a clean-shaven face. The juniors were looking towards the spot where the newcomer was bound to appear as he came higher, and they saw the man before he saw them.

The expression on his face struck them a little.

He was a young man, not over thirty, with a rather hard, clear-cut face, and extremely keen eyes set close together. His expression puzzled the juniors a little; there was something grim and dogged in it, something that told of a grim, hard determination. He was a stranger to them, though certainly he could not have been a stranger in the locality, or he would not have known his way up the rugged path on the cliff.

He clambered on to the plateau and stopped to breathe, and then he saw the juniors sitting on the chalk boulders, resting. He started violently as he saw them.

Apparently he had not expected to meet anyone on the rough cliff-path, or perhaps had not desired to meet anyone. He stood looking at them with a very unpleasant expression on his face.

Bob Cherry gave him an affable nod. The man looked anything but good-tempered; but Bob had good-temper enough for two.

"Good-afternoon, sir!" sang out Bob cheerily.

The man did not answer the greeting.

He had placed a bag on the ground, to relieve himself of the weight, and the juniors noticed, without especially heeding, that the initials on the leather were "J. S." They wondered a little at a man carrying a bag on a rough climb over the cliffs. The path up from the bay was not easy for a climber unencumbered.

"Hefty climb up, sir, what?" said Bob, not at all abashed by the bad manners of the stranger.

The man seemed to think better of his bad manners, however, and he smiled and nodded.

"Yes; it's longer than it looks from the sea," he remarked. "Is it far to the top?"

"You're just half-way up," said Bob.

"You know the path?" asked Wharton.

"No; I am quite a stranger here."

"It's rather risky if you don't know the way," said the captain of the Remove.

The man nodded, picked up his bag, and went on. The juniors looked after him rather curiously. It was perfectly plain that the man had intended to sit down and rest, and had changed his intention on seeing the schoolboys there.

Why he should have done so was a mystery.

He disappeared in a few moments from sight among the windings of the cliff path.

Bob Cherry grinned.

"The dear man doesn't seem to like good company," he remarked. "At least, he doesn't seem to care for ours."

"He's a bad egg," said Johnny Bull, sententiously.

"He said he was quite a stranger here. But he isn't, or he wouldn't know this path. He's gone right up—and a stranger would never know the way without stopping and picking his way jolly carefully. He's out of sight already."

Harry Wharton nodded.

"That's true," he said. "He's been over this ground before, that's a cert. I remember the first time I came up this path I was puzzled in a dozen places. That chap came right up to where we are, and he's gone right on without having to stop to think. He knows the ground as well as we do."

"The knowfulness is terrific," agreed Hurree Jamset Ram Singh.

" But why did the esteemed and rotten person tell us whoppers ? "

" Goodness knows ! "

" Hallo, hallo, hallo, here comes his bonnet ! " exclaimed Bob Cherry, as a hat flew by on the wind.

Bob made a jump and a grab at the whirling hat, but missed it, and it flew on beyond the little chalk plateau, and he did not come back. Probably he did not consider the hat worth a laborious climb down to the cliffs, and a still more laborious climb up again.

The Co. were not much interested in the matter, anyway, and, having rested, they rose and resumed their way down the cliff, dismissing the peculiar stranger from their minds.

" Where will you have it ? " roared Nugent minor. " Wherever you can put it ! " retorted Legge. The next moment the two fags were rolling on the floor in a terrific struggle, gasping and spluttering and breathing blood-curdling threats.

went careering down the cliff towards the beach.

Evidently the wind, higher up the cliff, had whisked the hat from the stranger's head, and whirled it away. With his bag in one hand, and doubtless holding on to the rocks with the other, he had been unable to save it.

The juniors half-expected to see the stranger returning for his hat But

THE FIFTH CHAPTER

NOT A SUCCESS !

" LEAVE the talking to me ! " said Dicky Nugent.

" That's you, all over ! " said Gatty.

" Just ! " agreed Myers.

The three fags were standing on the platform at Courtfield Junction, and the station clock indicated half-past three. The train was signalled—

the train that was to bring Mr. John Sutcliffe to Courtfield to meet, unexpectedly, three leading members of the Form he was to take at Greyfriars.

Outside the station waited the car.

It was not a common or garden taxi; it was a car from Courtfield Garage, specially engaged by Nugent minor & Co. to carry them and their new Form-master to Greyfriars.

Keen bargaining on the part of the fags had reduced the charge for the drive to five shillings and sixpence; which left sixpence over for a tip to the chauffeur.

The three fags waited eagerly, as the train came rolling in.

Myers was a little doubtful about this stunt; Gatty was not wholly confident. But Dicky Nugent was serenely confident. As it was his wheeze, he, naturally, thought well of it.

The train stopped, and at least fifteen or sixteen people alighted from it.

Dicky Nugent & Co. scanned them eagerly as they passed.

Most of them, evidently, could not have been schoolmasters. There were only two men in the lot who could possibly have been Mr Sutcliffe—though both of them, of course, could not have been that gentleman. The fags eyed the two warily and keenly, but could not make up their minds which of the two was their quarry.

"Well, we've got tongues in our heads," remarked Dicky Nugent. "We can ask."

And Dicky cut after the two gentlemen, who were going to the barrier.

"Excuse me, sir, are you Mr. Sutcliffe?"

"No."

"Bound to catch the wrong man first!" said Myers satirically.

"Well, the other man must be Sutcliffe," said Dicky.

And he rushed after the other man.

"Mr. Sutcliffe——"

The gentleman stared at him.

"My name is not Sutcliffe," he said, and walked on.

"Oh, my only hat!" ejaculated Dicky, in dismay.

Neither gentleman, evidently, was John Sutcliffe. The three fags gathered on the platform again, in doubt.

"Must have been one of the other johnnies that we let pass!" said Myers. "Gone now."

Dicky shook his head.

"Nothing of the kind. I looked 'em over—grocers and commercial travellers and farmers and a soldier and some girls. He's missed his train, that's what it is."

"Sure he was coming by the three-thirty?" asked Gatty.

"I heard Mr. Quelch tell Walker."

"Might have got out at Redclyffe and walked," suggested Gatty.

"Why should he?" said Nugent minor irritably. "It would be a jolly long walk from Redclyffe to Greyfriars."

"People do, though, sometimes. Might be a merchant who likes country walks."

"Oh, rot!"

Dicky Nugent refused to entertain the idea for a moment. If Mr. Sutcliffe had got out at Redclyffe, and walked by way of the Pegg road and Friardale, the scheme of meeting him at Courtfield was evidently N. G. Nugent minor, as the great chief of the Second Form, did not feel disposed to admit that any scheme of his could possibly be N. G. Therefore, Mr. Sutcliffe had not got out of the train at Redclyffe and walked!

"Lost his train, of course," said Nugent minor confidently. "He'll come by the next."

The fags waited for the next train.

They waited impatiently. But the train came in at last.

This time, they posted themselves by the barrier, and scanned each passenger carefully as he came by on the way out.

But this time, there was no one that could possibly have been taken for a schoolmaster.

Half the passengers were women, and there was a couple of schoolboys —Ponsonby and Gadsby of the Fourth Form at Highcliffe, who passed the Greyfriars fags with supercilious noses in the air. There was a stout farmer, there was a white-whiskered retired colonel, there was a man with a violin-case, and a Hebrew gentleman, and a fisherman, and two knutty youths. And that was all, and they passed out and left the fags with the platform to themselves.

"Well?" said Myers, with a touch of irony.

"Well?" said Gatty.

Dicky Nugent breathed hard.

Mr. Sutcliffe had not arrived by the three-thirty, and he had not arrived by the four o'clock train. It looked very doubtful whether he would arrive at Courtfield Junction at all. It was borne in upon Nugent minor's mind that Mr. Sutcliffe must, after all, have got out at Redclyffe and walked.

"Waiting for the next train?" smiled Myers.

"And the train after that?" inquired Gatty.

"If you fellows want to spend a half-holiday hanging around a railway station, there's nothing to stop you," said Nugent minor. "I'm going."

And he went.

Gatty and Myers followed him.

There was a somewhat heated argument with the driver of the car. His view was that he had been

GREYFRIARS RHYMES

BILLY BUNTER

(the fat boy of the school)

YOU'VE doubtless heard of "W. G."—
  Not Grace, but simply Bunter—
Who, though he eats enough for three,
  Is hungry as a hunter.
He pouches pies and scoffs jam-tarts
  A dozen to the minute;
In fact, when Bunter really starts,
  An ostrich isn't in it.

He follows on the new boy's trail
  As grimly as a warder,
And unto him unfolds a tale
  About a postal-order.
He cadges crowns, or even pence,
  "To be repaid to-morrow,"
And varies with his victim's sense
  The sum he hopes to borrow.

A fabricator, as a rule,
  Is much inclined to try us;
The "Peeping Tom" of Greyfriars School
  Gives points to Ananias.
He rolls out fibs in such a way,
  'Tis strange how he conceives them;
They have one drawback, sad to say—
  For not a soul believes them.

The good old days have taken flight,
  When kings were held to ransom;
Yet Bunter, though he's not a knight,
  Imagines he is handsome.
Says he: "Indeed, I'm wondrous fair—
  A fine and handsome lad I!
And pretty maidens everywhere
  Present me with the 'glad eye.'"

He thinks he is a ladies' man,
  And when Cliff House makes merry,
He joins the revels if he can,
  But keeps away from Cherry.
For Bob, in thought for Marjorie,
  Won't let a pig confront her;
He puts this down to jealousy,
  Does fat, misguided Bunter!

Thus Bunter figures in our eyes—
  A fellow always slacking;
Who never cares for exercise,
  And needs a world of whacking!
To sum him up in good round terms
  (I don't think I should risk it!)
Of all the meanest, craftiest worms,
  Why, Bunter takes the biscuit!

engaged for a five-and-six drive, and that he had waited half an hour over and above. However, that matter was settled more or less amicably for half-a-crown; and the three fags walked back to Greyfriars.

"After all, it will run to a jolly good tea in the Form-room," said Dicky Nugent on the way home. "We've got three-and-six."

Gatty and Myers brightened up. This was a solace; indeed, they began to perceive that it was not wholly a disaster, after all, that Mr. Sutcliffe had failed to arrive by the train at Courtfield Junction. A spread in the Form-room was a compensation.

Dicky Nugent & Co. were rather tired and dusty when they arrived at the school. Sammy Bunter was loafing around near the gates, and Nugent minor called to him.

"Sutcliffe blown in yet, young Bunter?"

Sammy chuckled.

"Long ago! You duffers were waiting for him at Courtfield, weren't you? He, he, he!"

"So he's come?" exclaimed Myers.

"Half an hour ago!" cackled Sammy Bunter. "He, he, he!"

Dicky Nugent & Co. stayed only to bang Bunter minor's head on the gate, and then walked off to the school shop, where the sum of three shillings and sixpence was expended on the good things supplied by Mrs. Mimble. The goods were carried off to the Second Form-room—where a feast of the gods was soon in progress.

THE SIXTH CHAPTER

IN THE CHALK CAVES!

"In this style, three-and-nine!" said Bob Cherry humorously. And the Famous Five chuckled.

Harry Wharton and his comrades had reached the bottom of the steep path down the cliff, and sand and shingle, broken by great chalky boulders, lay round them. And on a point of chalky rock lay a hat—obviously that which had blown from the head of the stranger who had passed them on the cliff. The wind had landed it there, till a strong gust should catch it and carry it away again.

"I suppose we shan't see that merchant again, and can't give him back his roof," he remarked. "But it seems a pity to leave it here—it's a good hat."

"My dear man, we can't carry other people's hats about on a half-holiday," said Nugent.

"Nunno! But—it's a decent lid," said Bob. "It must have cost the owner thirty bob or so. If there's a name in it, we might be able to send it home, if the johnny lives about here anywhere."

"He said he was a stranger here."

"But he wasn't, or he wouldn't have known the path up the cliffs, as Johnny pointed out, old bean."

Bob Cherry was looking into the hat to see whether there was a name or other indication of proprietorship within.

He gave a yell of surprise.

"Oh, great pip!"

"What the thump——" exclaimed Wharton.

"Ha, ha, ha! We can take this tile home to the owner," said Bob. "Who'd have thought it? Look!"

He held up the hat and the juniors stared blankly at the name stamped on the inside band.

"J. Sutcliffe."

"You remember, there were the initials 'J.S.' on the bag he was carting up the cliff," said Bob. "It's the new Second Form-master for

Greyfriars. So we can take his hat home with us."

"That would be the proper and politeful caper," assented Hurree Jamset Ram Singh.

Johnny Bull had a thoughtful look.

"I don't think much of the new master of the Second," he remarked. "A Form-master ought not to tell lies. He was telling us lies about being a stranger in this locality. Blessed if I know why, but he was!"

"He must be more or less a stranger here," said Harry. "I've heard that he was engaged from the Head's agency in London."

"But he knows the district; he's been here before, and knows the place quite well," said Johnny. "He couldn't have gone up the cliff as he did otherwise. He's an odd fish altogether. It was queer his being here at all. If he got out at Redclyffe to walk he would naturally take the Pegg road and the Friardale footpath; he's come eight miles out of his way by the beach and the cliff path."

"Might have liked a walk by the sea, old bean."

"It proves he knows the country well here. Fancy a stranger coming along the beach from Pegg, past the caves, and taking the chance of finding the path up the cliffs. If he hadn't found it he would have been cut off when the tide comes in. And it's no joke tramping over a mile of shingle with a heavy bag and then carting it up the cliff. It's not a natural proceeding for a new master coming to a school. Blessed if I make the man out at all!"

"Never mind! No bizney of ours," said Bob. "Who's going to carry this hat?"

"Findings keepings, old man. You carry it!"

"Come on, then," said Bob cheerily.

The juniors tramped along the shingle to the opening of the sea-caves. The tide was out to a great distance; there was no danger of the sea coming in yet. When the tide was in the water washed right into the caves, filling the open spaces with foam and spray.

According to legend the caves had been used by smugglers in old days. The great cliff was honeycombed with them, and the interior caves were out of reach of the tide, though, of course, cut off from access when the water was in the outer caves.

Nugent glanced out over the tumbling sea as the juniors reached the opening in the cliff.

"It's on the turn," he said.

"Lots of time," said Wharton. "I looked it out, of course, when we fixed on this excursion. The tide doesn't get in till dark—and we're not staying till dark."

"No joke to get shut in the caves by the tide," said Bob. "Some fellows were once, and they had a chilly night of it."

"No danger of that now. No danger except from the ghost of the smuggler, and we're not afraid of that."

"Ha, ha! No."

The Famous Five tramped into the cave.

"Hallo, hallo, hallo! We're not the first here to-day," exclaimed Bob, pointing to a footprint in a patch of sand within the opening of the cave. "That was made since the last tide."

The juniors looked at the footprint in silent surprise. The same thought was in all their minds. Only a few days previously they had made a strange discovery in the caves beneath the new wireless station on the cliffs and on the other side of Pegg village. Surely they could not be on the verge of finding another secret hoard of explosives beneath the massive Shoulder? The idea was absurd, and yet—the footprint! Whose could it be?

"Jolly few people come along here in the winter," exclaimed Wharton abruptly.

Bob Cherry raised his voice and shouted into the deep cave.

"Hallo, hallo, hallo! Anybody at home?"

His voice came thundering back in a thousand echoes. But there was no other reply.

"Whoever he was, he's gone," said Nugent. "Come on!"

Outside the cave the bright winter sunshine was sharp and clear. But once inside all was gloomy and shadowy. In hollows of the chalk lay pools of water left by the last receding tide, and the ground was almost carpeted by masses of dripping seaweed. The juniors glanced round them for other footprints, but the hard chalk showed no trace of any. They advanced a dozen yards up the rugged cave, and then Wharton turned on the light of his electric torch.

"Hallo, hallo, hallo! There's the giddy spook!" exclaimed Bob suddenly. "Jolly polite of him to be at home when we're calling."

A wild and wailing sound echoed through the caves.

"The wind!" said Harry.

"Of course! But it sounds jolly human, all the same. No wonder the fishermen believe the place is haunted."

"Hark!"

From somewhere in the dense darkness, at a distance from the juniors, came a faint and painful cry.

The chums of the Remove started and drew together rather quickly. It was an eerie, unnerving sound.

"My hat! Was that the wind?" asked Nugent, in a low voice.

"Must have been," said Harry, but his face was grave. "The wind plays all sorts of tricks in these fissures and crevices. Couldn't have been anything else."

"Of—of course not!"

But the juniors stood still for a few minutes, listening with almost painful intentness. That strange, eerie cry had startled them. But though the wailing of the wind in the hollows still sounded and echoed they did not hear again that peculiar cry.

Bob Cherry shook himself.

"Dash it all! Are we getting nervy?" he exclaimed. "Come on!"

And the juniors tramped on, their electric torches gleaming about them on the wet and rugged rocks; but in spite of themselves, their faces were grave now, and their voices, when they spoke, subdued. That strange cry, echoing from the heart of the chalk caves, still seemed to be ringing in their ears.

THE SEVENTH CHAPTER

THE NEW MASTER OF THE SECOND!

"WHAT'S he like?"

The feast in the Second Form-room was ending.

Sammy Bunter was not one of the invited guests, but he was there. In such matters Sammy was very like his major in the Remove.

"You've seen him, Bunter?" said Gatty.

Bunter minor nodded. He was not able to speak for the moment, his mouth being full of cake.

"Well, what sort of a merchant is he to look at?" demanded Dicky Nugent. "Anything like our old Form-master?"

Bunter minor shook his head.

"Hallo, hallo, hallo!" ejaculated Bob Cherry, while the Greyfriars chums were resting on the chalk boulders. "There's somebody else on the cliff-path." A stranger came into view, and he looked at the juniors with a very unpleasant expression on his face.

"Looks a beast—what?" asked Myers.

Another nod.

"Anything like Quelchy?" asked Gatty in dismay.

"Worse!" said Sammy Bunter, finding his voice at last, the cake having gone the way of all cakes. "Looks a jolly hard nut to crack, I can tell you. I heard him speaking to Mr. Quelch when he came in, and he's got a voice like—like—like an iron bar. Hard, you know. I'm jolly glad he's only a temporary beast. Shouldn't like to have a whole term with him."

"That sounds nice!" grunted Legge.

"Oh, that's only Bunter mi's rot!" said Dicky Nugent. "I dare say he's all right, and he would have been jolly pleased if he'd come to Courtfield Junction and found us waiting for him with a taxi—I mean a car. Do you know how he got here, Sammy?"

"In a taxi."

"Well, if he took a taxi from Redclyffe, he must be a silly ass," said Gatty. "It's three times the distance from Courtfield, and the fare would be enormous!"

"He didn't pay the man a big fare," said Sammy Bunter. "I saw him pay the taxi."

"You see everything, don't you?" jeered Gatty. "Just like your major in the Remove."

"Look here, Gatty——"

"Let that cake alone, you fat brigand. You've had half of it already!"

"If you're going to be mean about a slice of cake——"

"I'm going to rap your knuckles if you don't keep your paw off it!" said Gatty belligerently.

"He's close with money, just like you fellows with a cake," said Bunter minor, reverting to the subject of Mr. Sutcliffe.

"How do you know that, then?" asked Dicky.

"The taxi-driver wanted six shillings from Courtfield, and Sutcliffe made it five," said Bunter minor.

Dicky Nugent stared.

"From Courtfield?" he repeated.

"What rot!" said Gatty. "I tell you he never came to Courtfield. We waited on the platform for him."

"You missed him!" said Bunter minor.

"You silly owl, as if we should miss him."

"Well, the taxi came from Courtfield, anyhow," said Sammy. "I know the driver by sight; he's in the rank at the station there."

Myers chuckled.

"He must have been one of that lot in the first train, Dicky, after all. You missed him."

"You missed him, you mean!" said Nugent minor hotly.

"We all missed him," said Gatty pacifically; "but it's jolly queer. There wasn't a man who looked like a schoolmaster, except the two we spoke to, and they weren't Sutcliffe."

"He never came to Courtfield," said Nugent minor obstinately. "May have picked up an empty taxi on the road from Redclyffe."

"Rot!" said Legge.

"What?"

"He came to Courtfield all right. You fellows were looking for him with your eyes shut!" explained Legge.

Dicky Nugent jumped up with a war-like look.

"Oh, cheese it!" said Legge, without moving. "You can jolly well prove it if you like. Go and look at him. He's in his study now. He went there after seeing the Head. Look at him, and you'll see that he's one of the passengers you let pass you at Courtfield."

Nugent minor glared at Legge.

"I know he jolly well isn't!" he said. "I'll go and squint at him, and if he isn't, as I know he isn't, I'll jolly well punch your head when I come back, young Legge!"

"I'll be there when you do it," said Legge.

"Look here——"

"Order!" said Gatty. "Go and squint at the man, Nugent minor; that will settle it. Ask him if prep's at the usual time. That will be an excuse for butting into his study. Look here! I'll come with you!"

"Come on, then!" said Dicky. "You wait here, Legge. I'm punching your head when I get back!"

And Nugent minor left the Form-room with George Gatty. They proceeded to the masters' corridor, and Dicky tapped at the door of the study belonging to the master of the Second Form.

"Come in!"

It was rather a hard and metallic voice from within the study. It bore out Sammy Bunter's description.

Dicky opened the door, and entered with Gatty.

Both the fags looked curiously at the man who was to have charge of the Second Form for a couple of weeks.

He was sitting in an armchair before a glowing fire, smoking a cigarette. He was a man of rather slight, but strong and wiry build, with a hard face and penetrating eyes. Certainly he did not look the easy-going gentleman that the fags had hoped to see. Whether as a beast he was equal to Mr. Quelch, they had yet to discover; but they had little doubt that he was a beast.

"Mr. Sutcliffe, sir?" said Nugent minor.

"I am Mr. Sutcliffe."

"We—we're in the Second sir" said Dicky. "I'm Nugent minor, sir."

"Indeed!"

"This chap is Gatty, sir."

"Well?"

The new master did not seem especially pleased to make the acquaintance of these two important members of his Form.

The fags were staring at him hard.

They had never seen him before, and they were quite certain that he had not been among the passengers who had arrived at Courtfield by the three-thirty or by the four-o'clock train. They would not have forgotten that hard face with its strongly-marked features.

"I—I hope you had a good journey down, sir?" said Nugent minor.

"Thank you, I did!"

"We—we went to the station to meet you, sir——" Nugent minor thought that that was worth mentioning. Having taken so much trouble on the new master's behalf, the heroes of the Second were at least entitled to the credit of it.

"What?" exclaimed the new master.

He rose quickly from his chair, as if startled.

"We—we thought you'd like it," said Dicky, faltering under the hard stare of the Form-master.

"What do you mean?" exclaimed the new master harshly. "I don't understand you. What do you mean?"

"We—we went to Courtfield——"

"To Courtfield?"

"Yes, sir. To meet your train, sir," stammered Nugent minor.

Nugent minor, when he had propounded his scheme in the Second, had declared that the new-comer would be certainly pleased by such a kind attention. Even if he was not pleased, there was no reason why he should be displeased.

But there was no doubt that he looked displeased. He looked angry and annoyed.

For a moment, indeed, his angry look startled the fags, and they backed a little towards the door.

But the new master's face cleared the next moment.

"You went to Courtfield to meet my train?" he asked.

"Yes, sir. We—we thought——"

The new master smiled.

"Did you meet it?"

"Yes, sir—the three-thirty; but you didn't come by it," said Nugent minor, "so we missed you, sir."

"You need not have taken the trouble," said the new master. "As it happens, I lost the connection at Lantham, and came on by the next train. You may go, my boys."

Dicky Nugent gasped.

"You—you came on by the next train to Courtfield, sir?" he stuttered.

"Yes. You may go. I do not desire to be troubled by the boys of my Form till I am rested after my journey."

The two fags backed out into the passage. It was only too obvious that the new master did not want them in his study. Dicky Nugent drew the door shut, and stared blankly at Gatty.

"The next train!" he whispered. "He says he came on by the next train. We waited for the next train, and we know he never came in it."

"What on earth is he telling us lies for?" said Gatty, in wonder.

"Goodness knows."

The two fags returned to the Second Form-room. Legge greeted them with a grin.

"Well?" he asked.

"I was right!" snapped Nugent minor. "He never came to Courtfield by train. We've never seen him before."

"Only—only he says he did!" gasped Gatty. "He's told us lies. What has he told us lies for? He says he came on by the second train, after losing the first."

"Well, so he did, then," said Legge.

"He didn't! He doesn't know we waited for the second train; but we did, and he never came in it. We looked at every passenger as he went off the platform, and there wasn't one a bit like him."

"Rot!" said Legge.

THE EIGHTH CHAPTER

THE MYSTERY OF THE CAVE!

"HARK!"

Bob Cherry uttered that exclamation suddenly.

The Famous Five stopped, their hearts beating fast.

From somewhere in the gloomy depths of the caverns, far beyond the glimmer of their torches, a weird and wailing cry came.

It was like the wailing of the wind in the hidden hollows, and yet unlike. Anywhere but in the depths of the caves under the great Shoulder, the juniors would have been certain that that cry came from a human throat—that it was the cry of one in pain and despair.

As the loud echoes died down, the wailing cry came again from the hidden distance. Nugent gave a shudder.

"By Jove! I'll swear that wasn't the wind!" exclaimed Harry Wharton. "Suppose somebody's got lost in the cave? There's no end of winding fissures leading out of one cave into another. People have been lost here. Might be some poor beggar yelling for help."

Bob Cherry whistled.

"It's possible," he said. "We know somebody's been here since the morning tide—there was that footprint. We thought he had gone—but he may have got lost—whoever he was."

"In that case it's jolly lucky we came," said Nugent. "Let's look, anyhow. We may find a giddy lost tripper instead of a smuggler's treasure."

The juniors pushed in, in the direction from which the wailing sound had seemed to proceed—though in the midst of the hollow echoes it was difficult to ascertain the precise direction.

Fron one great hollow to another, fissures and "faults" in the chalk gave access—in some places with ample space, in others, with barely room for a fellow to squeeze through.

The cry was heard no more; and the chums of the Remove wondered whether their ears had deceived them, or whether they had overshot the mark and left the place they were seeking behind them.

They turned back at last, tramping and clambering from cave to cave, flashing their lights to and fro.

"There it is again!" breathed Bob.

The faint, painful cry awoke the echoes once more.

"We've passed the place," said Harry.

"But we've been keeping our eyes open," said Johnny Bull. "If there was anyone here we'd have seen him."

"Might have fallen into some pit—there are big holes in the chalk, in places."

"Better be careful—we don't want to follow him in."

Again and again, though at lengthy intervals, the juniors heard the cry; and they were fully convinced now that it was a human cry. The wind was wailing in the fissures of the rocks but they picked out that strange cry at once, whenever it recurred, from the wail of the wind.

They stared round them in bewilderment.

In the massive sides of the cavern there were innumerable fissures ; a day and a night would not have sufficed to explore them all. But it was inconceivable that anyone could have penetrated into one of the narrow fissures and remained there. Why should he have done so ?

" This is jolly well getting on my nerves," grunted Johnny Bull. " Blessed if I don't begin to believe that it's the giddy old smuggler haunting the caves, just as the fishermen say."

" The hauntfulness is not terrific," said Hurree Singh, with a shake of his dusky head.

" Listen ! "

" Oh, come on ! " exclaimed Wharton. " I'm certain of the direction this time—it's over there."

He tramped across the rugged floor of the cave, flashing his light ahead. Before him as he stopped rose the slanting side of the cave, great masses of rough chalk, split by countless cracks. He flashed the light into a dozen fissures one after another.

" Hallo, hallo, hallo ! Look ! "

Bob Cherry gasped out the words. His light glimmered on a dark spot on the chalk at their feet, and he pointed to it with a shaking finger.

" Here he is ! " shouted Harry Wharton suddenly. His torch revealed the bound and gagged figure of a man, lying almost at his feet ! The prisoner mumbled faintly as he saw the juniors, who lost no time in releasing the unfortunate man.

Wharton uttered an exclamation.

"Blood!"

"Good heavens!" stammered Nugent, his teeth chattering.

"What on earth has happened here this afternoon?" exclaimed Wharton. "There's been foul play of some sort."

He bent over the mark on the chalk. It was a bloodstain, as if some wounded man had lain there. And now that their attention was directed to the ground, the juniors found several more spots of dull crimson on the chalk. They cast startled glances into the deep shadows that surrounded them.

Wharton pulled himself together with an effort.

"Somebody's been hurt here, and quite recently," he said. "We've got to find him. There! Listen!"

The feeble, anguished cry came again, and it seemed to the bewildered juniors that it came from the solid chalk side of the cavern, where no opening was to be seen.

But Hurree Jamset Ram Singh gave a sudden shout. The keen eyes of the nabob had detected what had so far escaped the juniors' eyes.

"Look, my esteemed chums! There is a fissure here; it has been blocked up!" he exclaimed.

"Great pip!"

"Oh, so that's it!" exclaimed Wharton.

The Famous Five gathered close to the spot, throwing the light upon it, and examining it keenly. There was a cavity in the chalk, and the mouth of the opening had been blocked up. Boulders and fragments of chalky rock had been stacked in, so carefully that scarcely a rift was left, and the block looked like a part of the cavern wall.

Wharton drew a deep breath.

"That accounts for it," he said. "Whoever was crying out is blocked in there, shut up in a hollow of the rock. Somebody has been knocked on the head and buried alive in the chalk. What awful villain——"

"Hark!"

The weird cry came again, close at hand now. All the juniors knew now that it came from the recess in the cavern wall, so carefully blocked up by an unknown and ruthless hand.

"We'll jolly soon have him out!" said Bob between his teeth.

"Put your beef into it!"

The juniors set the torches down, with the light gleaming on the chalk wall, and set to work. With busy, eager hands they tore away the masses and rugged fragments that blocked the opening. Many hands made light work, and the barrier was rapidly torn away and the opening of the fissure revealed.

Wharton caught up his torch and plunged through as soon as the opening was large enough to admit him. Then he gave a shout:

"Here he is!"

On the chalk at his feet lay a man bound hand and foot and gagged with a handkerchief fastened across his mouth. His white, drawn face glimmered colourless in the light; his eyes stared wildly at the captain of the remove. Wharton understood now why the unfortunate prisoner of the cave had uttered that wailing cry, instead of shouting for help. The gag in his mouth prevented utterance of words. Only with painful efforts was the hapless man able to utter a sound at all. He could not speak, but he cried out faintly as he saw the schoolboys, and his dilated eyes beseeched them.

Wharton threw himself on his knees beside the bound man, and tore at the cords that fastened him.

THE NINTH CHAPTER

NOT NICE FOR THE SECOND

"I SAY, you fellows!"

It was roll-call at Greyfriars, and Billy Bunter rolled into Hall with the Remove. He blinked over the juniors and noted the absence of five members of the Form.

"I say, you fellows, Wharton's mob haven't come in," said Bunter, with a grin. "They'll be for it."

"Silly asses!" commented Peter Todd. "They've been out of gates all the afternoon. Where have they got to?"

Bunter chuckled.

"Rooting about in the caves at Pegg," he said. "Catch me spending a half-holiday rooting about filthy old caves. I say, Peter, I wonder if they've got cut off by the tide? He, he, he!"

"You fat image!" said Peter. "If they've got cut off by the tide, they're booked for a night in the caves. Is that anything to cackle at?"

"He, he, he!"

Billy Bunter appeared to think that it was something to cackle at, for he cackled unmusically.

"Tide isn't in till after dark to-day," said Redwing. "They won't stay late enough for that."

"Well, it's dark now," said Bunter. "I think it's jolly likely myself. I offered to go with them if they'd take a lunch basket. They refused. Now they'll be sorry I wasn't with them. He, he, he!"

"Silence!" called out Wingate of the Sixth.

Mr. Quelch had entered to take the roll.

Some of the Removites glanced towards the big oaken doors, expecting to see the Famous Five dodge in at the last moment and scuttle to their places in the Remove.

GREYFRIARS RHYMES

FRANK NUGENT

(a member of the Famous Five

MAY Fate befriend you, worthy Frank—
  The finest motives fire you!
Your character is void of "swank,"
  For which we all admire you.
You are a white man to the core,
  True blue and tender-hearted;
And all your chums would miss you sore
  If fortune found you parted.

When Wharton saved Frank Nugent's life
  Frank previously had licked him;
The cruel current's whirling strife
  Bade fair to claim a victim.
But Harry, though a fiery youth,
  Had pluck excelling passion,
Or Nugent would, in very truth,
  Have died in dreadful fashion.

Right bravely Wharton saved his foe—
  He was a splendid swimmer.
When Nugent thanked him, he did show
  Of gladness not a glimmer.
But Franky praised him all the same,
  Until the wrongs were righted;
And very soon, in friendship's name,
  The pair became united.

Frank's deep affection made him glad
  To serve his gallant leader;
And now he is the favourite lad
  Of many a "H.A." reader.
He figures in the Famous Five—
  A hero without question;
And keeps that brilliant band alive,
  With every bright suggestion.

In every wheeze he takes a part,
  At feeds you'll find him munching;
And Highcliffe cads have learned to smart
  By reason of his punching.
When in girl's garb he joined a ball,
  To Smith he did his grief take;
The Bounder was not pleased at all—
  His eye required a beefsteak!

In course of time poor Franky found
  His name was in bad odour;
And all the fellows on him frowned,
  From Vernon-Smith to Loder.
The rumour that he haunted pubs
  Was viewed with keen revulsion;
With Smithy, Frank had several rubs,
  And then received expulsion.

But Truth soon lifted up her head,
  And Smith's deserts weren't pleasant;
But let the dead past hide its dead—
  We'll think about the present.
The Bounder always was a worm—
  A bugbear to the nation;
But Nugent, till his final term,
  Will win our approbation!

But they did not appear, and Mr. Quelch began to take the roll.

Mr. Quelch's frown was quite formidable when he had finished. No fewer than five absentees had to be marked, and they were all members of his own Form. The Remove master's expression hinted that William George Bunter's surmise was well-founded, that the five culprits were "for it."

Mr. Quelch was not in a good temper. He was deeply annoyed by five members of his Form being absent from calling-over. Such a matter seemed a trifle light as air to the Remove fellows; but that was only one of the many matters upon which they did not see eye to eye with their Form-master. But that was not all. The new master of the Second had a severe headache after his train journey—at all events, so he declared—and the Head had asked Mr. Quelch to take the Second in prep that evening.

The Head had asked him very courteously, but a request from the Head was equivalent to a command. Mr. Quelch was not unwilling to oblige a colleague, especially on his first day at the school. But he had had enough of the Second Form for one day—too much, in fact.

Mr. Quelch was fed-up with the Second, though certainly he would not have expressed his feelings in those words.

Certainly the Second Form would have let him off the duty gladly, if they had known. Unfortunately, that did not rest with the Second Form.

Towards seven o'clock there were cheery faces in the Second Form-room, the happy fags being quite unconscious so far of their impending fate.

The rumour had spread that Mr. Sutcliffe had a bad headache after his journey, and that he was lying down on the sofa in the study. Dicky Nugent & Co. were not, perhaps, unsympathetic towards a gentleman who was suffering from a bad headache. But they really had no leisure to think about Mr. Sutcliffe, being occupied with thinking about their worthy selves.

If Mr. Sutcliffe was lying down with a bad headache, it looked as if there might be no prep that evening. That prospect was so joyful that the Second Form naturally had no consideration to waste upon their Form-master.

"No prep, very likely!" said Dicky Nugent blissfully. "If his napper's really bad, you know, he won't want us in prep—his first night here, too. Looks like a good thing for us."

"We don't mind if Walker takes us," grinned Gatty. "Walker will let us do as we like, so long as we don't make row enough to interrupt his reading."

"May be no prep at all."

"Hurrah!"

The Form-room door opened.

"Why—what!" ejaculated Dicky Nugent.

The grim face and lean, angular figure of Mr. Quelch appeared in the doorway. There was a sudden silence as the Remove master entered. The Second Form blinked at him.

"Take your places," said Mr. Quelch grimly. "Your new Form-master has a headache, my boys, and I am taking you in preparation this evening."

"You, sir?" stuttered Nugent minor.

"I!" said Mr. Quelch, more grimly than before.

And throughout the Second Form the happy satisfaction died out of every face.

THE TENTH CHAPTER

A STARTLING DISCOVERY!

HARRY WHARTON, kneeling beside the bound man in the fissure of the smugglers' cave, did not lose a moment. The man's eyes watched him like those of a wounded animal. From the blackness of despair the unexpected arrival of the Greyfriars juniors had brought the hapless man life and hope, and he seemed overcome. The Co. looked into the fissure over Wharton's shoulders while he released the prisoner. Their faces were pale and tense.

Wharton found it no easy task to release the bound man, and he opened his knife to cut the cords. The prisoner was bound with great care and skill, and whoever had fastened him up had evidently taken a great deal of trouble over the task. He could not move a limb, and the gag had been secured in his mouth by cords winding about his head. By desperate chewing and biting the hapless man had been able to shift it sufficiently to give utterance to feeble cries. Wharton removed the gag first, but the man did not speak; his lips were white and numbed, his teeth chattered. Wharton noticed that he lay on a thick travelling-rug, but the cold in the cavern was intense.

The bonds fell to pieces at last under the sawing of Wharton's pocket-knife, and the man was free. But he did not move.

"Let me help you up," said Wharton softly. "Lend a hand, Bob."

"What-ho!"

The fissure extended back about a dozen feet into the chalk, and it was not more than four feet wide. Blocked up as it had been with fragments of rock, it was as secure a prison as could have been devised. But for the cries of the prisoner, certainly the juniors would never have guessed that he was there; indeed, even while he was crying out, they had passed the spot two or three times unsuspecting. There was little room to move in the confined space, but Wharton and Bob Cherry grasped the man and lifted him to his feet. He gave a shrill cry of pain.

"Cramp," said Bob. "Keep your pecker up, sir. It will pass off when you get moving."

"Lift him out," said Harry.

The man was a good size, fairly tall in build. Johnny Bull lent a hand, and the three juniors lifted him out of the fissure and bore him into the cave. The man's eyes gleamed as he caught sight of the daylight in the far distance down the cave and the gleam of the tumbling sea in the sunset. It was the sight of freedom to him.

Who he was, how he had come to be imprisoned in the cave, the juniors could not even begin to guess. It was an amazing mystery to them so far. The man looked a respectable, middle-aged gentleman, rather tall in build, with a bald spot on his head. His clothes were good, but they were obviously very tight for him—he looked as if he was dressed in the clothes of a man slighter in build than himself. There was a bruise on his head, and on his colourless cheek blood was dried where it had run down from a cut.

The man stirred at last; his breathing became more regular, his face showed a little colour, and he rubbed and chafed his hands to restore the warmth. Several times he tried to speak, but his numbed lips refused to form the words. But he succeeded at last.

"Heaven bless you!" were his first words.

"Thank goodness we came here this afternoon, sir!" said Harry. "Thank goodness we found you!"

"I think you have saved my life. I should have frozen to death if I had remained there the night. And that wretch told me I should remain! He promised to send word where I could be found to-morrow. But—but I should have frozen to death before the morning; I am sure of it!"

He shuddered.

"As soon as you're able to walk, sir, we'll help you along to Pegg," said Bob. "You can get a bed at the Anchor, and a doctor, or a trap to take you home. It's only a mile, and we'll help you."

"Heaven bless you!" said the man again.

There was another long silence, but the hapless man was evidently recovering a little. He pressed his hand to the bruise on his head.

Wharton was thinking it out.

"One of us had better cut in to Pegg and telephone for the doctor from the Anchor," he said. "Dr. Pillbury can get across there in his car by the time we get this gentleman there."

"Good egg!" said Bob.

"I'll go," said Nugent.

And Frank Nugent hurried down to the mouth of the cave and scudded away over sand and shingle towards the fishing village, where the lights were already beginning to gleam out over the bay.

"Thank you for helping me like this," said the rescued man faintly. "You are schoolboys, I suppose?"

"Yes, sir; we belong to Greyfriars."

The man started.

"Greyfriars School?" he exclaimed. "I was going there."

"You were going to Greyfriars!" exclaimed Wharton, in astonishment.

"Yes."

The man was silent again, breathing hard; and the juniors watched him in great surprise. Their interest in the stranger deepened when they learned that he was going to their school.

"I came from London to-day," the man went on, after a long pause. "I should have gone to Courtfield Junction; but owing to that—that villain—I got out at Redclyffe to walk. He represented himself as a Greyfriars master—a falsehood, as I know now." He pressed his hands to his head and groaned. "Fool that I was! He must have been watching me, and entered into conversation with the intention of deceiving me and robbing me!"

"You've been robbed?" asked Bob.

"Everything! Even my clothes and papers, even to my boots and hat. He gave me his own in exchange, the dastard!"

"But why did he change clothes?" exclaimed Wharton, in astonishment. "He's given you a good suit of clothes, though it's rather too small for you."

"I cannot understand that. I cannot understand it at all; for I had little to make this crime worth while—a watch, a pin, a few pounds. It is amazing that he should have committed the crime for so little. We talked in the express; he told me he was a Greyfriars master, and he seemed to know a good deal about the school—and I had no doubts. As I was going to the school I was interested in what he could tell me about the place. He looked a well-dressed and respectable man. He told me there was a short cut from Redclyffe, which people belonging to Greyfriars were in the habit of using instead of going on to Courtfield."

"It's a jolly long cut!" said Bob.

"Thank you for helping me," said the rescued man. "You are schoolboys, I suppose?" "Yes, sir; we belong to Greyfriars." "Greyfriars School!" exclaimed the man. "I was going there. I am the new master, Mr. Sutcliffe!"

"I did not know that. I took him for what he represented himself to be. I got out at Redclyffe to walk to the school with him, leaving my trunk to go on to Courtfield. He said that the short cut lay by the beach, and I was glad enough to see the sea——"

"The awful rotter! The way is on the Pegg road, not in this direction at all," said Johnny Bull.

The man nodded.

"I guessed afterwards, of course, that he was tricking me into a lonely place. But I suspected nothing then; it would never have occurred to me that I was worth deluding and robbing. I had told him in our conversation that I was poor and glad of a temporary post as a master in a school. He knew I had a little—a few things and some books in my bag—a few pounds in my pocket. What man in his senses would risk penal servitude, and perhaps the gallows, for so little? It was not as if he were some desperate tramp; he was well-dressed and looked well-off. I cannot understand it. But when we were passing this cave he told me the legend connected with it, and suggested entering. I preferred to get to the school as soon as possible, so declined; and then, to my amazement, he whipped out a pistol and ordered me into the cave."

"My hat!"

"Even then I supposed it was some ghastly jest. But as I refused to obey he struck me down with the butt of the pistol. I was half-stunned;

he led and dragged me into the cave. Then I knew that I was in desperate hands. He was stronger than I, and he had the pistol; I was at his mercy. He forced me to change clothes. Why, I cannot imagine, for his clothes were more expensive than mine—twice the value at least—and mine did not fit him; they were too large for him. His, as you see, are too small for me. He took even my hat, though it was too large for him, and he had to pad the lining with something to keep it on. Unless he was mad, I cannot understand it. But he was sane enough."

The juniors listened in amazed silence.

"Then he bound me, as you saw—bound me very carefully—and placed the gag in my mouth, and blocked me up in the fissure. I supposed that he was burying me alive. I was frantic with terror, but I could not speak. But he told me that he was simply shutting me up here to keep me safe till he was clear away, and that to-morrow morning he would send word to the headmaster at Greyfriars where I was to be found."

The man shuddered.

"Blessed if it doesn't sound like a lunatic!" said Bob Cherry. "He doesn't seem to have gained much, and he will go to prison for this for years."

"It is inexplicable. From what he said, it appears that he will not be clear away till to-night at least; and now I am free I can set the police on his track. He must be still in the vicinity."

Johnny Bull uttered an exclamation.

"It's the man! The man we saw in——"

"What?"

"The man with clothes too large for him, and a hat too large, that blew off! Look here, sir, what's your name?"

"John Sutcliffe."

Bob Cherry gave a shout of amazement.

"Mr. Sutcliffe! The new master of the Second at Greyfriars?"

"Yes."

"Great Scott!"

THE ELEVENTH CHAPTER

LIGHT AT LAST!

HARRY WHARTON AND CO. stared blankly at the man they had rescued.

The discovery was simply amazing.

Bob Cherry made a dive for the hat he had been carrying, and which he had dropped and forgotten. He picked it up and brought it to the man sitting on that chalk boulder.

"Is this yours?"

Mr. Sutcliffe took it and stared at it.

"Yes; that is my hat. My name is written in it."

"Then we've seen the man!" shouted Bob.

"I knew he was a bad egg!" said Johnny Bull sententiously. "I told you fellows so."

Wharton's eyes blazed with excitement.

"We know the man by sight. We know the way he went," he exclaimed. "We can jolly well put the police after him. The man who was wearing your hat was the man who shut you up here, that's certain."

"You—you saw him?"

Wharton explained. The new master of the Second nodded when he had finished.

"That's the man, undoubtedly," he said. "He must have passed you going up the cliff path after leaving me here. A man with strongly-marked features and very sharp eyes, rather close together——"

"That's the man," said Bob. "His clobber was too large for him, and his hat blew off on the cliff for the same reason. The bobbies will know the sort of man to look for with so many witnesses to describe him."

"But what he did it for is a giddy mystery," said Johnny Bull. "He must have had some reason, but I'm blessed if I can get on to it."

Mr. Sutcliffe shook his head.

"I can't understand it," he said. "The exchange of clothes was to his disadvantage; the rug he left with me was worth more than the money he took. He has gained nothing, or next to nothing, yet if I had died in the cave of cold it would have been a hanging matter. But I think I can move now, my dear boys, if you will help me."

"What-ho!"

Mr. Sutcliffe rose feebly to his feet. Harry Wharton took one of his arms, Bob the other. Most of his weight fell on them as they led him from the cave, but the juniors were strong and sturdy. It was high time to be moving, for the winter dusk was thickening, and the tide was coming in.

Out of the gloomy cave the juniors tramped away over the sand and shingle towards the glimmering lights of Pegg.

The unfortunate master dragged more and more heavily on the juniors. At last the four of them lifted him bodily and carried him along. Even with four strong pairs of arms to bear the burden it was no easy task getting him to the village. As they came in sight of the Anchor Inn Frank Nugent came running to meet them.

"All serene!" he exclaimed. "There's a room and a bed got ready. I've phoned to the doctor, and he's coming over in his car as quick as he can. He will be here by the time we get the chap to his room."

"Good!"

A curious crowd at the Anchor surveyed the juniors and the injured man as Mr. Sutcliffe was carried in. He was taken up and placed on a bed, and by that time the doctor's car was heard in the cobbly street. Dr. Pillbury came up, and Harry Wharton & Co. explained to him, and willingly enough handed Mr. Sutcliffe over to the medical gentleman's care.

"Leave him to me," said Dr. Pillbury. "I will give him a lift to Greyfriars in my car when I've attended to him, and I will speak to the police. You boys had better get back to school."

"I was thinking so, sir," said Wharton, with a smile. "They will be wondering what on earth's become of us."

And a few minutes later the trap from the Anchor was bowling away by the shadowy lanes, with the Famous Five in it, and it soon reached Greyfriars.

Harry Wharton & Co. walked across to the House, feeling quite cheery. They had reason to be pleased with their exploits that afternoon, and there was no doubt that Mr. Quelch would excuse them for missing call-over when they explained what had happened. Only, as Bob remarked, they would have to be sure to start in with the explanation before Quelchy started in with the cane.

"I say, you fellows——"

"Hallo, hallo, hallo!"

Bob Cherry greeted the Owl of the Remove with a cheery smack as Bunter rolled up to meet them in the lighted hall.

"Yow-ow! So you're not drowned?" exclaimed Bunter.

"Not quite," said Bob. "Do we look drowned?"

"The drownfulness is not terrific, my esteemed idiotic Bunter."

"Bunter was going to bag your study if you were drowned," explained Peter Todd.

"Oh, my hat! Why, you fat villain!" exclaimed Nugent.

"Ha, ha, ha!"

"But where on earth have you been?" asked Peter. "Quelchy's got his rag out."

"That's all right. Quelchy is going to smile sweetly when we tell him the stunt," said Bob cheerily. "Come on, you chaps, and get it over."

And Bob started for the Remove master's study.

"Quelchy's not there!" called out Peter. "He's taking the Second in prep. The new master's lying down with a giddy headache."

Harry Wharton & Co. stopped dead.

"The — the what?" stuttered Wharton. "What did you say, Peter?"

"Quelchy's taking the Second——"

"I don't mean that. You said——"

"The new master's lying down with a headache," said Peter in wonder. "Why shouldn't he?"

"What new master?"

"Man named Sutcliffe."

"Man named Sutcliffe!" repeated Bob Cherry faintly. "D-d-d-did you say a man named Sutcliffe?"

"Yes, ass. Haven't you heard that there was a new boss coming to-day for the Second Form?"

"But he hasn't come!"

"He has," said Peter.

"He has come?" repeated Wharton. "What do you mean, Toddy? Are you trying to pull our leg, or what?"

"Blessed if I make you out," said Peter blankly. "Mr. Sutcliffe is in his study now. He's got a headache after his train journey, and Quelchy is taking his Form in prep. What is there surprising in that?"

The Famous Five looked at one another.

Had Peter told them that Pontius Pilate or Julius Cæsar was lying down with a headache in the Second Form-master's study it could not have surprised them more.

"Good heavens!" gasped Wharton.

The discovery was staggering. Like a flood of light, the truth came to the captain of the Remove.

The Famous Five knew now where to look for the man who had robbed Mr. Sutcliffe and blocked him up in the fissure in the smugglers' cave!

They knew where to look for him—in the Second Form-master's study, under the name of the man he had robbed!

"Great pip!" breathed Bob Cherry.

"The great pipfulness is terrific! The esteemed scoundrel is here—at Greyfriars!" ejaculated Hurree Jamset Ram Singh.

"Let's go and see Wingate," said Harry. "We'd better tell him first."

"But what——" exclaimed half a dozen voices.

But the Famous Five did not heed them. They hurried away to Wingate's study, where the captain of Greyfriars listened, with eyes growing wider and wider, to a tale that fairly made him jump.

THE TWELFTH CHAPTER

CATCHING THE CRACKSMAN!

TAP!

The hard-faced man who was known at Greyfriars as Mr. Sutcliffe, the temporary master of the Second, frowned darkly.

He had been smoking a cigarette

"What the——" Gentleman Jim rose quickly to his feet as the prefects, followed by Mr. Quelch and Mr. Prout, and Harry Wharton & Co., entered the study. The cracksman was cornered! "Hold him!" exclaimed Wingate.

before the fire, in a contented and satisfied frame of mind.

So far all had gone well for the schemer. Mr. John Sutcliffe, alias Gentleman Jim, the cracksman, was safely installed at Greyfriars.

Never had Gentleman Jim handled a "job" so easily.

Greyfriars was a "crib" well worth "cracking," in the language of Gentleman Jim. But it was not an easy crib to crack. "Inside information," so important to a gentleman of his peculiar profession, had been hard to come by.

A dozen times the rascal had visited the neighbourhood, staying for two or three days at a time, studying the locality, picking up what information he could, in various disguises. Gentleman Jim knew the country round Greyfriars like a book now. But he had still been at a loss for "inside information." But that day he had resolved to chance it, and then his good luck—Gentleman Jim was generally lucky—had befriended him once more. A chatty and unguarded gentleman in the train——

The cracksman had known at a glance that Mr. Sutcliffe was a schoolmaster. He had known that he was going to Courtfield, the station for Greyfriars. He had surmised that the master might have some connection with Greyfriars School, and he had entered into talk with him with a view to extracting, if possible, some of that " inside information " he so keenly desired. The cool and wary rascal had turned a chatty and unsuspicious gentleman inside out in a few minutes, and then the scheme had come into his head.

A temporary master engaged for a couple of weeks from an agency—utterly unknown at Greyfriars. It was " pie " to Gentleman Jim, as he would have expressed it.

The whole thing had been almost too easy. It had only required nerve, iron nerve, and a grim, relentless determination. Those qualities Gentleman Jim possessed in abundance.

In the Form-master's clothes, with the Form-master's papers and credentials, the bag marked with the Form-master's initials—he was Mr. Sutcliffe, the new master. He had walked by solitary paths to Courtfield, where he had bought a new hat to replace the one that had blown off on the cliff, and taken a taxi to the school from the station.

Only one hitch had occurred—the little scheme of the Second Form fags to meet their new master at the junction.

Dicky Nugent had given the new master a shock of which he never dreamed, when he came to the study with Gatty.

But there had been no trouble. Trouble certainly might have transpired had the man attempted to take the Second Form in prep. Even Sammy Bunter would have discovered that he was no genuine Form-master.

But a severe headache after a long railway journey—that was good enough. That saw the impostor through the first evening. And the next day he was to be gone. He was waiting only for the school to sleep—by two in the morning, at the latest, " Mr. Sutcliffe " would have vanished from Greyfriars School for ever. To save his neck, he would leave a message where his hapless victim was to be found. That lack of " inside information," which had promised to make the cracksman's job difficult and dangerous, mattered nothing now. Installed in the House, unsuspected, the job had become child's play.

So the reflections of Gentleman Jim were very pleasant and agreeable as he smoked his cigarette before the study fire.

But he frowned as the tap came at the door.

The story of a severe headache ought to have kept him clear of visitors. Some fag, perhaps, bothering him again. But he had his part to play, and he called out calmly :

" Come in ! "

The study door opened, and Wingate of the Sixth entered. Gwynne of the Sixth, and Walker, and Mr. Quelch followed him in. Behind them was the stout form of Mr. Prout, and behind Mr. Prout was Gosling and Harry Wharton & Co.

The cracksman rose quickly to his feet.

" What——" he began.

Gentleman Jim was generally very much on his guard. But he was not prepared for the sudden spring with which George Wingate reached him, and he went tumbling over in the grasp of the captain of Greyfriars, almost before he knew what was happening.

The rascal was on his back on the study carpet, with Wingate on him. He knew, then, that the game was up, and desperately strove to get at his revolver. But he had no chance. That sudden attack had been made to prevent him from getting at the revolver, and it was successful.

"Hold him!"

Gwynne and Walker were grasping the rascal; and Wingate's grip was like iron. Mr. Quelch added a tenacious grasp; a moment more, and Mr. Prout and Gosling had hold of the man.

Wingate took charge of the revolver while the cracksman was still struggling frantically but helplessly in the grasp of so many hands.

"There's the revolver," said Wingate. "Lucky those young beggars warned us about it!"

"Let me go!" panted the struggling rascal. "What does this mean? What—what——" He gasped for breath.

"Scoundrel!" said Mr. Quelch icily. "It means that some boys of this school have found your victim, blocked up in the cave at Pegg—that Mr. Sutcliffe is now here, in my study—that the police have been telephoned for, and that you will be handed over to them."

The cracksman spat out an oath.

"And it means that we've got you safe, and you can't use a weapon," said Wingate. "It means that you're going where you belong, you villain—and that's prison!"

"Hear, hear!" chortled Bob Cherry from the passage.

"Secure his hands!" said Mr. Quelch. "Take care; he is a dangerous scoundrel! Make him secure!"

The cracksman still resisted feebly; but his hands were bound together, and then his struggles ceased. Wingate pitched him into the armchair.

He sat there, panting, his eyes glittering like a snake's. And the Greyfriars prefects remained with him, watching and guarding him, till Inspector Grimes arrived from Courtfield with a constable; and in the midst of a buzz of excitement from all Greyfriars he was taken away.

. . . . . .

It was a nine days' wonder at Greyfriars.

The Famous Five, of course, came very prominently into the limelight.

Mr. Sutcliffe was the recipient of much sympathy. He stayed only a few days, cared for in the school hospital; the shock he had received had made him quite unable to take up his duties at the school. The Famous Five saw him off, when he went, very cordially. He had lost his temporary engagement at Greyfriars; but he told them that the Head had kindly insisted that he should be put to no loss in the matter, so that was all right. Everyone, in fact, was content with the way the matter had turned out—excepting the cracksman who was in prison awaiting trial.

But most content of all were the Second Form.

"Sorry for the old bird, of course," said Dicky Nugent to his comrades. "Sorry and all that. But we really didn't want him."

"We didn't!" agreed Gatty. "But now he's gone. so everything in the garden's lovely!"

"So long as we don't give Quelchy an excuse for butting into our Form-room again," said Myers.

And the Second Form were careful to that extent. And until a new master arrived to take the Second, Walker of the Sixth read his novels in the Second Form-room, and Dicky Nugent & Co. had the time of their lives.

THE END

Harry Wharton's Picnic!

By **BOB CHERRY**

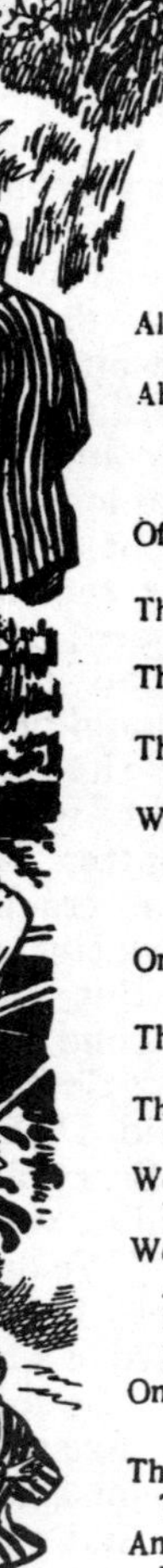

Bunter's eyes are glistening
  With thoughts of grub galore!
And Bunter's ears are listening
  Outside our study door!
Already he is pondering
  On methods that are dark;
Already he is wondering
  If he will taste the quality,
  And join the gay frivolity,
  The cheerfulness and jollity
Of Harry Wharton's picnic on the Sark.

Though we have not invited him,
  He joins us all the same;
The picnic has delighted him,
  He wants to share the game.
The sun is shining brilliantly
  In welcome to our barque;
We ply the oars resiliently
  And start with careless revelry,
  With gay, light-hearted devilry,
  With sprightliness and chivalry
On Harry Wharton's picnic on the Sark.

The little waves are glittering
  In answer to the breeze,
The birds are gaily twittering
  Their music in the trees,
We find a spot convenient
  Within old Popper's park.
We know he won't be lenient,
  And if he comes up presently,
  He'll look at us unpleasantly,
  His wrath will fall incessantly
On Harry Wharton's picnic on the Sark.

The sausages are spluttering,
  The kettle is in song,
And Billy Bunter's muttering—
  When Popper comes along!
He looks at us disdainfully,
  And we regret our lark,
He wields a dog-whip painfully
  And sets about us viciously,
  So we retire judiciously;
  Thus ends, but not deliciously,
Our first unhappy picnic on the Sark.

THE FIRST CHAPTER

ALL OUT!

Down the centre of the broad French highway roared the car, held unerringly to the crown of the road despite its leaping speed. Little wisps of morning mist dancing in the sunlight were slashed to shreds by the racer's spinning wheels, losing themselves in the blurred slipstream of disturbed air, dust, and grit streaking out behind.

By CLIFFORD CAMERON

A great yarn of motor-racing, in which an affair of honour is fought out to a finish in a death-defying duel of speed!

Settling himself more comfortably in the cockpit, Roy Grant tilted his head a trifle sideways and peered past the insect-starred windshield at the road ahead, the mask of caked dust and oil-spume on his face splitting in an exultant grin as he watched the tall poplar trees lining the highway streaking towards him at terrific speed.

The dust that had mingled with the engine-blown oil on Roy's face could no more hide the youthfulness of his features than it could conceal the rakish speed-born lines of the car he was driving. That dust had been picked up in four-and-twenty laps of the eight miles circuit of the Grand Prix de l'Ouest, the great French road-race, and Roy had one more lap to go before his day's practice over the course should be completed.

He shrugged down in his seat as the sudden determination came to him to make this last lap the fastest he had ever done, and his right foot pressed just a little harder on the throttle pedal. His revolution counter told him that he was now travelling at 125 m.p.h.

With a quick movement he pulled his soiled goggles off his eyes, squinting through half-closed lids as a gale of air swept suddenly into his unprotected pupils. Then he reached for a clean pair of goggles dangling loose around his neck, snapped them into place on his head, and tensed ready for a bend in the road ahead.

From windows set high in the white-washed walls of a little cluster of cottages flanking that bend, swarthy French peasants watched Roy's car hurtling towards them. He stormed up to the turn faster than anything they had ever seen before, then his foot shifted crisply from the accelerator pedal and stamped the brake.

Tortured fabric screamed in the car's brake-shoes, and the madly spinning tyres danced in torment on the road. As if grabbed by a giant's hand, the racer slowed, and Roy's left hand dropped like lightning from the steering-wheel to the gear-lever, changing into second with faultless precision. Next instant he was in the heart of the bend, and putting all his strength into his arms as he forced the car round.

The peasants at the high cottage windows shrank back instinctively as they watched the car skid for a split second. They had just a fleeting vision of the racer's tail wagging, then the machine was through the bend, and the raucous bellow of its exhaust was slamming back from the cottage walls. " How he drives, ce fou Anglais ! " those peasants muttered, looking into one another's startled faces.

Where the houses flanking the bend fell away, Roy changed up into top gear, flogging his machine to its limit as the road opened up dead straight in front. And so he drove on, putting everything he knew into handling the car, taking straights and bends at limit speed until a line of small, open-fronted replenishment pits alongside the road showed before him.

Little clusters of men, busy around rakish racing cars standing in front of these pits, turned to watch Roy's car as it stormed up to them, and there were some who snapped the triggers of stop-watches as he went by. Roy passed them all, still at top speed, but a hundred yards down the road he slowed the car and drove sedately back to a pit flaunting a banner marked " Titan Motor Co."

As he stopped the racer and switched off the engine, a stocky man in tweeds jumped over the pit-counter to meet him. It was old Dave Blair, racing manager for Titan cars, which was the make Roy was driving.

Dave had the reputation of being the most taciturn man in the motor-racing game, but just now his gnarled face was beaming, and he was babbling congratulations as he helped Roy from his driving seat.

" Five minutes fifty-four seconds for that last lap ! Over eighty miles an hour, and the record's only seventy-eight ! Great, son, great ! " He patted a beefy fist into Roy's back, then went on : " How's she goin' ? Everything O.K. ? "

Before Roy could answer, the excited Dave had left his side and was running an experienced eye over the dials on the instrument board of the car, feeling the heat of the tyres, and giving instructions to the mechanics under his charge.

Helping himself to a cooling draught of lemonade from a jug on the pit-counter, Roy watched the enthusiastic old man with good-natured amusement.

" She's going great guns, Dave," he said. " And if I can make her last out during the race on Saturday I shall fancy my chance of winning."

" Fancy your chance ! " Dave Blair wheeled at the words. " Listen, son, if you can go on Saturday like you've been goin' this mornin', you've got the race in your pocket."

"I'm inclined to agree with you, Mr. Blair."

The remark, quietly spoken by someone standing just behind Roy's back, made the youngster's attempt to gulp a mouthful of lemonade end in a splutter. It was the first intimation Roy had had that someone was behind him, and he almost jumped with surprise. Turning, he found himself face to face with a tall, swarthy figure dressed in spotless white racing overalls, and his startled gaze met two cold eyes staring amusedly into his own. He recognised the man as Count Séliman, chief driver of the French team of Voileau cars, and probably his most serious rival in the forthcoming Grand Prix de l'Ouest.

"Congratulations, Grant," the count said in perfect English. "A very fine run of yours this morning. Five minutes fifty-four seconds for that last lap, wasn't it?"

For a moment Roy was too surprised to speak. Then:

"Tha—thanks," he stammered. "Er—very good of you, count, though I'm sure you could do better with the car."

Séliman's smile grew.

"Kind of you to say so. Of course, in a race, perhaps—extra experience, and that sort of thing. You're only a beginner, aren't you? That makes a difference in an actual race. All the same, yours was a very creditable performance for the practice. It'll be interesting to see how near you get to me on Saturday, won't it?"

For a moment the man's cool assurance took Roy's breath away, and he was wondering if he had heard aright. Then the full meaning of the count's last remark sunk home. The man was so cocksure that he was going to win that he imagined Roy's only interest in the race would be seeing how near he would be behind Séliman's Voileau at the finish of the event!

Old Dave Blair was the first to break the awkward silence.

"Maybe it'll be just as interesting to see how near you get to Grant's Titan!" he grunted. Then: "Come on, Roy, let's get the car away"—and he deliberately turned his back on the French crack.

The smile vanished from Count Séliman's face and a hard glint came into his eyes. For a moment it looked as if he would reply, then he turned on his heel and strode off in the direction of his own racing camp.

"What did you turn on him like that for?" Roy asked Dave when the count was out of earshot.

"Because he's the most poisonous snake that ever got behind a steering wheel," Dave replied shortly. "I don't know much about him, but what I do ain't pleasant. Besides, look at that ugly mug of his, and the nasty way he has of creeping up so quiet nobody can hear him coming. Didn't you notice he did it just now? Him and his 'interesting to see how near you get to me'! Huh!" Old Dave's face was a picture of disgust.

"If half the tales I've heard about Séliman are true," Blair went on, "he ought to have been warned off every race-track in Europe. They say he killed Varazzio, the Italian, at Monza through deliberately skidding a car in front of him so that Varazzio had to charge off the track to miss him. And I've heard he was behind that car-nobbling at Monaco, when the Gordon team had to withdraw at the last minute because someone filled their oil-sumps with emery powder the night before the race. Then there was——"

A sudden uproar from the Voileau camp made him break off what he was saying, and both he and Roy turned to see what the disturbance was about. What they saw made them clench their fists with rage.

A tall man in white overalls, easily recognisable as Count Séliman, was gripping an elderly mechanic by the collar of his overalls and punching the man unmercifully in the face. High above the mechanic's yells of terror and pain came bursts of execration from the count, speaking rapidly in French, abusing the mechanic for some mistake in his work on the count's car.

Before the watching Englishmen's eyes, the count drove home a final blow that left the mechanic unconscious and limp in his grasp, and the enraged driver flung the man from him like a sack. The mechanic lay still where he had fallen, while his comrades stood round helplessly.

Just for a minute, Roy was too astounded to act. Then, galvanised to action by the count lunging a kick at the prostrate figure on the ground, he began to run forward, shaking off a restraining arm Dave laid on his shoulder.

In a few strides he was beside the count, had grabbed his arm and whirled him round so that they both stood face to face.

" Leave him alone, you cad ! " Roy said, in an ominously quiet voice, " or I'll——"

He broke off to escape a wild blow the count aimed at him—and what happened then was so swift that it left the onlookers dazed ! One minute the count was on his feet and aiming a punch at Roy's face, the next he was lying on the ground with a bewildered expression on his face, where a white weal was blushing a sudden red.

There was dead silence, while nobody moved. Then the count spoke, and his words came from between clenched teeth.

" You'll pay for this, Grant ! If you think you can strike the Count Séliman without paying for it, you must be taught your mistake. My seconds will call on you to-morrow." He started to rise to his feet, and some of his mechanics rushed to assist him. He brushed them aside. " Out of my way, idiots ! " he snarled. " Get on with your work—and take this pig on the floor out of my sight. As for you, Grant, you will hear more of this from my seconds." And he clicked his heels together in a stiff little bow.

Roy felt a touch on his shoulder, and turned to find Blair at his side.

" Come away, son," the old man said. " We don't want any trouble from the gendarmes, and Séliman seems to have had enough for one day."

Roy allowed himself to be led away, glaring back at the count with undisguised disgust.

THE SECOND CHAPTER

CHALLENGED !

BACK at the Titan pit, where they were watched by many curious eyes, Roy found his voice.

" Sorry, Dave, but you'd have done the same if I hadn't got there first. Someone had to, didn't they ? "

" Of course," Dave grunted, patting the boy's shoulder reassuringly, " but what was Séliman saying about ' hearing from his seconds ' when I arrived?"

Roy told him, word for word, all that Séliman had said. When he had finished, the old man's face was grave, and he gave a low whistle.

" You know what that means, don't you, son? He's going to challenge you to a duel! The dirty, murdering crook! It's said he has killed two men in duels already, and I suppose he wants to add you to the list for the sake of ' his honour '—such as it is!"

" A duel!" Roy echoed. " My hat! Does he mean it? Why, I've never handled a sword or revolver in my life!"

" Don't worry, boy," Dave reassured him. " He'll probably think better of challenging you when he cools down a bit. It wouldn't do any good to what little reputation he's got left if it got round that he's been issuing challenges to duelling novices. Besides, duelling is illegal, even in France, and though the police can't always interfere early enough to stop the fights, they'd mighty soon give us protection from a man like Séliman."

" Anyhow, let's forget it. We've got plenty of work to do on the car, and I'm feeling hungry, too."

And so the matter was dropped—until later.

. . . . .

By the time Dave and Roy were having dinner that night in the private room of the hotel where they had made their quarters, the subject of the duel had been practically forgotten in the interest of preparing the Titan which Roy was to drive in the big race.

But just as Dave was pouring out coffee to round off the meal, two strangers were announced by a white-faced, excited waiter, who explained that the callers would neither give their names nor state their business. After a hurried consultation, Dave advised Roy to invite the strangers in.

The men whom the waiter ushered in were Frenchmen in immaculate evening dress, and one of them, who appeared to be spokesman, made the necessary introductions.

" Monsieur Grant," he said, addressing Roy, " allow me to introduce Monsieur le Marquis de St. Alaire, while I am Le Duc de Gavine. We are friends of Monsieur le Comte

What happened to Count Séliman was so swift that it left the onlookers dazed. One minute the count was on his feet and aiming a blow at Roy's face, the next he was lying on the ground, bewildered. " You'll pay for that blow, Grant! " said the count between clenched teeth.

Séliman; you will understand, of course, why we have called?"

"I can't say I do," Roy replied. "Please sit down and tell me your business." And he proffered chairs. His face was a picture of surprise when the Frenchman haughtily waved the seats aside.

"Monsieur," the spokesman of the callers said, "we are the count's seconds. He has asked us to explain to you that he requires satisfaction for the insult you gave him on the race-course this morning. By the laws of duelling, you, as the challenged person, have the right to choose the site and the weapons. The latter I will leave entirely to you, but as you are a stranger here, may I suggest the Panchères Wood, which is quite near here, as the best meeting-place? And, say, dawn to-morrow as the best time?"

The explanation of the strangers' call was so unexpected that Roy could not reply for a moment. Then he heard Dave Blair speak.

"Gentlemen," the old man said, "I am afraid you are wasting your time. If Count Séliman has a quarrel with young Mr. Grant here, I am sure Mr. Grant will be pleased to fight him in a decent way any time the count wishes. But it'll be with fists, and not with swords or pistols!"

The Frenchman gave no sign that they had heard Dave. Both continued to favour Roy with a haughty stare, until, finally, the Duke of Gavine remarked:

"We are still waiting for your answer, monsieur!"

"You've had it!" Roy replied hotly. "If Séliman wants to fight, I'll take him on any time, with or without gloves. I know nothing about duelling, and the count knows it."

"The count has thought of that," the Duke answered, and a thin smile played at the corners of his lips. "He therefore has requested us to suggest—although, of course, it is an irregularity—that the duel should be fought with racing cars."

"Racing cars?" Roy could not keep the amazement he felt out of his tones.

"Exactly! Shall we say three laps of the Grand Prix de l'Ouest course, yourself and the count to start together, and the object of the race to see which of the two of you can crash the other off the road!

"Come, now, what do you say? I must warn you, of course, that a refusal on your part must be accepted as a sign of cowardice, and that the count will not allow it to go unknown that you have refused to give him satisfaction after insulting him. He will publish——"

"Who cares what he publishes?" Dave Blair had risen to his feet, and was standing up to the Frenchman in a towering rage. "Get out of here, you idiots; we haven't time for your silly challenges and sillier talk. Get out!"

"One moment, Dave!" Roy, too, had risen, and now he was very grave and quiet. He addressed the Frenchmen: "Gentlemen, you may take back word to the count that I accept his challenge, and that we will fight our duel in racing cars. We will meet at five-thirty to-morrow morning at the pits on the course. Good-night."

Not another word was spoken as, to Dave's utter astonishment, Roy held open the door for the Frenchmen, acknowledged their stiff little bows, and then closed the door again after them.

"You crazy kid!" was all Dave could say when at last he found his voice.

. . . . . .

" Get out of here ! " exclaimed Dave Blair to the count's seconds. " We haven't time for your silly challenges and sillier talk. Get out ! " " One moment, Dave ! " said Roy. " Gentlemen, you may tell the count that I accept his challenge—the duel to be fought out in racing cars ! "

Dawn was just breaking when the shrill clamour of a bedside alarm-clock woke Roy next morning. With a sleepy grunt he turned on his side and switched off the bell, and then was suddenly and instantly wide-awake as he realised the full significance of the early call. Within an hour or two he was to pit his skill and daring against Count Séliman in a duel to the death with racing cars !

It seemed that last night's happenings must have been only a nightmare —until he realised the grim reality of it all. He remembered the long argument he had had with Dave after the count's seconds had gone ; how the old man had tried by every possible argument to dissuade him from the speed duel, only to be won over at last by Roy explaining that a refusal to meet the count would be accepted by Séliman as a sign of cowardice.

" After all," Roy had said, " the firm can't have any objection. I'll use my own Titan—it's only just been tuned up, and it's nearly as fast as the car I'm driving on Saturday. Of course, the firm would kick up the very dickens of a row if they knew I was driving at all in anything as dangerous as this is going to be, but nobody need ever know the duel was anything but ordinary race practice."

By such arguments Roy had finally won Dave over, though the old man's assent had been very grudgingly given.

As he bathed and dressed, Roy could not prevent a queer sinking feeling coming over him. It wasn't that he was afraid, but this business of fighting a man for his life was something he could not stomach.

Roy was just buckling on a stout body-strap to help brace his muscles against the jarring of the fierce drive in front of him when Dave, fully dressed, burst into the room. The racing manager looked anxious, and his worried expression grew as he saw Roy's body-strap.

"So you're going through with it, boy?" the old man said. "Why don't you drop the idea? I could fix it with the local police to stop the duel, if you don't want to call it off yourself."

"Thanks, Dave, but it's no use." Roy gave the old man's shoulder a reassuring pat. "I've got to go through with this now, but everything's going to be all right, so don't worry. Let's go down to the car."

Not another word was exchanged as they walked out of the hotel and through the deserted streets to the old barn which had been converted into a garage for the Titan cars. There they found two mechanics waiting for them, and through the open door of the barn could be seen Roy's racer, its streamlined bulk hidden under a grey dust-sheet.

Working in silence, the mechanics pulled off the dust-sheet and wheeled the car out into the early morning light. Oil and petrol tanks were filled, tyre pressures tested, and then Roy climbed into the driving seat. He switched on the engine, nodded to the mechanics to show that he was ready, and the two men bunched at the tail of the car, putting their beef behind a lusty shove.

As the car rolled forward Roy let in the clutch. The engine sucked thirstily, coughed once or twice as it half-fired, and then suddenly burst into full-throated song. Roy throttled down and let the machine tick over until the engine should warm up.

"Five o'clock, Dave," said Roy, with a glance at the shock-proof watch on his wrist. "We've only got half an hour."

Blair nodded gloomily.

"I'll go and get the tourer," he replied, and turned into the garage. Presently he emerged at the wheel of a Titan touring car, into which the mechanics climbed after locking the barn doors.

With a sudden roar from his car's exhaust, Roy accelerated forward, Dave following in his tourer, and they drove slowly round the outskirts of the town to the line of pits in front of the grandstands on the Grand Prix de l'Ouest racecourse.

Séliman had already arrived, and was busy with a knot of mechanics on his Voileau. The French car, painted blue in its national racing colour, looked viciously fast. A supercharger bulked at its streamlined nose, half covered by a metal cowling, and the narrow, low-built bodywork raked back to a pointed tail. From its exhaust gouted puffs of blue smoke as the count, seated in the cockpit, revved up the engine in short bursts.

Roy pulled up in front of the Titan pit, and presently two men detached themselves from the little cluster around the Voileau. Roy recognised them as his visitors of the night before—the count's seconds.

"You're on time, m'sieur," the Duke of Gavine said, as he reached the Titan pit. "And are these your seconds?" He indicated Blair and

Anderson and Hewett, the mechanics, with a wave of his hand.

" They are," Roy explained.

" Then let us discuss details, gentlemen. Are you agreed to starting at five-thirty, and that your principal and mine shall race for three laps ? "

Blair and the mechanics nodded dully.

" Good ! " The duke turned to his companion, " That is quite in order, eh, Marquis ? Then let us get back."

He extended a hand to Dave, which the old man took, while St. Alaire did the same with Anderson and Hewett. Roy they both ignored. Then they turned and strode swiftly back to the Voileau pit.

" Well, that's that," muttered Dave. He turned to Roy. " How are you feeling, boy ? "

" Pretty good," Roy lied. Actually he had a queer tightening around his heart, and the sinking sensation in his stomach was growing more pronounced. He pulled himself together with an effort. " I wish it was time to start," he burst out.

He glanced at his watch again. The hands pointed to twenty-five minutes past five. He looked at Dave, and the old man, seeing the youngster's nervous tension, laid a hand on his shoulder.

" Drive slowly up to the starting-line, Roy—it'll help you get a grip on yourself," Blair advised. " Just think of it as the start of the Grand Prix, and you'll be O.K."

Letting in the clutch and engaging bottom gear, Roy felt instantly more self-assured, and the gentle acceleration of his car as he moved off helped drive his unpleasant emotions still farther away.

As he passed the Voileau pit, the count was just moving off, too, but Roy noticed that the Frenchman took care to keep behind him as they ran gently to the starting line marked in white across the course.

The two drivers stopped their cars, with engines running, so that their front wheels just touched the line, and one of the count's mechanics took up his place nearby with a stop-watch in one hand and a little white flag in the other.

Dave and Roy's mechanics, who had followed in the tourer, ranged themselves around the Titan.

" Good luck, Roy," Dave muttered, " and don't take any more risks than you need. Just remember that you're every bit as good a driver as Séliman —and watch out for his dirty tricks."

Roy shook hands with his manager and the two mechanics in turn. Then, at a signal from the man with the starting flag, he settled down in his cockpit, and drew his goggles more comfortably about his eyes.

He could feel a cold, damp clamminess all over his body, and his tongue seemed parched and dry. He was just wondering whether the count was feeling the same sort of uneasy foreboding, when, with a suddenness that he had not expected, the starter's voice cut across his thoughts.

" Ready ? " he heard the man call. Then, in a silence broken only by the muffled drone of the two cars' exhausts, came the counting of the passing seconds : " Ten, nine, eight, seven, six, five, four, three, two, one—GO ! "

Down flashed the white flag.

On the instant, two highly tuned engines burst into their full-throated war-song, tyres howled and scrabbled a little on the road, hands snicked levers through the gears—and the duel was on !

THE THIRD CHAPTER

THE SPEED DUEL !

THE sudden excitement of the start drove all thoughts from Roy's mind save that of getting his car under way without loss of a split second.

From the corner of his eye he could see the Voileau's bonnet come nosing up alongside, all glittering chromium plate and burnished blue enamel. Instinctively, he trod the throttle pedal harder, as if this was the start of a race and he duelling for the lead with a friendly rival.

Whoom-raaaah ! came a bellow from the count's car as its driver snicked into second gear, and zoooomp ! came the Titan's answer as Roy, too, changed gear.

Steadily, the Voileau crept up to the Titan. The count was putting all he knew into his driving, determined to get level with Roy's car before they reached a corner showing down the road ahead. Inch by inch, the Voileau gained. Now it was spinning its speed-blurred wheels at Roy's elbow, now they reached the Titan's louvred bonnet—and then the cars were level, and hurtling down the road wheel to wheel !

Slowly the gap between the racing speedirons narrowed, forcing Roy to pull his car away from the other and to the side of the road. But the more he drew away, the farther the count edged over, until finally the Titan was a bare twelve inches from the grass-fringed edge of the road.

In a flash, Roy realised the purpose of the count's move. The duel was on in earnest, and Séliman was trying to crash the Titan off the road !

Frantically he sought for greater speed, striving to get ahead of the Voileau crowding him off the road. But the count's car was his match for speed, and clung on grimly beside him. For a fleeting second Roy took his eyes off the road to glance at the Voileau's driver. Count Séliman, shrugged down in his seat and with his hands tensed on the steering-wheel, was eyeing him through his goggles, and Roy thought he could see the ghost of a sardonic smile playing around the other's lips.

He turned away. Two hundred yards ahead, the road bent round a knoll of trees in a dangerous corner, and Roy tensed in his seat as he prepared to take the curve. His left foot jabbed the brake sharply, and as if by magic the Voileau shot ahead.

" He'll never get round ! " Roy gasped, amazed at the way the count was storming into the turn. " He's braked too late—— ! "

Next instant he was reaching frantically for his hand-brake, and his left foot was jamming the foot-brake into the floor-boards. In front of him, the Voileau was sliding across the road, the count half risen in his seat as he fought the steering-wheel—and Roy was storming up to his rival at 100 miles an hour !

As he stood hard on his brakes, it flashed across Roy's mind that the count's skid had been deliberately planned. Only a driver of the count's ability could have done it so cleverly ; but Roy also knew that Séliman was far too good a driver to have attempted to take the bend so fast.

The awful screaming of the Titan's tyres sounded high above the warring of the engine as Roy locked the brake-shoes solid with their drums. The steering-wheel shuddered under his hands like a living thing, and he gripped it the tighter as he realised that he could not stop in time to prevent smashing into the back of the sliding Voileau.

With a terrific crash the two cars met, the Titan's nose striking the Voileau's side with a force that lifted the French car clean off the ground, and as Roy fought to keep his own car under control, he saw the Voileau completely overturn.

On either side of the road tall trees were sliding past—there was no escape there. But in the short seconds that had passed since the Voileau's first sign of a skid Roy's brain had been working frantically, and at the very moment when the Titan should have slammed into the Voileau's tail Roy piled all his strength into a great effort to turn the steering-wheel.

Bucking under the strain, the Titan swung broadside-on across the road. It was only by hanging on to the steering-wheel that Roy prevented himself being shot out. The car gave a sickening lurch, then shot forward into the trees at the roadside.

That was Roy's chance—and he took it. Somehow—but exactly how he never knew—he managed to keep enough control over the Titan to head the car between two gaunt trees. He crashed down a young sapling, then shot through the edge of the knoll of trees on to a patch of grass bordering the road beyond the bend. He was just in time to see Count Séliman's Voileau rocket out of the corner and streak away. Séliman was leaning back in his cockpit, a mocking leer on his face as he looked behind to see how his trick had succeeded.

At sight of him something snapped inside Roy's brain. The terrible strain of the past few seconds had taken toll on his keyed-up senses, leaving him momentarily weak and dazed, but now a great wave of rage swept over him, giving him the energy of a madman.

With a single lunging movement he swept the gear-lever of his car into second gear. The engine was still running, for the car had not yet stopped moving, and now, as Roy stamped the throttle wide, the Titan leaped forward across the grass, plunged over the low bank at the roadside, then shot in pursuit of the Voileau.

Roy had gone fey—he was seized by that strange absorption in a single purpose which comes every now and then to a racing driver whose nerves have been overstrained. There was room for only one thought in his mind, and that was to catch Séliman.

Like a howling fury of vengeance the Titan swept in pursuit. A glance at the speedometer told Roy that he was travelling at ninety miles an hour, and still accelerating like a bullet. He caught a glimpse of the Voileau disappearing at half-speed round a bend ahead, then he was storming into the same bend—and without slackening speed!

In a cooler, saner moment he would have thought it impossible to take that corner at such speed. The tyres of his car screamed in protest, and the machine swung giddily sideways. Next moment Roy was through the bend and thundering down on the Voileau.

Above the uproar of his own machine Séliman caught the racket of the oncoming Titan, and shot back a startled glance. Then he was fighting grimly to get his Voileau under full speed, ready for what instinct told him was to be the fight of his life.

But he was too late. Before the Voileau could pick up speed the Titan was alongside, and Séliman had a glimpse of Roy's grim, set face.

Without a glance at his rival, Roy reined in the Titan to keep pace with the Voileau. Then he began to edge closer to the count's car, copying the trick Séliman had taught him. Nearer and nearer he steered his thundering racer, until bare inches separated the spinning hub-caps of the two cars.

They were on a straight stretch of road now, and as the two cars hurtled along it Roy moved over closer and closer to the Voileau. Inch by inch he forced the count to the side of the road, until the Voileau's wheels were brushing the grass banks—at 120 miles an hour!

All the colour had drained from the count's face, leaving it set and white. For the first time in this speed duel he was scared—scared because he knew that here was a new Grant, and that he was going to have to fight this duel out to its bitter end.

Side by side the two cars roared around a gentle curve in the road, the count's brain working furiously to think out a plan of campaign that would leave his rival no chance of an escape. Hurtling beside him, Roy watched and waited, determined to forestall any treacherous move the count should make.

They were now approaching the bend where Roy had so thrilled the peasants at their cottage windows during his practise run the day before, and along the straight road leading to it the count had a chance to make use of his Voileau's greater all-out speed. Slowly the French car drew ahead, and Roy, knowing that his car was already at its limit, had perforce to watch it go.

That Séliman had a very good reason for outstripping the Titan Roy could guess, and he braced himself more firmly in his seat, ready to see what the next move would be. Something warned him that the climax of the duel was at hand, and as the two cars slammed up to the cottage-fringed turn together that climax came.

Prepared as he was, the suddenness of the count's manœuvre all but caught Roy off his guard. Roy glimpsed Séliman shooting a glance back over his shoulder to see how far the Titan was behind, then the Voileau seemed suddenly to come back at him as the count stamped on his brakes.

With a gasp, Roy trod his own brakes, changing gear in the same moment. Immediately the Titan slowed, with a jar that sent Roy lurching forward across his steering-wheel, the blow on his chest knocking nearly all the breath from his body.

From the Titan's tyres came the scream of rubber gripping the road. Brakes whined in their drums, and the engine boomed out like a hound in leash. Still slowing, the Titan stormed up to the back of the Voileau, but the suddenness of the count's manœuvre had prevented Roy braking in time to avoid hitting his rival's car.

Frantically Roy flung his steering wheel to the left, and the Titan's nose came round in response. He felt the tail wag, heard the crunching of metal as the Titan's offside front mudguard struck the tail of the count's car, then he was alongside the Voileau, and skidding half sideways across the road, and missing the cottage walls by inches only.

With a bump that sent the car bounding into the air, one of the Titan's front wheels just touched a wall at the roadside. For a split second Roy thought his machine was turning over, then the Titan fell back with a crash, sending him sprawling sideways in his cockpit.

Above the din of his own car Roy heard the sudden snarl of the Voileau as the count changed gear and accelerated violently to escape from the bounding, lurching Titan beside him. And at the very same moment the Titan, released from the drag of its brakes as Roy's foot slipped from the brake-pedal, shot across the road.

With a crash the two cars met, the Titan's nose striking the Voileau's side with a force that lifted the French car clean off the ground. Roy had the merest glimpse of Séliman rising in his seat, and of the Voileau overturning with a tremendous crash, then bouncing twice before it lay still, a heap of smoking ruin.

All this Roy saw while he still fought to keep his own car under control. The Titan was lurching wildly under him, and as he pulled himself back into his seat with an effort he reached for the hand-brake, tugging on it with all his strength. With a jolt, the Titan came to rest.

Almost before the car was at a standstill Roy had leaped over the side and was running to the wrecked Voileau. The count was lying half out of his cockpit, one side of his overalls spattered with dust from the road, and a raw wound showing on the side of his head. Bending down, Roy placed an ear against Séliman's chest.

At first he could hear nothing but the thumping of his own heart, and the roaring that filled his speed-deafened ears. Then he made out the faint palpitations of the count's blood-stream, and knew that the man was alive.

Working swiftly, Roy stripped off his shirt, tearing it into bandages, which he wound around the ugly gash in the count's head. Then, placing his hands under Séliman's armpits, he dragged the unconscious man to the Titan, setting him beside the driver's seat in the cockpit.

Slipping down beside the count, Roy started up the engine. Then, with one arm around Séliman to hold him upright, he started the long drive back to the pits, in his heart the great hope that he would be able to get the count to medical aid in time to save his life.

. . . .

The Grand Prix de l'Ouest was at its height, and the great crowds of spectators watching the cars hurtle around the eight-miles circuit were delirious with excitement. Only five laps to go, and two cars, a British Titan and a French Bugatti, were fighting out the result on their own, with the rest of the field left miles behind.

At the Titan pit, old Dave Blair was dancing with excitement like a cat on hot bricks. His car, with Roy at the wheel, was one of the two leaders, and he knew that the Titan still had speed in hand!

Every time the Titan and the Bugatti swung past him he watched anxiously for the "All right" signalled by a wave of Roy's mechanic's hand. And when they passed him on the last lap, he signalled back with a yellow board mounted on a wooden pole—the prearranged signal for "all out!"

From the grandstands opposite, another figure signalled, too—a figure swathed in bandages, with legs stretched out on a surgical chair. Dave grinned happily as he saw the bandaged arm raised in salute. It was Count Séliman, willing Roy on to win.

Back into Dave's memory came a scene in a hospital ward—himself, Roy, doctors, nurses, and some of the count's friends grouped around a bed in which lay Séliman. And Séliman had opened his eyes, painfully raised a hand, and said, "Thanks, Grant—I'm sorry." That was all, though Séliman's eyes had said all the rest there was to say.

But now the crowd was roaring anew, and Dave craned forward from his pit counter. Hurtling towards the grandstands and the finishing line was a racing car, and the sun flashing on its paintwork shone on green—the green of Britain's national motor-racing colour!

It was the Titan, winning, and as it thundered by Roy waved a gauntleted hand first to Dave, then to Séliman.

A minute later, Dave was helping Roy and his mechanic from the Titan's narrow cockpit, while Press photographers and officials pressed forward to congratulate the young driver on his success. Someone hung garlands of flowers around the shoulders of the winning car's crew, and a news-reel cameraman thrust a microphone into Roy's hand with a request for him to speak a few words.

With a single gesture Roy waved them all aside, while he turned to Dave.

"Everything all right?" he asked anxiously.

"All right!" echoed Dave joyfully. "Why, you young mug, you've just won the biggest road-race in France in a Titan car and you ask me if it's all right!"

Glowing with enthusiasm, the old racing manager pumped Roy's hand in his own beefy fist. Then he leant forward to whisper something in the boy's ear.

"It's all O.K. about Séliman, if that's what you mean," he said. "The whole affair's hushed up, and nobody knows that it was anything but an ordinary accident that cracked Séliman up You can forget everything except that we've won the Grand Prix de l'Ouest, and now we're going' to have a clean-up in every other big race this year."

Dave was right They did!

THE END

The 'Tec of St Tony's

BY KAYE CAMPSON

The mystery of the missing school cups! How and by whom were they stolen from St. Anthony's School? It is a problem that gets everyone guessing—except Frank Dare, the 'tec of St. Tony's!

THE FIRST CHAPTER

THE STOLEN CUPS !

DOWN on the green cricket-field the click of a willow bat echoed sharply as it struck a leathern ball.

There came the pad of running feet, and a cheer that echoed up the hill like the cry of a flock of sea-gulls, in the hot sunshine of high summer.

From a grey, ivy-clad tower, a bell musically chimed the hour of four o'clock, and a scatter of rooks rose, circling and cawing softly, above the age-old buildings that were grouped about a cool, cloistered lawn.

On the slope of that hill, Frank Dare stirred himself and sat up, turning a length of grass meditatively between his white, even teeth.

He laughed shortly, but there was little mirth in the sound.

Beside him a figure stirred lazily, and one sleepy eye looked out from beneath the shadow of a wide-brimmed straw hat, which was tilted over the lounger's face.

" S'matter ? " asked the sleepy one. " Has Jackson hit a boundary ? You seem about as happy as a tragedy queen this afternoon, Frank. Yet, if I were in your place, I should be dancing for joy. You're leaving St. Tony's. And yet I've got another year to do in this lost and forgotten hole before I go up to Cambridge and really become conscious."

The Hon. Thomas Ethelbert Delaney rose to his feet, and dusted down an immaculately-cut blue jacket and a perfectly-pressed pair of silver-grey flannels, which were famous as the pride and joy of St. Anthony's School.

He was a middle-sized youth, with a round, good-natured face, upon which an aristocratic Grecian nose sat with a faintly comical air.

It was his habit to refer to himself as the " Last of the Delaneys."

He said that his " ancestahs," as he called them, revolved in their graves with astonishing velocity every time he got " swished " by a low-down, common person, such as a mere Housemaster.

But that was the Hon. Tom's

special form of humour. And in all St. Tony's there was not a better loved or more popular fellow.

He suddenly turned towards Frank and his good-natured, faintly comic face was twisted with shyness.

" I—look here," he burst out. " I know all about it, Frank. It's tough, your having to leave because your dad did not leave enough money to keep you at school! Perfectly awful! But I thought perhaps that, since we've been pretty thick together for the last three years, you wouldn't mind—you'd understand—I mean you wouldn't be all proud and ghastly if I——"

With uncertain hands, he pulled a wallet from his pocket.

" For goodness' sake, don't jump on me!" he exclaimed. " But I wrote to my comic old dad about you last week, and he sent—I mean, he asked me to ask you if you'd accept a loan——"

Frank Dare suddenly let out a yell of laughter, and grabbing his dear friend by the waist, thudded him impolitely to the ground.

" You ass!" he said. " You fat-headed, Roman-nosed, good-natured, idiotic goop! If there was anyone in this world I'd accept a loan from, it would be you—or your good old dad. But I'm not asking for loans. I'm going to find a job—can you get that into your thick head? I'm going to *work* for my living. I'm not going to live on other people's money."

He sat on the chest of the last of the Delaneys and bounced up and down.

" And that's that!" he said. " I just can't say thank you, Tommy. But there's no reason for anyone to worry about me at all. Mother's got enough to live on. All I've got to do is to look out for myself."

" Then look—look out for my ribs," gasped the Hon. Tom plaintively. " Get off, you elephant! Why don't you apply for a job in the police—you're hefty and awkward enough. Go and see old Warden Keyes. He's one of our old boys, and he'll probably recommend you for point duty, or something."

Frank Dare rose up, laughing.

" The amount of sense you talk when you're not thinking is just the outcome of not thinking what you're talking about," he said. " Warden Keyes is the greatest detective that ever happened, Tommy. He's marvellous! I've read all about his life, and I'm proud to have gone to the same school as he did! By jove, if that fellow would offer me a job, I'd stand on my head with delight."

" Then, for goodness' sake, ask him!" said the last of the Delaneys, rising and dusting himself down. " You've always been keen on amateur detective work. I still remember that pot of treacle I lost, which you traced to Baggy Porson's study. Dashed smart bit of work, I call that—I mean the good old sleuth, and what not. Dash it all, I'll go up to Warden Keyes myself and tell him all about you!"

As he spoke, both were approaching the big circular tent in which all the school trophies were on view, ready for presentation that evening.

All round the tent a dozen or so fags were standing on guard. Fifty yards away was the Head himself, a bent, silver-haired figure, deep in conversation with a tall, keen-faced man of perhaps half his age.

" There's Keyes," said the last of the Delaneys, starting forward. " Now, my hat, I'm going to do you a bit of good, Frank. Now——"

He was stopped suddenly by two

For a moment the Head stood transfixed as he stared at the cup plinths. "Bless my soul!" he exclaimed. "The cups have gone." It barely seemed possible that the cups could have been stolen when a circle of boys had guarded them! But where were they?

muscular arms which whipped about his waist. Both his feet whirled in the air. And Frank Dare's voice spoke grimly, close to his ear.

"If you don't want to be shot, or bludgeoned, or cut up into little pieces and thrown to the fowls of the air," said Frank, "you'll keep your tongue still! Shut up, Tommy! If you go whooping to Keyes now, you'll spoil all my chances in the future. I'm going to study up this business, and go and see him when I know something about it. So be quiet, will you?"

With a muscular heave, he swung his friend past two grinning fags who were on duty outside the tent doorway.

Inside the warm, stuffy interior of the tent, Frank let the last of the Delaneys go. And then stood grinning and staring round the dim interior.

Almost at once, however, his expression changed. In the centre of the tent were a couple of trestle-tables on which the silver and gold school cups had been piled.

The cups at St. Tony's were famous —and enormously valuable.

But now those trestle tables were empty! There was nothing on them except for the plinths on which the cups had stood.

"Well, well," said the Hon. Thomas, following his companion's look. "It seems that we've arrived too late. Dash it all, the balloon has already ascended. But I didn't think the Head was going to do the presentation until six o'clock this evening. S'funny ——"

"Funny!" echoed Frank.

He glanced all round the tent, and bent a look beneath the tables.

There was nothing there at all. A puzzled frown came over his face, and he darted to the door, swiftly questioning the two fags on duty.

"When were the cups taken out?" he asked. "Where have they been put for the Head to present them?"

Blank astonishment showed in the two youngsters' eyes.

"Taken out, Dare?" gasped one of them. "But they haven't been taken out, Dare! The Head hasn't told us to bring them out yet."

For a moment Frank hesitated, glancing back into that empty tent.

"Don't rag!" he snapped. "Those cups and trophies were taken out a little while ago. Where are they? Look here, who's been in here? Have any of you kids left your posts?"

"Oh, *no*, Dare!" gasped the other boy. "We've been here all the time. Lots of people have been in and out, of course. But the cups haven't been moved——"

His voice broke off in a yell of amazement as he craned aside and glanced into the tent.

His cry caught the attention of the Head, who immediately came across to see what the trouble was. And behind the Head came the tall, well-dressed figure of Warden Keyes.

Frank Dare stood aside in the tent opening.

"I'm sorry, sir," he said, as the Head glanced at him. "But there seems to be some mistake. The school cups have been removed. I don't know if it was by your orders, sir."

"It certainly was not, my dear Dare," said the old man, looking puzzled. "But are you sure? I certainly gave no orders—dear me! Bless my soul!"

For a moment he stood transfixed in the tent opening, staring at the empty tables within. Behind him, Warden Keyes stepped up swiftly and glanced over his shoulder.

"Do you mean that the cups have been removed without your knowledge, sir?" asked Keyes, in a low, vibrant voice. "But I understood that you had a circle of boys on guard."

The Head took off his glasses and polished them on a silk handkerchief. He perched them back on his nose, and assumed quite his grimmest expression.

"I certainly had," he snapped. "But I fear that they must have disregarded my orders. The cups have gone, Keyes. Bless my soul, they have —— Dear me, they've gone! There's nothing in the tent. Here, Smithson—Parker—Jobling. Stand before me. Fetch your comrades. This is serious —most serious indeed."

Messrs. Smithson, Parker and Jobling scuttled in a scared manner around the tent. They fetched the rest of the fag guards, and the whole lot lined up in two rather self-conscious and frightened rows.

Frank Dare and the Hon. Thomas Delaney glanced at each other. The Hon. Thomas raised his eyebrows.

"One of these youngsters is going to catch the seat of his trousers against a cane, dear old boy," he murmured. "Dash it all, the little beggars have been skidding off to buy ice-creams from the tuck-shop. And someone's swiped the trophies."

But it appeared that the last of the Delaneys was far from the truth. The fags swore that they had been on duty all the time without leaving their posts. They backed each other up solidly.

And those at the door were certain that none of the visitors who had entered the tent had come out again carrying anything suspicious.

At the end of the examination, the Head was beginning to get testy and heated. But Warden Keyes stepped forward suddenly and took charge of the situation.

" Excuse me, sir," he said. " Forgive me—but I have had considerable experience of matters such as this. I trust these boys. I do not doubt that they have been in their places all the time."

He shrugged his shoulders.

" The value of that collection of cups was in excess of a thousand pounds," he said coolly. " That would make a good haul for any clever, professional thief. The robbery has been well planned."

His fine eyes half closed, and his clever, lean face set like a rock as he walked into the tent and glanced round.

" But how ? " he murmured. " *How ?* I came in to look at the cups myself half an hour ago. They were all here then. And I haven't been more than twenty yards away from the place ever since. The youngsters have been on duty—I noticed them."

He swung about suddenly and linked his hands behind his back.

" Will you entrust this matter to me, sir ? " he asked the Head.

" My dear Keyes," said the old man. " Of course—of course ! But this is most distressing. Bless my soul, I can hardly believe that it's possible. It seems a miracle ! "

" Spades ! " snapped out Warden Keyes. " Get spades, you two ! "

He gestured towards Frank Dare and Tom Delaney.

" Hurry now ! " he snapped. " No one can have got out of here with the cups. They're somewhere here still, or I'm a Dutchman."

Frank ran, and the last of the Delaneys ran beside him. They went into the hut in which the cricket groundsman's tools were kept.

But here, Frank suddenly stopped with a queer expression on his face.

" You take the spades, Thomas," he said. " You take them. I've got something to do. I've got an idea ! "

And much to the Hon. Thomas' amazement, he ran straight out and made his way towards the big refreshment marquee.

THE SECOND CHAPTER

CAPTURED BY CROOKS !

THE last of the Delaneys perspired. He rested his aching back and regarded Mr. Warden Keyes with a most unfriendly eye.

For half an hour on end, the last of the Delaneys had been digging and turning over turf with a spade. Around him, a crowd of his schoolfellows toiled in the same manner within that canvas circle of the trophy tent.

Warden Keyes moved amongst them and examined the broken ground carefully. He called for greater and greater efforts.

The Hon. Thomas Delaney made no protest, but his expression showed that he thought this occupation both exhausting and rather unnecessary.

Also, he was puzzled at the fact that Frank Dare was nowhere to be seen. Frank had always been such a keen amateur detective. His absence was puzzling.

It would have puzzled the last of the Delaneys a whole lot more if he had been able to follow his friend's movements step by step.

Frank went the round of all the tents that had been erected on the school cricket ground. He left the hubbub which centred around the scene of the robbery altogether.

And for a long time he roamed about the half-deserted cricket-field, deep in thought.

He was so occupied, indeed, that he hardly noticed the fact that the spade workers had finished their task.

Warden Keyes called them off when the whole circle of grass beneath the trophy tent had been turned over.

Meanwhile, the cricket match had been finished. Parents and boys were assembling at the grand-stand for the usual speeches and prize-giving which followed this match at the end of the summer term.

And as they assembled, a lorry drove up with half a dozen workmen, who streamed out across the grounds and asked permission to take the trophy tent down.

Warden Keyes nodded assent. He had questioned quite a hundred people already and had been over every inch of ground that that tent covered. The method of the robbery was still a mystery.

Undoubtedly, the cups had been removed. Undoubtedly there had been a gang amongst the visitors who had managed to spirit those trophies away without the guardian fags noticing anything unusual.

Keyes called the fags together as the tent was being pulled down.

He questioned them without getting much result.

Baffled, he walked amongst the parents and visitors, in the hopes that he might see someone whom he knew to be a suspicious character amongst them.

And as he did so, the tent was let down and folded up.

It was carried to the waiting lorry and loaded on board. But, as that lorry drove away out of the grounds, a figure scorched after it on a bicycle.

It was the figure of Frank Dare. And he pulled up with a quick skid beside the last of the Delaneys, as he passed.

" Tommy," gasped Frank. " Tommy, get your bike ! Come on, follow me as best you can ! I've suddenly seen the whole thing ! I've got the right idea, I believe ! But come on ! "

" Whoa ! " gasped the Hon. Thomas. " Wait a minute ! Look here, Frankie, don't be such a comic, mysterious sleuth. I say, look here ——"

But Frank Dare had gone. His bicycle-tyres fairly whizzed through the dust. And the last of the Delaneys was left staring after him rather in the manner of a stranded codfish.

Frank Dare, however, kept up full speed. Soon the school grounds were left far behind him, and he was following the path of that lorry to the near-by town.

Its greater speed carried it well ahead, of course. But Frank knew the address of the tent contractor, and so he went there without hesitation.

But when he arrived, he found the yard empty.

There was no lorry in there at all, and no one on duty. For a moment, he felt that the trail had come to a dead end. It was hopeless. But then he saw a farmer rattling along in a trap, and he dashed up to stop the man and ask questions.

A minute later, Frank was on his machine again and following the directions he had been given. The lorry had passed the farmer about half a mile ahead.

By questioning again and again, Frank kept to its trail, and finally traced it to a town about ten miles distant. There, he cycled round in a manner that looked somewhat aimless.

But he looked into every yard he passed. And, at last, his search was rewarded when he saw the lorry standing on an empty piece of waste ground, which was flanked by an unoccupied, neglected-looking house.

"Tommy," gasped Frank as he scorched up on his bicycle, "get your bike and follow me as best you can! I've suddenly seen the whole mystery!" And the next moment Dare was speeding after the disappearing lorry.

Frank Dare leant his machine against an outer wall, and ranged round that house like a bloodhound. He listened carefully and thought he heard voices from inside.

Then he found a ground floor window which answered to his pressure.

Silently he lifted it and climbed inside.

Whereupon, a thousand lights seemed to dance before his eyes and he pitched headlong across the floor. A stinging, crushing blow struck him on the back of the head.

And he remembered no more—until he realised that a half circle of grim-looking men were surrounding him.

He tried to start up, but found that he was bound to the chair in which he was sitting.

His head throbbed wildly and he felt sick and ill. Then one of the men spoke in a low, grim voice.

"College kid, boss," he said. "Here's his cap; I found it on the floor. He must have followed."

A man, who was slightly better dressed than the rest, looked at the cap which was held up and nodded coolly.

"Well, this is where he stops following," he snapped. "Tie his mouth up. Have you got the car ready, Lefty?"

A small, rat-faced member of the group, who also suffered from a squint, grinned and nodded.

"O.K., boss," he said. "We've clamped the false sides on the lorry and we've got the stuff neatly boxed up. Ready to go?"

Frank opened his mouth to speak, but before he could do so a cloth was whipped round it and tied behind his neck.

Then the men trooped out of the room, and he was left there to strain wildly at his bonds, and stare up at the small, narrow window, which gave the only light that the place contained.

The room was bare and unfurnished. He realised now that it was not the one by which he had entered.

Obviously, he had been carried inside the house and lodged somewhere above.

Fear gripped at his heart. Tied up and deserted here, he had no chance of making a sound to draw anyone's attention. The house was not occupied.

Weeks might go by—perhaps months, before he was found.

Death by slow starvation faced him. The only person he had spoken to when leaving the cricket ground was Tom Delaney.

And Frank knew that the Hon. Thomas was neither quick in action nor unusually bright when it came to thinking out unusual problems.

He tried to pull himself together and overcome the wild throbbing that beat within his head. He tore and wrenched at his bonds. He jerked about and tried to overturn the chair, with the idea of getting his face close to the floor and rubbing that gag away from his mouth.

But then he found that the chair was tied to a ringbolt in the wall. It would not move more than a few inches.

And the footsteps of the gang sounded fainter and fainter as they went down several flights of stairs within the quiet dark recesses of the house.

But then, suddenly, there came a wild yell and those footsteps echoed in a mad scramble. There was a crash of revolver firing.

THE THIRD CHAPTER

DARE'S DEDUCTION

TWICE and three times a revolver fired and more yells followed.

There was a babble of voices and a crash, as of someone falling against a line of balusters and ripping them out.

Then came a commanding, ringing voice, which Frank recognised with a thrill of relief.

It was the voice of Warden Keyes, snapping out jerky orders as though he were leading a fight.

More crashes echoed up through the dark house, together with a volley of swearing.

There was a last scrambling rush, and a bullet whined through the door of Frank's dark room, flattening itself amidst a shower of plaster against the wall, a foot above his head.

Then two figures rolled in, fighting madly. Frank saw that one was the last of the Delaneys—and that the other was the squint-eyed member of the gang.

A third figure followed and dived upon them like a hawk. In a second that fight was over.

And Warden Keyes, breathing heavily, knelt upon the squint-eyed man's chest, ripping off his own necktie and handing it to the Hon. Thomas with an order to bind the man's hands.

It was only a second later that the last of the Delaneys let out a wild howl as he caught sight of Frank tied up in the shadows.

Ten seconds after that Frank was free, but swaying giddily on uncertain feet as the detective held him up.

" Have you got them—all of them?" he gasped. " And the boxes, Mr. Keyes ? The cups were in the boxes."

The detective stared at him in amazement, but turned aside to yell sharp orders through the door, where policemen could be seen struggling with those of the gang who had not yet been fully brought under control.

And then he turned back to Frank and there was admiration and astonishment in his smile.

" Steady, youngster," he said. " Sit down for a minute and don't talk. You've had a nasty knock. Quiet now, and I'll tell you my part of the story first."

He nodded towards Delaney.

" Your young friend came and told me that you'd scorched off," he said. " So we followed as quickly as possible in my car. We lost your trail completely. And only because young Delaney saw your bicycle propped up here did we realise that you must be inside. Of course, we entered, and we were fortunate enough to meet the gang face to face. I recognised the leader—and he recognised me."

Keyes chuckled shortly.

" These fellows are all the same," he said. " They're too impulsive in a tight corner. I'd nothing to go on.

There was a last scrambling rush on the stairs, then suddenly the door flew open and two figures rolled in, fighting furiously. Frank saw that one was Delaney and the other was the squint-eyed member of the gang. Help was at hand !

I'd not the faintest evidence that you were kidnapped, and I couldn't arrest that fellow because he's only been out from his last stretch of imprisonment for a couple of months, and there was nothing against him. But he pulled a gun directly he saw me."

"And, by jove, Mr. Keyes was wonderful," panted Tom Delaney admiringly. "He dived straight at that gun, Frank. I swear the bullet couldn't have missed his head by an inch. But then he got the fellow down. I sailed in, just to keep the pot boiling, and I yelled fit to bust for the police. Luckily, there was a Robert on duty near by. He started playing tunes on his whistle——"

Warden Keyes laughed shortly.

"Well, well," he said. "All that doesn't matter very much. The great thing is that we've got the gang. But how did you know about them, youngster? What on earth gave you the idea that they'd got the cups? And, above all, how did they *get* them?"

Frank Dare looked up with a faltering smile.

"The cups were in the tent roof, sir," he said. "I didn't realise it until almost too late. I *knew* that those cups couldn't have been taken out. I knew that if you didn't find them buried under the grass, they must be somewhere in the tent. And then it suddenly occurred to me that the trophy tent was the only one which was *lighted* inside. There were small lamps hung over the trestle tables."

A look of genuine admiration came over the detective's face.

"Go on, youngster," he said quietly. "And what did you think the lamps meant?"

"They wouldn't have meant anything, sir," said Frank, "if they had been in *all* the tents. But since they were in only one, it was obvious that that one tent was unusually dark. Now in the ordinary way canvas tents are not dark. The canvas is semi-transparent. It lets in a lot of light."

"I'm beginning to see," said Keyes in a low tone. "By jove, I'm beginning to see. Youngster, that's one of the smartest pieces of deduction I've ever known. I'll frankly admit I didn't think of it. And you mean—"

"I mean," said Frank, "that the tent had a false roof—a double roof. I'll bet it had, sir. One of the gang waited inside until there were no other visitors present. Then, by a special pulley, he let down the false roof and chucked the cups inside it. He pulled it up again—and walked out as innocently as possible."

"Great jumping Jehosophat!" exploded the last of the Delaneys. "Frank, you're a marvel. I see the whole idea. The cups were hung up inside that double roof, and the gang came and pulled down the tent and carried it away, cups and all. My hat, it's that double roof which made the tent dark, so that they had to have lamps inside there."

Frank Dare shrugged his shoulders.

"Oh, well," he said, "that's how I looked at it. I'm afraid I wasn't very bright. The beggars were actually carting the tent away before I'd tumbled to the whole idea."

It was whilst he was speaking, however, that a couple of policemen toiled into the room, carrying between them two or three small packing cases.

Gold and silver glinted within those half-opened boxes.

Keyes patted Frank on the back and nodded the policemen out of the room.

" Well, there's the end of your story, young man," he said. " And a very fine story it is. By jingo, that was as smart a piece of work as I've ever known in all my career. You've got a head on you, my boy. And you oughtn't to go wasting it in some stuffy bank or office when you leave school."

" He's leaving *now*, sir."

The words came from the Hon. Thomas Delaney, who looked rather pink in the face, and whose eyes refused to meet those of the gesturing Frank.

" I don't care," went on the Hon. Thomas. " You can do what you like to me afterwards, Frank, but I'm going to speak up now. Mr. Keyes, Frank's leaving the school to-day because his dad's—his dad's died, and there's no money left. Frank's got to work for his living. The frightful ass wouldn't accept any kind of loan from me, but he's mighty keen on being a jolly old sleuth-hound and what-not. So I thought I'd tell you. I know he'll probably break my neck for doing so, because the silly ass is as shy as a giddy schoolgirl, and——"

" And I certainly will, Tommy," breathed Frank wrathfully. " I'll scrag you when I've got over this headache."

But Mr. Warden Keyes took him gently by the arm.

" This is interesting," he said. " It's so interesting that we'll have a little chat, my young friend. I don't mind admitting that pressure of work has made me wish I had a bright, keen assistant during the last few weeks. I couldn't think of anything better than choosing a fellow from the old school. And I couldn't think of any fellow better than you. Come along now, we'll chat this over, and then I'll go and see the Head."

Gaspingly Frank Dare was led away to chat.

And next morning, when he left the school, amidst a cheering crowd of the fellows who came to see him off, his bags were labelled to a certain address in Baker Street, London.

Curiously enough, Mr. Warden Keyes lived in Baker Street also. And that was the beginning of the famous firm of Keyes and Dare, private investigators, at the mention of whose name every crook in Europe is said to tremble like a leaf.

AN ODE TO AN ORATOR!

by

MONTY LOWTHER

UNDER a spreading chestnut tree
   That fathead Skimpole stands;
The chump—a silly ass is he—
   Has a volume in his hands
About Determinology,
   Which no one understands.

He shouts, as all good speakers do,
   He roars and bangs his fist;
The listeners are looking blue
   And urge him to desist
(A thing not done by any true
   Determinologist).

" This is, my friends, no time for mirth!"
   Shouts Skimpole, blithering.
" A message of tremendous worth
   In simple words I bring.
It's—down with everything on earth;
   Yes, down with everything!"

" Hear, hear!" shouts Digby. " I suppose
   We'd better start with you!"
An egg takes Skimpole on the nose
   And makes him shout " Yarooh!"
The crowd all chuckle, " There he goes!"
   As he drops out of view.

And now a prefect wanders by,
   A frown is on his face;
He gives the crowd his gimlet eye,
   And they fall back a pace.
He says, " If you want thrashing, why,
   You've come to the right place!"

Then Skimpole cries, " I beg to state
   That I shall not obey
Such orders as you may dictate;
   I do not own your sway!
The prefect system's out of date,
   And down with it, I say."

The prefect, with a thoughtful frown,
   Whips out a cane, and—well,
Poor Skimpole startles half the town
   With his terrific yell.
Again the first thing that's put down
   Is Skimpole of the Shell!

A Powerful Story of the Pacific

By JOHN G. BRANDON

The CALL of the SEA!

Young Bill McBride was on a school outing when he saw the sea for the first time . . . . There was one boy who did not return home from that outing . . . . Bill had answered the call of the sea!

THE FIRST CHAPTER
"BLUE-GUM" BILL McBRIDE

"BLUE-GUM" BILL McBRIDE stood upon the South Reef beach at Menada, looking sadly at the *Arawanna* gradually being broken up on the coral reef beneath her by each huge Pacific comber that raced in with a deep boom and a smother of foam upon the reef.

The small port of Menada is perched upon the north-easterly point of the Island of Celebes, one of the outflung posts of the great Dutch East Indies, and it is the seat of the Dutch Administration of the island.

Menada, also, is the jumping-off ground for that horde of tough, sun-baked and hard-fisted adventurers who sail their small craft the length and breadth of the wide, island-dotted Pacific Ocean, carrying copra, *bêche de mer*, shark fins, pearl shell, and any old thing they can pick up to make a living. When there are no real honest cargoes to be picked up, then they carry Mannlicher rifles in piano cases and Chinese coffins, and run them up the Sumatra coast for the rebellious Achins to have another go at their hated Dutch masters with.

These, and a thousand and one odds and ends of contraband, all slipped in and out of Menada, to the anger of the Dutch authorities.

And at the age of nineteen one of the worst offenders in the whole of the Dutch East Indies was that long-legged, red-headed and ham-fisted young Australian known, from his hardness of frame, as "Blue-Gum" Bill McBride.

A Sydney-sider, Bill was born and schooled up in the back-blocks of the Parramatta River, and the less said about the quality of his education the better. Each morning, after he'd milked a dozen cows, he rode fifteen miles in to school from the well-nigh barren patch upon which his stout-hearted Scotch parents were endeavouring to make their living. Schooling over, he rode the fifteen miles back, milked the cows again, then took up a seven-pound axe and gave a hand at dropping blue and red gum trees thirty to forty feet high. At fourteen years old young Bill could fell a gum tree faster than could his father, over whom, even then, he stood a head and a half taller.

But at school Bill was somewhat of a dunce, and all he ever brought home in the shape of medals he wore on his hide, administered by an earnest but irascible old Scotch master who was a sound believer in the old adage: "Spare the rod and spoil the child." Whoever in his school *might* be spoiled, it certainly was not going to be lanky young Bill McBride.

And then, suddenly, came the end of school. A beneficent government brought a host of up-country school children to Sydney for educational purposes. And on that day, for the first time in his life, "Blue-Gum" Bill McBride saw the sea. As he stood staring at it like someone in a trance, he saw, too, something majestically cleaving the blue waters of the harbour. A great tower of gleaming, sun-lit canvas, with her house-flag flying at the main, and from her spanker halliards the Union Jack—a six-thousand-ton, five-masted, full-rigged clipper ship of a famous line. And as she came up into the wind below Goat Island, before letting go both anchors with a rattle, Bill McBride heard the call of the sea.

There was one boy who did not return home from that outing. Before the police could lay hands upon him, Bill McBride was outward-bound from Sydney to Papiete, in Tahiti, upon an ancient, but seemingly imperishable schooner called the "Arawanna."

He was under the command, though he did not know it at the moment of offering his services, of the redoubtable Captain Jim Burston, a relic of the "good old days" of the Pacific. The fiercest-tempered, hardest-fisted old buccaneer who ever sailed the seas.

And so commenced those four years in which Bill McBride, under the ancient buccaneer and contraband-runner, sailed the Pacific from Singapore to the Kermadec Islands. Four years in which he filled out from a long, lanky lad into one of the most powerful men in the Pacific; a man who, put to it, had broken the hearts—and very nearly the necks—of some of the most notorious toughs in the Islands.

Four years of constant danger, of wild, tropic storms, of running the gauntlet into ports where gunboats lurked in wait in every channel, with orders to sink them on sight.

The Dutch authorities' hatred of the old contrabandist was so great that they would have stooped to any depths to see him finish his days in prison—or up against a stone wall. And, great as was their hatred of the old captain who had so long defied them, it was no whit less for the young lieutenant Captain Burston had trained to follow in his footsteps—the most daring young raider in the Dutch East Indies and Malay Archipelago.

As Bill's eye fell on Van Hartog and his merry men walking past the end of the alley, he dived into a doorway and crouched there until they had passed.

And then, up in the Banda Sea it happened. A strangely faint voice from the open skylight one night brought Bill McBride down into the cabin on the run, to find his skipper stretched out upon the settle, his old face strangely grey.

"Bill," the old man said quietly, "I'm making my last port. It's a stroke of some sort. I've lived pretty hard, and I dare say I've earned it."

"I'll run for Sourabaya," Bill said. "There's a doctor there——"

The captain waved the suggestion aside feebly.

"Run nowhere, Bill. Doctors can't do anything for me, I know. All I want to say is that the old tub is yours, boy, and everything on her. Look after her; she's old, but she's good for a long time yet. She's been home and a good bit more to me for nearly forty years; just as you've been a good companion to me in the last four. You're going to make the man I knew you would that first night I clapped eyes on you in Sydney Harbour. I've put some pretty hard things up to you, but you've stood the test every time. I've never known you do a mean or a dirty thing to anyone, and I've never seen you flinch when death's been flying all round us, free for the asking."

He drew a long, quivering breath and Bill could see he was in pain. The captain picked up a small packet that lay by his side.

" I want you to have this, Bill," he said. " That and the old Arawanna and the bit of ready money that's on board are all I've got But I don't want you to ask what's in this packet or even open it until the day comes when you're flat broke and can't see a ray of hope anywhere. Sew it into your clothes and leave it there till then. Promise."

Bill took the packet from the limp fingers and gave his promise. The old eyes, now filming fast, wandered about the cabin, taking farewell of objects that had been his silent companions for years.

" There's one thing I'm proud of," he said suddenly. " I've made a *real* sailorman out of you, Bill. You're not the sort who would stack the old girl up and leave her bones to bleach on some darned coral reef or other."

Again there came a silence, then suddenly the white head turned to him again and Bill saw that there was the ghost of a twinkle in the old, tired eyes.

" Bill," he said, " I was nearly forgetting another last bequest I've got to leave. When you run into Menada again, give that fat hound of a Port-Kommanden—the one who had me locked up in the calaboose—a good kick in the pants for me. What was his name? Van Hartog. Don't forget, boy. Make a job of it."

And Bill, in a choking voice, said that he would not forget.

Another silence, then the old, sunbronzed hand groped for his.

" I'm making—port—Bill. 'Bye—lad! Good—luck."

THE SECOND CHAPTER

BILL BUTTS IN!

There was a mist in the blue eyes of Bill McBride as he stood watching the old Arawanna slowly but surely being broken upon the cruel coral teeth beneath her. With the huge rollers breaking in after the typhoon that had driven her to her fate, it was only a matter of minutes now before she sank.

All that he had in the world would go with her, with the exception of the clothes he stood up in. A sleeveless singlet that showed the knotted muscles of his arms and a pair of ancient duck pants that clung to him like a sheath. And then, as he watched, the bow lifted high, then dived below—for ever. Without a word Bill turned and stumbled through the burning sand into the palm and mangrove belt that fringed the beach. He could not see very well at that moment; there was a blur over his eyes.

Near the front edge of the palm-fringe the sound of voices stopped him. He moved behind the stump of a big coco-palm and waited. For one thing, he could have sworn that he had heard the Arawanna mentioned. Moreover, it had been in that strange mixture of pidgin English that Dutch officialdom almost always uses to address its Sikh police. The mention of the Arawanna was not so good!

Were they already aware that the old schooner was ashore? Were they trying to snap him up on some pretext or other before he could pick up another craft? Instinct warned Bill McBride to lie doggo for a while and watch events.

He saw the police range up and down the beach searching for any sign of flotsam, but Bill knew it was too early for any to show up yet.

And then, in the shade of a big palm, his fat face glistening with perspiration, Blue-Gum Bill saw his worst enemy—Kommanden van Hartog. He was in charge of the search, and Bill knew that if the Dutchman laid hands upon him he would get a rough time. A long term in some stinking Dutch prison or the chain-gang, for a certainty—if they didn't make a quicker end of him than that. It was time to get a move on and find a hide-out.

When darkness fell he'd chance the sharks and swim out to one of the British-owned schooners if there were any in. Not one of them would give him up to the Dutch.

Out of the palm-belt upon the port side he slipped, and raced like a greyhound for the first bit of cover—the junk wharves and buildings of some Chinese trader.

In less than two minutes Bill was lost to sight in and out a dozen yellow-inhabited alleys.

From the end of one of them he got a sight of the small harbour. Lying out in the stream was the Dutch patrol-gunboat Amsterdam, and coming ashore from her in a swift motor-launch were three or four of her officers. No friends of Bill McBride, any of them. For the second time he ducked well out of sight.

The sun was blazing down now upon his bare head ; but for the thick red thatch of hair that covered it he would have stood in danger of being sunstruck. His clothes, such as they were, saturated with hours and hours in sticky salt water, were now dried upon him and stuck to his skin. Gingerly he pulled them from his hide for a bit more freedom. Under his singlet, still upon the bit of lanyard about his neck, he felt old Captain Burston's mysterious packet. It had stuck to him through it all.

" Looks like as if you're going to be opened pretty soon," he said. " If a man can be up against it harder than I am this minute, then he's in a bad state."

He was in the very act of fingering it when his eye fell upon a group of men hurrying past the end of the alley—Van Hartog and his merry men ! Bill dived into an adjacent doorway and crouched there until they had passed.

Slipping out of it again, Bill raced for the jungle fringe. He'd have to take to the inland a bit—till dark, at any rate. Maybe at some plantation bungalow he could get a bit of grub.

Out of the edge of the clearing he came suddenly upon a low, native-built, palm-thatched bungalow. Behind it he could see stretching a well-ordered cocoa plantation. There was someone on the wide veranda, too—a white girl and—yes, a Dutch policeman. The policeman was bawling at the girl, and she was crying. From where Bill was the sound of her convulsive sobbing drifted across to him. What in blazes was this game ?

Blue-Gum Bill didn't know much about girls, but he could see that this one was young and very beautiful, and that she was as good as she was beautiful, he was certain.

That the Dutch policeman—Bill could see that he was sergeant—was bawling questions at her in such English as he could speak, proved that the girl was British. He was questioning her over something, and doing it as brutally as he knew how. Bill's big fists began to clench as hard as a cannon-ball. Something would have to be done about this !

With his natural gift for decisive action the instant he had made up his mind about anything, he *did* that something. From out of the jungle edge came a series of cries that might have come from a person in mortal agony. The sergeant swung round, peering intently at the direction from which the ghastly sounds had come.

A second series brought him across to the jungle-edge and into it.

His hand dived for his pocket when he caught sight of the tattered figure that stepped from behind a tree, cutting off his retreat.

" *Verdammed* Britisher," he growled.

Bill's first upper-cut took him squarely under the chin and, heavy as he was, lifted him nearly a foot from the ground. Then a sweet right-hand swing spun him around like a top, and he dropped flat upon his face—out to the wide world.

In a couple of minutes Bill had stripped him to his shirt, lugged him across and tied him securely to a palm trunk. Then he donned the sergeant's duck uniform and in it went across to the veranda.

The girl's astonishment at this new-comer once over, Bill soon got the story of her trouble from her; one that made him regret that he had not given the sergeant a double dose whilst he was about it. But he was not the *real* villain of the piece, and that person would get *his* if Bill swung for it.

It was a simple, sad story the girl had to tell. The orphaned daughter of a dead planter, suddenly left alone and penniless, she had taken a post as companion to an invalid Dutch woman whose husband was a big friend of Van Hartog. Her employer suddenly succumbing to illness, the girl had had to suffer the unwelcome attentions of Van Hartog. She had tried to leave the place, but her money had been withheld and she had not a penny or a friend in the world. To hold her securely, a charge of theft had been trumped up against her, and she was terrified that Van Hartog would have her thrown into prison.

Bill's big hand patted her upon the shoulder as consolingly as he knew how.

" Don't you worry, little lady," he said. " You've got a friend, all right. I'm not much to look at, but before Bill McBride lets you down somebody is going to get all mucked up ! "

She stared at him in astonishment.

" McBride ! " she gasped. " If you are McBride, the gun-runner, they are hunting for you everywhere. It was known last night that your schooner was in these waters and nearly dismasted. There is a reward of two thousand *guilders* offered for you, alive or dead."

Alive or dead! That didn't sound any too good to Bill.

" Oh, please, go, and save yourself," the girl urged him. " I must get along as best I can."

But Blue-Gum Bill McBride shook his head.

" That's not my way, lady," he said quietly. " When I start anything, I *finish* it."

" But Van Hartog will be here just after sunset," she warned agitatedly. " I heard him tell the sergeant so. He will find you here and——"

" He'll find me here, all right," Bill said grimly. " And when I'm through with him he'll wish he hadn't. Don't you be scared—stand on me. But if you could find me a bite to eat——"

THE THIRD CHAPTER

HARTOG GETS HURT !

It was late afternoon when Bill, fed, and like a giant refreshed, drew that little packet from about his neck and opened it. With this girl in the trouble she was, this seemed to be about the time, if it was ever going to do any good at all, that it began doing it. As he undid the last piece of wrapping, something in cotton wool gleamed up at him—something that made him catch his breath. *It was a huge red pearl!*

Bill knew enough of the stones to know that in his hand was as sure

Bill's upper-cut took the sergeant squarely under the chin and, heavy as he was, lifted him nearly a foot from the ground. Then a right-hand swing spun him round, and he dropped flat upon his face—out to the wide world !

a thousand pounds as though he held it in good bank-notes.

For a long time he sat staring at it while many thoughts raced through his mind. When he got up his jaw was set with the determination of a man who has made up his mind to do something—do it—or bust !

" I'm going down into the port," he told the girl. " Don't worry about me. I'll get through and back, somehow. While I'm gone, pack as many of your clothes as you can get into a bundle that I can carry. Keep the door locked and don't let anyone in until I come." From the pocket of the sergeant's tunic he took a small automatic pistol. " If Van Hartog shows up before I get here, you know what to do. Hold him up with this until I arrive. So long—and don't be scared."

It was nearing dusk when Bill got back. In his pocket were bank-notes for six hundred pounds, all a pearl-buyer would pay him for what was perhaps the finest red pearl in the world. The old shark had rooked him right and left, of course ; Bill knew that. But a man with two thousand *guilders* on his head, dead or alive, hasn't time to stick around bartering. And, anyhow, there was this girl ; she had to be got out that night, somehow or another. And as he had slipped back cautiously from the port, Bill had worked out a plan. It was a bit risky with a young lady on hand, and that gunboat out there ; but, again, beggars can't be choosers.

Waiting in the bungalow for nightfall, Bill came across a bundle of malacca canes standing in a corner. He picked one out and gave it a testing swish. Good little stick ; just the ticket for something he had in view !

It was dark, and Bill was beginning to get a bit restless, when a rickshaw raced up to the front of the bungalow. From the shelter of some curtains he watched Van Hartog lumberingly descend. He looked about him for a moment, then hurried into the house.

A door closed behind him as if by its own volition, and the hard barrel of the sergeant's automatic was rammed suddenly into his fat stomach.

" Come in, *m'neer*," an ice-cold voice greeted him, a voice that made him start and suddenly tremble. " I've been waiting for you."

One grab for his gun Van Hartog made. It was torn out of his hand with a wrench that made him cry out. Down upon his fat carcase descended the malacca cane, every cut like the slash of a sabre. In an iron grip he writhed, trying in vain to bite and kick. Steadily that merciless flail came down upon him until the smart white duck uniform he wore was a tatter of blood-stained rags, its wearer a huddled, moaning mass.

" Now get up ! " Blue-Gum Bill ordered ; and, as well as he could, the stricken Van Hartog lumbered up upon trembling legs.

He was indeed a pitiable-looking object.

" I've got a legacy for you," Bill went on grimly. " One I promised faithfully to see you got. Turn around."

Sobbing, the unhappy Van Hartog did so. Then Blue-Gum Bill took a kick with one of the sergeant's heavy boots that sent Van Hartog flying up against the opposite wall.

" That's from old Captain Jim Burston," he said, " and you may think yourself lucky he didn't leave you a hundred ! You'd have got 'em all—every one ! "

He roped the panting, sobbing Kommanden up to a bed-head, and left him to think things over. Outside the girl was waiting, her bundle beside her. Bill tossed it into the rickshaw and helped her in, then pushed his gun into the rickshaw boy's startled face.

"You get down to the wharf as fast as you can make it," he commanded, "and if you let out one squeak that you've as much as *seen* this lady, or me, next time I come to Menada I'll blow your head right off your shoulders! Savee?"

Bill jumped in and seated himself beside the girl. From inside the room the sound of convulsive sobbing floated out to them. Bill grinned quietly to himself.

"What has happened to him—Van Hartog?" she asked.

"'Me,'" answered Blue-Gum Bill McBride, positively if not grammatically. "I've happened to him, and it hurt!"

Steadily that merciless flail came down upon Van Hartog, writhing in Bill's iron grip, until the white duck uniform he wore was a tatter of rags.

It was upon the pier that the last chapter of Bill's getaway was enacted. A long shadow moved along in the dim wharf lights, followed closely by a shorter one. A policeman was standing on guard by where the fast motor-launch of the gunboat was tied up. Something took the man under the ear, and a moment later he was tied and gagged securely. Bill hid him in an old customs shed where he was certain he would not be found until morning.

Out into the dark water the nose of the motor-boat shot, jumping at once into high speed. Out past the gunboat she belonged to, out to windward of the reef that stretched across the mouth of the little harbour.

"It all hung on the good luck that the patrol had not her searchlight on," he told the girl. "If she had, we'd have had to run it under her quick-firers."

Then Bill stepped on the gas, and the light craft fairly flew from wave-top to wave-top down the Celebes Straits.

It was after a long silence that he turned suddenly to her and pressed a packet into her hand.

"That's yours," he said shortly.

"Mine?" she asked wonderingly.

"Yours. It—er—was all a frame-up, that about your dad not leaving you any money. I—I heard all about it while—while I was down in port this afternoon. A swindling lawyer had got it, and was hanging on to it," he lied valiantly. "But I made him pass it over. Threatened to shoot him if he didn't."

"But——"

"There isn't any 'but,'" he hurried on quickly. "There's only just the money—five hundred pounds in all. That'll see you O.K. for a bit when you get to England. We'll pick up the steamship 'Malaya' sometime about daylight. She'll be making down the Celebes and then up for Singapore. Captain Andy Melrose is a friend of mine; he'll see you're all right for home."

"Home," she echoed.

"England. We colonials always call England 'home.' In a sort of way, it is. Pretty good place, too, I reckon. I'm hoping to see it myself one of these fine days."

. . . .

It was as Bill stood up in his boat waving a farewell hand to a figure at the stern-rail of the fast-retreating Malaya that a year-old and still green and sad memory came into his mind.

"That's what you'd have had me do with the red pearl, skipper," he said softly. "For all your blustering and raving, that's what you'd have done yourself, and without hesitating a minute. And, anyhow," he concluded half-defiantly, "we Britons have got to stick together, and that's a fact!"

BILLY BUNTER'S BOOBY-TRAP!

By FRANK RICHARDS

Revenge on " that beast Quelch " was the motive for Billy Bunter's booby-trap. But not for the first time, Bunter learns that there's many a slip 'twixt cup and lip!

THE FIRST CHAPTER

BEASTLY FOR BUNTER !

"OH, my hat ! " murmured Bob Cherry.

Some of the Remove fellows grinned.

The Remove—the Lower Fourth Form of Greyfriars—were in class. It was a hot afternoon Mr. Quelch, their Form-master, was imparting valuable instruction of an historical nature. But to many of the juniors he seemed to be just droning ! Somehow, their thoughts wandered to the cricket field, or the river, or the shady woods. Some of them were feeling quite drowsy. Lord Mauleverer almost nodded off. Billy Bunter quite nodded off ! Hence the grin that spread from face to face in the Remove.

For the silence, hitherto broken only by the drone of Quelch, was now also disturbed by a rumbling sound—which might have been the mutter of distant thunder ; but was, in fact, the snore of Billy Bunter.

Snore !

When Bunter slept, he snored ! That rumbling sound, familiar in the Remove dormitory, was unfamiliar in the Remove Form-room. So it was not so easily recognised by Mr. Quelch as by his pupils. All the Remove knew that Bunter had nodded off, and was beginning his nasal solo. But Mr. Quelch glanced out at the open window, wondering if that whirring rumble portended a thunderstorm !

Snorrrrrre !

Once started, Bunter was going strong. His fat chin drooped on his podgy chest ; his little round eyes were closed behind his big round spectacles. Slumber's chain had bound him ; and he snored, in happy disregard of Quelch and English History.

" The silly ass ! " murmured Harry Wharton.

"Poke him, somebody!" whispered Frank Nugent.

"The pokefulness is the proper caper!" breathed Hurree Jamset Ram Singh, the dusky junior from India's coral strand. "The esteemed Quelch will be terrifically infuriated."

Johnny Bull, who was nearer to Bunter, made a movement. There was no doubt that Quelch would be wrathy if he discerned a fellow asleep in class. He was far from being aware that his valuable instructions had a soporific effect on his Form. The discovery would not have pleased him a little bit.

"Please do not talk in class!" rapped Mr. Quelch. "Bull! You may sit down."

"Oh! Yes, sir!" stammered Johnny Bull.

"The window had better be closed," said Mr. Quelch. "I think there is going to be a thunderstorm! Wharton, you may close the window."

"Oh! Yes, sir!" gasped Wharton.

He left his place and closed the window.

But the sound that Mr. Quelch had mistaken for the rumble of distant thunder was heard even more distinctly after the window was closed. Bunter, deeper in happy slumber, was putting on steam.

Snorrrrrre! Rumble!

Mr. Quelch closed his book with a snap. He became aware of an epidemic of grinning in the Form. He realised that something was "on." And he realised that that whirring rumble was near at hand. He frowned. He came nearer to his class, and his gimlet-eyes searched over the Form. And then he knew.

"Bunter!" rapped Mr. Quelch.

No reply.

"BUNTER!"

Snore!

"Upon my word!" ejaculated Mr. Quelch. "The boy is asleep—actually asleep! BUNTER!"

Snore!

Mr. Quelch laid down his book. He picked up a pointer. The expression on his face was one that the fabled Gorgon might have envied. Bunter needed waking up! His Form-master was going to wake him.

All eyes were fixed on Mr. Quelch as he came along to Bunter's place, pointer in hand.

"Bunter"

Snore!

Rap!

"Yarooooooh!" roared Billy Bunter, suddenly, as the pointer smote. He woke up then! He woke up quite suddenly!

"Bunter——"

"Ow! Beast!" roared Bunter. "Rotter! Yah! Leave a fellow alone! 'Tain't rising-bell yet!"

"Ha, ha, ha!" yelled the Remove. Billy Bunter, evidently, had awakened under the impression that he was in bed in the dormitory.

"Bunter!" almost shrieked Mr. Quelch. "Silence in the Form! Bunter!"

"Oh, crikey!" The hapless Bunter realised where he was. He rubbed his eyes, set his big spectacles straight on his fat little nose, and blinked at his Form-master. "Oh! I—I—I wasn't asleep, sir!"

"You were not asleep!" gasped Mr. Quelch.

"Oh, no, sir!" groaned Bunter. "I—I may have had my eyes shut! I—I listen better with my eyes shut, sir! I—I heard every word you were saying."

"You were snoring!" hooted Mr. Quelch.

"Oh, no sir! I never snore," stuttered Bunter. "The fellows keep on making out that I snore, sir! But I don't! I—I stayed awake one night, sir, to see whether I did—and I—I didn't!"

"Ha, ha, ha!"

"Silence! Bunter, you were fast asleep, in Form, and you have not heard a single word——"

"Oh, yes, sir—every syllable!" gasped Bunter. "I wouldn't miss a word, sir—I'm so keen on grammar."

"Grammar! This lesson is English History!"

"Oh, lor'! I—I mean history, sir! I—I wonder what made me say gig-gig-grammar! I—I meant to say history, sir! I—I haven't missed one syllable, sir!"

"Indeed!" said Mr. Quelch, in a grinding voice, "then in that case, you will give me the dates!"

"I—I haven't any, sir!"

"Wha-a-t?"

Quelch had been giving important historical dates to his Form. Bunter had missed them, and he was not even aware of the dates to which his Form-master was alluding. His fat thoughts ran on quite another kind of dates. Just before class he had been eating dates. There were still traces of them smeared round his extensive mouth.

"I really haven't, sir!" gasped Bunter. "You—you can search me, sir—I swear I haven't."

"Is this boy out of his senses?" exclaimed Mr. Quelch. "Bunter, give me the dates at once."

"I've eaten them, sir."

"Ha, ha, ha!" shrieked the Remove.

"You—you—you have what—what?" stuttered the Remove master.

"I ate them before I came into class, sir!"

"You ate them!" repeated Mr. Quelch, like a man in a dream.

"Yes, sir! I—I haven't any left! We ain't allowed to bring tuck into class, you know, sir! I finished them before I came in."

"You—you incredibly stupid boy!" exclaimed Mr. Quelch. "Do you imagine that I am speaking of edible dates? I am alluding to the dates I was giving out to the Form—historical dates."

"Oh!" Bunter realised that there was a misapprehension. "I see! I—I mean—oh, lor'!"

"Give me the dates at once, Bunter! To begin with, the date of the Spanish Armada."

Billy Bunter blinked at his Form-master almost in anguish. He had not the remotest idea of the date in question. But he had to answer; so he made a shot at it. It was by no means a bull's-eye!

"Nineteen-fourteen, sir!" gasped Bunter. He remembered vaguely that some big event had happened in 1914. He hoped that it was the Spanish Armada!

But Mr. Quelch's expression told him that it was a bad shot. He tried again in a hurry.

"I—I mean 1815, sir."

"You—you—you mean 1815!" gurgled Mr. Quelch. Bunter evidently remembered Waterloo year, though not in connection with Waterloo!

"Yes, sir—I—I—mean, no, sir——"

"Bunter! After class you will write out, 'The Spanish Armada came in the year 1588,' five hundred times."

"Did—did—did it, sir?" gasped Bunter. "That's not in my book, sir."

"What?"

"It says in my book that it came only once, sir——"

"Boy!"

"But—but it does, sir!" gasped

Bunter, feeling that he had got this right, at least. "I—I'm almost certain that the Spanish Armada came only once, sir. I—I don't see how it could have come five hundred times."

"Ha, ha, ha!" came in a yell from the whole Form.

"Silence!" roared Mr. Quelch. "This boy's stupidity and impertinence are not a laughing matter. Bunter, you will write out five hundred times that the Spanish Armada came in 1588."

"Oh, lor'!"

"And now stand up! Bend over the form!"

"Oh, crumbs!"

Whack!

"Whoooop!"

Whack!

"Yaroooooooop!"

Whack!

"Whooooo-hoooooop!"

"You will now give attention to the lesson, Bunter," said Mr. Quelch. "And if you fall asleep again——"

Mr. Quelch did not finish. He left the rest to William George Bunter's imagination.

But Billy Bunter was in no danger of falling asleep again! Those three hefty whacks were more than sufficient to keep him awake. He was not feeling sleepy now. He could not even keep still! He squirmed on his form, and seemed to be understudying the young man of Hythe, who was shaved with a scythe, and could do nothing but wriggle and writhe!

THE SECOND CHAPTER

SOME SCHEME!

"I SAY, you fellows!"

Billy Bunter blinked into No. 1 Study. The Famous Five had finished tea, and were discussing whether to go down to the nets, or to push a boat out on the Sark, when the fat face and glimmering spectacles of the Owl of the Remove appeared in the doorway. The Famous Five looked merry and bright, as was natural when classes were over on a bright summer's day. But Billy Bunter looked neither merry nor bright. Bunter was worried.

"Hallo, hallo, hallo!" roared Bob Cherry. "Enjoying life, old fat bean?"

"Done your lines?" asked Harry Wharton.

"I haven't finished them," said Bunter, shaking his head. "Quelch told me to take them in at six. It's nearly six now. I simply can't get them finished in time."

"How many have you done, then?"

"Two!" confessed Bunter.

"Ha, ha, ha!"

If Bunter, at a minute to six, had done only two lines out of five hundred, it was fairly certain that he would not get that "impot" done in time.

"Blessed if I see anything to cackle at!" said Bunter peevishly. "I asked Toddy to do the lines for me, but you know how selfish Toddy is; he wouldn't. I say, you fellows, Quelch will come up for those lines, if I don't take them down to him. He said he would. He will bring his cane with him."

"Better put some exercise books in your bags!" suggested Johnny Bull.

"Oh, really, Bull! Now look here, you fellows. I want you to help me; it's up to you, after all I've done for you, you know."

Bunter rolled into the study, and planted a heap of foolscap on the table, pushing aside the tea-things. The tea-pot tipped over into the

" Mind that table-cloth ! " shrieked Nugent. But his warning came too late. Bunter did not mind the table-cloth ! With a smack of his hand he up-ended the ink-bottle over the foolscap. " There, that's all right," he said.

butter-dish, and spilled its contents into the jam. That did not matter to Bunter—it was not his butter and jam.

" Look out, fathead ! " exclaimed Frank Nugent.

" Oh, really, Nugent ! Don't waste time jawing," said Bunter. " You've got a bottle of ink in the study cupboard, Wharton."

" How do you know what's in the study cupboard, you fat villain ? "

" I didn't look into the cupboard after class for the toffee," said Bunter hastily. " I never heard Nugent mention it. I hope I'm not a fellow to listen to what fellows say to one another. Besides, there wasn't any toffee there, and I never ate it, and I left it just as it was when I found it——"

" Oh, crumbs ! "

" Never mind the toffee. For goodness' sake, don't start making a fuss about a measly stick of toffee. I want that bottle of ink."

" To wash down the toffee ? " asked Bob.

" Ha, ha, ha ! "

" Will you listen to a chap ! " howled Bunter. " It's striking six now ! Talk about King Henry the Eighth fiddling while Constantinople was burning. Look here, I'll get the ink if you're too lazy to move."

Billy Bunter dived into the study cupboard, and reappeared with a large bottle of ink, more than half full.

He put it on the table and jerked out the cork. The chums of the Remove watched him, in astonishment. What he wanted with the ink was a mystery to them. There was no time left to write his impot, and anyhow he did not need a bottle of ink for that purpose. Apparently some deep and mysterious scheme was working in the fatuous brain of the Owl of the Remove.

" Now, you knock that bottle of ink over, Wharton ! " he said.

Harry Wharton jumped.

" Knock it over ! " he ejaculated.

" Yes, over my impot ! See ? Mop the ink all over it—smother it, soak it, drench it all over ! Just leave the two lines I've written, to show that the impot was done before you knocked the ink over it. Then I can take it down to Quelch."

The Famous Five gazed at Bunter. Slowly his masterly scheme dawned on their minds. The top page of foolscap was already adorned by two lines of writing in Bunter's scrawl and Bunter's spelling :

" The Spannish Armader caim in 1588."

" The Spannish Armader caim in 1588."

Those two lines were to be left, to show that the imposition—which had not been written—had been written. Spilt ink was to disguise the fact that the rest was a beautiful blank. Lots of ink would be required, but there was lots of ink in the bottle.

" My only hat ! " gasped Harry Wharton.

" Buck up," said Bunter urgently. " I want to get to Quelch before he comes after me. You see, if I told him I upset the ink over the paper after writing it, he mightn't believe me. He's doubted my word before ! It's rather ungentlemanly to doubt a fellow's word ; but the fact is, Quelch is no gentleman. Look how he jumped on me this afternoon, when I told him I hadn't been asleep. Practically made me out a liar ! "

" Oh, scissors ! "

" But it will be all right if I tell him I dropped in here to speak to you, and you—like a clumsy ass, you know —knocked the bottle of ink over on my impot. If he asks you, you can tell him so. See ? "

" And tell him you asked me to ? " roared Wharton.

" Eh ? No ! Of course not, you silly ass ! Tell him it was an accident, of course. You can tell him anything you like, old chap, so long as you stuff him. So long as he believes the lines were written, it will be all right. In fact, I think you'd better come to the old codger's study with me, and explain. It would sound better."

" I'm to come with you to Quelch, and tell him a string of thumping lies because you've been too jolly lazy to write your lines ? " gasped the captain of the Remove.

" Yes, old chap ! I'll do as much for you another time. I say, get on with it ; there's no time to lose. You haven't knocked the ink over yet."

" And I'm jolly well not going to, you howling ass ! "

" Oh, really, Wharton ! Well, look here, I'll knock it over——"

" Mind that table-cloth ! " shrieked Nugent.

But he shrieked too late. Bunter did not mind the table-cloth ! It was not his table-cloth ! He had no time or inclination to think of trifles like that ! With a smack of his fat hand, he up-ended the ink-bottle over the foolscap. Ink swamped out in a flood. The top sheet was inundated

" Look here, Cherry," said Bunter. " All you've got to do is to tell that old idiot Quelch that you upset the ink over my impot. The silly old ass——" Bunter broke off suddenly and blinked over his shoulder—to see Mr. Quelch standing in the doorway !

at once. So was a goodly portion of the table-cloth.

" There, that's all right," said Bunter. " Give it time to soak through, and old Quelch won't be able to see that there wasn't any writing. It would have been better for you to knock the bottle over, Wharton. Then you'd have been telling the truth when you told Quelch you did it. But you're not quite so particular about the truth as I am, I know."

" You—you—you blithering bandersnatch," gasped Wharton, " I'm not going to tell Quelch anything of the kind. You can tell your own fibs."

" Oh, really, Wharton ! Ten to one Quelch won't believe me if I say I had the accident ! A fellow expects his pals to back him up," said Bunter, warmly. " I say, Bob, if Wharton's too jolly mean to help a fellow out, you'll do it for me, won't you ? Old Quelch—— "

" Shut up ! " gasped Bob Cherry.

From where he sat, Bob had a view of the Remove passage through the open doorway. In that passage an angular figure appeared ; the figure of Henry Samuel Quelch, the master of the Remove. Evidently Mr. Quelch was on his way to Bunter's study, as the fat junior had not delivered the goods ! But at the sound of Billy

Bunter's voice in No. 1 Study, Mr. Quelch suddenly stopped and looked in.

Bunter was not aware of it. Bunter, of course, had no eyes in the back of his head.

" Look here, Cherry, you do it—you're not so funky as Wharton! What are you making faces at a fellow for, you ass? Look here, all you've got to do is to come down with me to Quelch, and tell the old idiot that you upset the ink over my impot—once it's soaked through he will never know there wasn't any writing on it, and we shall pull his leg a treat! The silly old ass—— "

The horror in the faces of the Famous Five made even Billy Bunter realise that something was amiss! They were gazing at the doorway—now filled by the angular figure of Mr. Quelch—as if a grisly spectre had appeared there.

Billy Bunter blinked round over a fat shoulder, to see what it was that horrified them so.

" Oh, crikey! " he gasped. He almost fell down at the sight of the Remove master.

Mr. Quelch stepped into the study.

" Bunter! I heard you——"

" Oh, lor'! I—I wasn't calling you a silly old ass, sir! " gasped Bunter. " I—I was speaking of another silly old ass, sir——"

" What? " roared Mr. Quelch.

" I—I—I mean——" gurgled the hapless Bunter.

" You have not written your lines, Bunter! Your imposition is doubled. You will stay in on Wednesday afternoon, and write a thousand lines. For your attempted deception, and the disrespectful expressions you have used, I shall cane you——"

" Oh, lor'! "

" Follow me to my study, Bunter! "

" Oh, crikey! "

In the lowest of spirits, Billy Bunter followed the Remove master to his study. He entered that study in fear and trembling. He left it looking as if he was trying to shut himself up like a pocket-knife! And for a good hour afterwards, Billy Bunter's remarks were limited chiefly to " Yow! " and " Ow! " and " Wow! " The way of the transgressor was hard!

THE THIRD CHAPTER

HELPING BUNTER!

GROAN!

That dismal sound was heard from the Remove Form-room on Wednesday afternoon. It fell on the ears of five fellows who were approaching along the Form-room passage in a rather cautious manner.

It was a half-holiday, and a glorious summer's afternoon. Billy Bunter, detained till he should have written out his thousand lines, sat at his desk in the Form-room—and groaned! Mr. Quelch had marched him in at two o'clock. Now it was half-past two; and Bunter had not started writing. He just groaned.

" Poor old Bunter! " murmured Bob Cherry, and he opened the Form-room door. Billy Bunter blinked up in surprise at the sight of the Famous Five. They came in rather quickly, and Harry Wharton closed the door after they were in. It was strictly forbidden for any fellow to speak to a fellow under detention; and it was necessary to be wary.

" I say, you fellows—— " Bunter blinked at the chums of the Remove hopefully. " If you've got any toffee——"

Toffee would have comforted the hapless Owl of the Remove.

" Fathead! " said Bob. " We've come to lend you a hand. We're going to take a page each—and we can make a scrawl like yours, if we try hard——"

" Many hands make light work ! " said Frank Nugent.

" But too many cooks spoil the absurd broth," remarked Hurree Jamset Ram Singh, " and that is a boot on the other leg."

" Get on with it," said Johnny Bull. " If Quelch catches us here——"

" Oh, good ! " said Billy Bunter, in great relief. " If you do two hundred lines each, old chaps, that will make the lot——"

" And what are you going to do, you fat villain ? " hooted Johnny Bull.

" I'll watch you, old fellow."

" You slacking bandersnatch, get on with it. You do the top page, and leave the rest to us," said Harry.

" Well, look here, be a bit careful with your writing " said Bunter. " If Quelch is to think that I did it, your usual rotten scrawl won't do, you know."

" You blinking, blithering, fatheaded, foozling frump," said Bob Cherry. " It's only because your fist is a spider-leggy scrawl that the wheeze will work at all. If it was anything like handwriting, we couldn't do it."

" Oh, really, Cherry——"

" Shut up, and start ! "

" Beast ! "

Having thus expressed his gratitude, Billy Bunter started. Greyfriars fellows sometimes helped one another out with lines ; and in Bunter's case, it was quite easy—it was only necessary to produce a smeary, smudgy, shapeless scrawl, and it would be recognised as genuine Bunter caligraphy at a glance !

" I say, you fellows——"

" Shut up, Bunter ! "

" But you'll have to spell properly," exclaimed Bunter peevishly. " If I spell right, and you fellows spell wrong, Quelch will spot it at once. You're spelling 'Spanish' with only one 'n'."

" Oh, my hat ! "

" And you're spelling 'Armada' with an 'a' at the end ! " said Billy Bunter, " and look how you're spelling 'came'—c-a-m-e ! That won't do."

" Ha, ha, ha ! "

" Blessed if I see anything to cackle at ! We've got to have the same spelling all through——"

" Better put it in Bunter's spelling," chuckled Bob Cherry ; " it will look more genuine ! "

" Ha, ha, ha ! "

And the Famous Five re-started, and proceeded to write, like Bunter, " The Spannish Armader caim in 1588." Certainly that looked more like Bunter's work than their own ! Whether Mr. Quelch would be satisfied with that new style in orthography, was another matter. Still, he was not likely to suspect any fellow but Bunter spelling like that.

Taking great care to produce a smeary, smudgy, almost illegible scrawl, the Famous Five got on with it. Bunter proceeded more slowly. Bunter did not like work.

" I say, you fellows——"

" Shut up ! "

" But, I say, sure you haven't got any toffee about you ? "

" Yes—shut up ! "

" Or any butterscotch ? "

" Shut up ! "

Snort, from Bunter.

" I think you might have brought a fellow something, when he's in detention. I must say you're a mean lot ! After all I've done for you, too ! Look here, one of you cut out and get some toffee."

"You fat owl——"

"I'll pay for it, if that's what you're worrying about," said Bunter, scornfully; "I'm expecting a postal order shortly——"

"Will you dry up?"

"I'll stand toffee all round, if one of you fellows will cut down to the tuck-shop and get it," said Bunter generously. "All you've got to do is to pay for it—and I'll settle when my postal order comes——"

"Shut up!" hissed Bob Cherry.

"Beast!"

In the kindness of their hearts, the chums of the Remove were giving up a portion of their half-holiday to help Billy Bunter out of detention. But they were rather repenting of their kindness, by this time. Really, Bunter was not a very pleasant fellow to help. However, they got on with it, and the lines grew and grew and grew, like the little peach in the orchard. Lines galore ran from the pens of the Famous Five, but not from Bunter's. Bunter wrote one line and took a rest—he wrote another line, and took a longer rest—another, and a still longer rest. Bunter would have preferred to sit and eat toffee, while the other fellows did the lines; and he reflected sadly on the selfishness of human nature!

It was rather unfortunate for the kind-hearted juniors that Mr. Quelch was also experiencing kindness of heart that golden summer's afternoon.

Mr. Quelch was seated in a deck-chair in the quad under his study window. A shady elm cast a grateful shadow. In the distance, white-clad figures dotted the cricket-field. A volume of Sophocles was open on Quelch's knee. Quelch was enjoying life—in his own way, though what enjoyment he found in Sophocles would have been a mystery to his Form. Several times Mr. Quelch's thoughts strayed to the junior detained on that glorious afternoon, and at last he laid down his book on the chair, went into the House, and rustled along the passage to the Form-room. Utterly unaware of the assistance Bunter was receiving, Quelch did not guess on how many ears the sound of his footstep fell and what dismay it caused.

"Hallo, hallo, hallo!" ejaculated Bob Cherry suddenly. "What——"

"Oh, my only hat!"

"If that's Quelch—"

"I say, you fellows——"

Footsteps approached the door of the Remove-room. For a moment the Famous Five sat transfixed. Then they jumped up and crouched low behind the desks. If Quelch only glanced in from the doorway! They vanished from sight as the door opened.

"Oh, lor'!" gasped Billy Bunter.

Mr. Quelch stepped in. The expression on his usually grim face was quite kindly.

"Bunter!"

"Oh, crikey! I—I mean yes, sir!" stuttered Bunter.

"If you have made due progress with your task, Bunter, I shall excuse you the remainder," said Mr. Quelch. "Let me see——"

He came across to the desks. Five juniors, crouching low, hardly breathed. Mr. Quelch glanced at the sheet that lay before Bunter. Then, in surprise, he glanced at the half-written sheets that lay on adjacent desks. Apparently, Bunter had started on a good many sheets of foolscap at once, and finished none of them—which was a rather unusual way of getting on with an imposition! Mr Quelch was surprised! Perhaps he was suspicious!

" Bunter, if anyone has been here assisting you——"

" Oh, no, sir ! " gasped Bunter. " Nobody's been here, sir, and they're not here now ! "

" What ? " ejaculated Mr. Quelch.

" There—there's nobody in the room, sir, except you and me, sir ! " gasped Bunter. " They—they're miles away ! I—I think they went up the river——"

" Who ? " roared Mr. Quelch. " Of whom are you speaking, Bunter ? "

" Eh ! Oh, nobody, sir ! I—I mean——"

Mr. Quelch had been a little suspicious. Now he was a lot ! With a grim expression on his face—from which all the genial kindness was now banished—he peered over the desks. Then he had an interesting view of five breathless juniors crouching in cover.

" Oh ! " ejaculated Mr. Quelch.

In grim silence the Famous Five rose to their feet. The game was up now with a vengeance. Mr. Quelch looked at them. Grimmer and grimmer grew his visage. The silence, for a moment, could almost have been cut with a knife. Then the Remove master spoke.

" Wharton, Cherry, Nugent, Bull, Hurree Singh ! It appears that you

With a grim expression on his face, Mr. Quelch peered over the desks. Then he had an interesting view of Harry Wharton & Co. crouching in cover. " Oh ! " ejaculated the Remove master. " It appears that you juniors desire to write lines on a half-holiday ! "

desire to write lines on a half-holiday. Very well. Each of you will write two hundred lines from Virgil, and take them to my study when written. Bunter, you will write the whole of your imposition, and not leave the Form-room until it is finished."

Mr. Quelch gathered up the written sheets, crumpled them together in his hand, and walked out of the Form-room. Harry Wharton & Co. gazed at one another. Bunter blinked at them accusingly.

"Well, you've done it now!" he said.

The Famous Five did not reply. Their feelings were too deep for words. They sat down to Virgil.

"I say, you fellows——"

"You piffling, pie-faced porker," hissed Bob, "if you'd kept your silly mouth shut, Quelch wouldn't have spotted us!"

"Look here, what about my lines?"

"Shut up!" roared Johnny Bull, so ferociously that Billy Bunter jumped and shut up.

With dismal industry Harry Wharton & Co. ground at Virgil. It was long before they finished, but they finished at last. By the time they had done two hundred each, Bunter had done nearly a dozen! They gathered up their lines and went to the door. Bunter blinked at them.

"I say, you fellows—you're not going! What about my lines?"

"You silly owl!" roared Bob Cherry. "Do you think that chicken will fight, after Quelch has spotted us?"

"Well, I think you'd better chance it," said Bunter warmly. "I've done only eleven—no, ten—out of a thousand! I'm not sticking in here all the afternoon to please you fellows! I should be finished by now, if you hadn't come butting in! What the thump did you come in at all for, if you come to that? It's up to you now, and I can jolly well say—yaroooooop!"

Five pairs of hands were laid on William George Bunter at once. He was swept off his feet, and he sat down on the Form-room floor.

Bump!

"Whoooop!" roared Bunter.

And the Famous Five departed, leaving him roaring.

THE FOURTH CHAPTER

BUNTER ALL OVER.

BILLY BUNTER opened the door of the Form-room and peered out cautiously into the passage, through his big spectacles.

The coast was clear, the House almost deserted on that sunny half-holiday. Bunter rolled out.

It was half an hour since the Famous Five had gone. They were playing cricket now—regardless of Bunter! Equally regardless of Bunter, Mr. Quelch was seated in the deck-chair under his study window in the quad, enjoying life with jolly old Sophocles! Everybody, in fact, was merry and bright, with the exception of William George Bunter—the victim, as usual, of selfishness and injustice! But the worm will turn! Bunter, being a good deal of a worm, was turning!

His eyes gleamed behind his spectacles! He had done a total of fifteen lines out of his thousand. A whopping was due if it was not finished. As the whopping was a certainty in any case, Bunter considered that he might as well leave nine hundred and eighty-five lines unwritten, as any smaller number! He was fed up with lines. He was thinking of something more agreeable—making that awful beast, Quelch, sit up, for detaining him!

He headed for Quelch's study.

On that glorious summer's afternoon, it was practically certain that Quelch, like everybody else, would be out of doors. But Bunter was cautious. He tapped lightly at Quelch's door when he reached it, ready with an excuse if his Form-master was there. He opened the study door, and blinked in. As he had quite expected, the study was vacant.

He rolled in, and shut the door after him.

Swiftly Bunter clambered through the window, and his fat little legs swung from the sill. In his haste he was quite unaware that Mr. Quelch was seated in a deck-chair underneath, deeply immersed in his beloved Sophocles!

The window was wide open on the quad. Nobody could be seen near it. It did not occur to Bunter's powerful brain that anybody might be sitting below it outside.

Bunter grinned.

From under Mr. Quelch's writing-table he subtracted the waste-paper basket. Taking a shovel from the fender, he groped with it in the chimney. Shovel after shovel of soot was hooked down, and deposited inside the waste-paper basket. Soot flew about the study, and settled on books and papers. Bunter did not mind. Nobody was going to know that he had been there—so that was all right! Ragging Quelch was an amusement which most Remove fellows would have likened to twisting the tail of a tiger in the jungle! But it was said of old that fools rush in where angels fear to tread. Bunter had thought it all out, with great astuteness.

He placed the door ajar, stood on a chair, and arranged the basket of soot on the top of the door, resting against the lintel. Anybody opening that door from outside was absolutely certain to get the basket of soot on his napper!

Bunter grinned with glee.

That, he considered, would serve Quelch right! And he would never know that Bunter had had a hand in it. Bunter had a safe alibi—a fellow under detention in the Form-room could scarcely be suspected of playing tricks in the Form-master's study. Bunter was going back to the Form-room. He was going to be there, at a safe distance, when the crash came! Quelch could suspect whom he liked—he was hardly likely to suspect Bunter.

Of course, having fixed the door in this masterly manner, Bunter could not leave the study by the door. But that was all right—all he had to do was to drop from the open window, and scuttle into the House again by the nearest door!

In a couple of minutes he would be safe back in the Form-room; safe and sound, and unsuspected.

Bunter could not help feeling pleased with this stunt. Other fellows thought it too risky to rag Quelch. Bunter was the man for such things.

He emptied Mr. Quelch's inkpot into the soot in the basket—a final artistic touch. Then he rolled to the window. It was time to go. He blinked from the window. Mr. Prout was to be seen in the distance, but his back was turned. The coast was clear. Still, it was as well to be rapid. Once he showed himself at the window he had to be quick.

And he was quick. Swiftly he swung himself into the window, and his fat little legs swung over the sill, and he dropped—on Mr. Quelch's head!

Mr. Quelch, the master of the Greyfriars Remove, had often been surprised—for life is full of surprises—but never had Henry Samuel Quelch been so surprised as he was now.

Deep in Sophocles, his head bent over that entrancing author, he was suddenly aware of something—he did not know what it was—crashing on him from above.

For one wild and whirling moment Mr. Quelch had the impression that it was an earthquake or that the skies were falling.

But it was neither. It was Billy Bunter!

Bunter was as surprised as Quelch.

When he swung over the window-sill he had naturally expected to drop on the ground. It was quite surprising to drop on something that reeled and rolled and roared!

Crash! Bump!

Mr. Quelch, in a dumbfounded state, sprawled over, and Billy Bunter sprawled headlong over him.

"Oh! Ow! Ooooooogh!" spluttered the amazed Remove master. "What—how—oh—ah—urrrrgggh!"

"Oh, crikey!" gasped Bunter.

He sat up dazedly, too astounded and confused to realise what he was sitting on. Only he noticed that it felt bony. Later he discovered that it was Mr. Quelch's face.

"Wurrrrrgggh!" came from under Bunter's fat form. "What—who—what—urrgh! Moooooooooh!"

"Oh, lor'!"

A sinewy hand grasped Bunter and hurled him aside. An angular figure rose from the earth with a crimson face, gasping and spluttering. Bunter sat on a collapsed deck-chair and blinked at his Form-master. He had wondered dizzily what he had fallen on. Now he knew. It was Quelch!

"Bunter!" almost roared Quelch.

"Oh, lor'! Oh, crikey! It—it isn't me, sir! I—I mean—oh, crumbs!" gurgled Bunter.

"You—you—you have been in my study, you—you—you have jumped from the window—on—on my head! You—you—you—Come!" Mr. Quelch grasped Bunter by the collar and hooked him to his feet. "Come! I shall cane you—I shall cane you with the utmost severity! I—I—Come!"

Mr. Quelch whisked into the House. Bunter, spluttering, whisked along with him—with an iron grip on his collar! Quelch was taking him to his study to be caned. Billy Bunter's fat heart almost died within him, and he quailed as he remembered what awaited Quelch when he reached his study.

"I—I—I say, sir——" squeaked Bunter.

"Come!"

"But—but—b-b-but—I—I say, sir, d-d-don't go to your study—oh, lor'—oh, my hat—I say—oh, scissors!"

Mr. Quelch reached his study. The cane was there, and he was anxious—in fact, eager—to reach the cane. Bunter struggled to hold back.

"I—I say, sir, d-d-don't open the door—oh, jiminy!"

Grasping Bunter by the collar with one hand, Mr. Quelch hurled open the door with the other and strode in, yanking Bunter.

Crash!

What happened next Quelch hardly knew. For the second time something unexpected descended upon him. This time it was not a fat schoolboy; it was a waste-paper basket crammed to the brim with inky soot! It up-ended on Quelch's head, fairly bonneting him. Soot smothered him—and Bunter. Soot descended on both of them in clouds, in volumes, in swamps. They were of the soot, sooty!

"Urrrrrgggggh!" gurgled Mr. Quelch, staggering in the doorway, suddenly transformed into the blackest of negroes. "Wurrrggh! Grooogh! Ooogh!"

"Ug-gug-gug!" spluttered Billy Bunter, nearly as sooty as his Form-master. "Oooooogh! Woooogh! Ooo-er—oh, crikey—goooooogh!"

"What the—ooogh! What—ooooch!"

"Ow! Wow! Groooogh!"

"Bunter, you—you have—groogh—you have—ooooch!"

"Oh, lor'!"

Billy Bunter fled. He left a trail of soot as he fled. Mr. Quelch did not pursue him. He wanted to skin Bunter. He yearned to skin Bunter. But skinning Bunter had to wait till he had had a wash and a change. The skinning process came later.

. . . .

"Hallo, hallo, hallo! What's that ghastly row?"

Groan!

Harry Wharton & Co. came in cheerfully after the cricket. Sounds of woe greeted them as they came up the Remove staircase. They gazed at Billy Bunter. He was leaning on the banisters on the Remove landing, uttering deep and dismal groans.

"Licked?" asked Harry Wharton.

"Ow! I say, you fellows—wow! That beast Quelch took me to the Head—wow—I've been flogged—ow—he made out that I fixed a booby-trap for him in his study—oooooh—just because I was there, you know—wow—and fell on his head when I got out of the window—yow-ow!"

"Ha, ha, ha!"

"I say—wow—the Head laid it on—yow-ow! I shan't be able to sit down for weeks—yow-ow-ow!"

"Ha, ha, ha!"

Groan!

"Buck up, old fat bean!"

Groan!

"Come into our study to tea."

Bunter ceased to groan.

"We've got a cake——"

Bunter brightened.

"And two kinds of jam."

Bunter smiled.

THE END

BILLY BUNTER'S POSTAL ORDER!

By ***FRANK NUGENT***
(of the Greyfriars Remove)

THE news was like a thunderclap!
It spread like a devouring flame!
The whole school reeled, and every chap
With eyes, refused to credit same,
When Bunter's postal order came!

That postal order, as you know,
Has won considerable fame.
We lent him money terms ago,
Which we've been waiting to reclaim,
When Bunter's postal order came.

But days and weeks went speeding by,
And our fond hopes grew weak and lame;
Still Bunter raised the some old cry,
Still carried on the same old game,
And then—the postal order came!

'Twas in the postman's bag of tricks,
Addressed to William George by name,
A handsome tip of two-and-six;
And even earthquakes seemed quite tame
When Bunter's postal order came.

In stunned amazement, startled, dumb,
The school heard Vernon-Smith exclaim,
"Don't spend it now it's really come,
But keep it in a gilt-edged frame!"
When Bunter's postal order came.

But saving, Bunter thinks, is wrong,
To gorge and guzzle is his aim;
He kept that order just as long
As he could find the tuckshop dame,
When Bunter's postal order came.

And then, of course, he ate his fill;
But when that half-a-crown was spent,
He said, "Lend me a bob until—"
We raised our boots with grim intent,
And Bunter—like his order—went!

The GREEN CAT!

By EDMUND BURTON

Out of a tragic disaster to a British torpedo-boat springs a thrilling adventure for Midshipman Clive Chester, the sole survivor—an adventure which plunges him into a sinister war between two Chinese secret societies!

THE FIRST CHAPTER

THE SOLE SURVIVOR!

DONG, dong, dong!

The great copper bell of Canton boomed the hour of three.

Under the blazing sun the calm blue waters shimmered. A single British torpedo-boat rode at anchor some distance off-shore, the White Ensign fluttering at her stern—a solitary emblem of the Motherland's might in an Oriental setting.

Midshipman Clive Chester, ever a strong swimmer, was revelling in his favourite pastime, watched by a little group of other "snotties" leaning on the rail as he turned and twisted in the water, displaying for their benefit a new stroke of his own invention—a peculiar overarm-cum-trudgen stroke which drew his gleaming body through the shimmering sea at a remarkable pace.

Presently he shot away towards the shore, and had reached a point a considerable distance from his floating home, when a sudden shattering noise made him turn his head in amazement. He was just in time to see the torpedo-boat open like a paper bag and, with flames shooting from her hull, slip downwards into the depths!

A few shattered pieces of wreckage

floated on the surface where she had been riding so proudly a minute before ; but that was all to tell the tale. Not a survivor had escaped, apparently, owing to the appalling rapidity of the vessel's end.

" Great Heaven ! " Clive breathed as, raising himself in the water, he took stock of his surroundings. " What can have happened ? They were about to test that new torpedo-tube, and—yes, that must have caused it. Something went wrong, and—good lor' ! They're wiped out, poor chaps ! "

It was an extraordinary predicament, surely, one in which, it is safe to say, a midshipman of His Britannic Majesty's Navy had never found himself before. But Clive was level-headed, and he lost no time in trying to succour any who might be left, small hope though there seemed to be of this.

He hailed one of the native boats which was speeding to the scene of the disaster and, climbing aboard, directed the Chinaman to help in the search. But it was all in vain. Quite plainly their assistance would not be required, for even the strongest swimmers would surely have been drawn under by the suction, unless they had had time to get well away—which, with the sole exception of Clive himself, they certainly had not.

Sadly he gave orders to be landed on the quay, and the owner of the sampan turned the craft about. The Chink looked at the white lad clad only in bathing costume, and dumbly indicated a great square of sacking which was lying at the bottom of the little vessel.

Clive, interpreting the fellow's meaning, stooped and picked this up, wrapping it round his body which had now dried in the hot sunshine.

It was a strange garment for a British midshipman to be forced to wear, but it was better than none at all under the circumstances. And still wearing the sacking, he presently stepped ashore, sitting down on a thick coil of rope to think out his unenviable position.

Few, if any, of those who passed paid attention to him. They seemed to be busy with other matters. Presently, lifting his eyes, Clive noticed that some kind of disturbance appeared to be in progress—a sort of political meeting.

There were men gathered in groups, wildly gesticulating, whose voices sounded like the squealing of so many guinea-pigs—the peculiar squeaking of the heathen Chinee when stirred out of his habitual Oriental calm. A little way to the right of this crowd, a gang of coolies were having a " free-and-easy " with the aid of sticks and cudgels. Possibly these composed the " opposition party," Clive imagined, but he could not understand what it was all about. Indeed, his heart was too sad and his mind too occupied at that moment to take a great deal of interest in anything beyond the terrible disaster which had come as a bolt from the blue sky above.

Then, suddenly, he became conscious of a voice addressing him in perfect English. Looking up again, he perceived that a richly-appointed palanquin had stopped a few yards away, and that a well-proportioned Chinaman of the higher caste was gazing in his direction.

" I am sorry to hear of this terrible accident, young man," the splendidly-attired personage was saying. " I am the Mandarin Fu Wan. The boatman who rescued you stopped my palanquin just now and told me of your plight, for he knows that I have always been friendly with the British. Pray come here ! "

Wonderingly, Clive rose and approached the conveyance which the bearers had set down on the quay. He stared at the richly-clad occupant, looking closely at the latter's face and feeling reassured, somehow.

Clive had been over two years on the China station, and had learnt enough to distinguish the rabble from the patricians; and the visage of the Mandarin Fu Wan was undoubtedly a prepossessing one.

His eyes, though slant and narrow, were honest ones, and he had far more expression in his features than is usual with men of his nationality. What was more, the expression was a good one.

"This is a strange plight for a member of the British Navy to find himself in," the Chinaman continued, "and I must do my best to better it. Will you honour me by accompanying me home, young sir? I can put you up for the present, until you know what you intend to do."

Clive was nothing loth. Anything, indeed, was better than travelling about Canton clad only in a bathing costume and a piece of sacking, and without more ado he muttered his thanks, taking his seat beside the mandarin in the palanquin.

"I have spent some time in your great country," Fu Wan explained, as the pair were borne through the tortuous streets, "and I have been well treated by your people; so anything I can do to assist an Englishman in trouble is done willingly and with extreme pleasure. I was educated in one of your universities; hence my speaking in your own tongue. There were no other survivors from your ship, I believe?" he added irrelevantly.

Clive shook his head sadly.

"None," he replied in a low tone; "it happened too quickly, whatever it was. One minute she was floating on the surface, with a crowd of fellows watching my swimming stunts; the next, she had vanished."

"Terrible, terrible!" murmured Fu Wan. "That is the worst of being too progressive. It makes men deal with things which may as easily destroy themselves as their enemies. We Chinese are not too progressive, and in that, I imagine, we are wise."

"But surely, sir, you admire the Western methods of progress—you who have lived among us and had an opportunity of studying matters first hand?"

"Oh, yes—I admire your people and their greatness," the other admitted, "but yours is a different temperament from ours, you must remember. What suits the Britisher does not suit the Chinaman."

For a few moments there was silence whilst the journey continued beyond the confines of the town and into much pleasanter surroundings.

"But China—Canton especially—is stirring just now," Fu Wan resumed musingly. "You may have noticed a disturbance on the quay as I came along?"

"I did—yes."

"It is one of many. There is considerable unrest at the moment, and there may be trouble later. Ah! Here we are now!" The mandarin stopped his palanquin and climbed down, followed by Clive. "Pray come with me, my young friend!"

They had halted before a pair of great red double-doors, which presently were opened from the inside, and the couple passed through into one of the most gorgeous buildings it had ever been Clive's lot to enter.

The hallway was a riot of inlaid marble and lacquer-work, whilst soft silken hangings draped the walls and doorway leading from this to other parts of the house.

The colouring was rich, but not gaudy. It was the dwelling of a man of excellent taste, for, with all the many blended hues, nothing clashed nor offended the eye.

A servant in white livery appeared suddenly in one of these doorways, bowing low.

" Sing will give you some proper raiment, my friend," Fu Wan said. " Accompany him to my son's wardrobe, and choose what you desire. My son is at present away, so all he has is yours for the time being. When you are ready, please follow the servant to my apartment."

Like one in a dream Clive passed along the many corridors in the wake of the white-liveried Sing. The man spoke no word, but it was plain that he knew exactly what was required of him. He brought Clive to a richly appointed bedchamber, and here a miscellaneous collection of beautiful clothing was spread out for his benefit. It was all, to the romantically inclined middy, just like a page torn out of the " Arabian Nights."

He selected a tunic of green Shantung silk, with a monogram on the breast pocket, together with some underwear of very soft material, and a pair of beaded, felt slippers. Then, having surveyed himself quizzically in the long mirror, he nodded to his guide.

Sing plainly understood and bowed low, turning on his heel and conducting his charge through another long corridor, where he presently knocked upon the portals of a richly lacquered door. Then he stood aside and Clive found himself again in the presence of his benefactor, the Mandarin Fu Wan.

Tea was set for two on a small table to one side of this sumptuous apartment, and the fine-looking Chinaman motioned his guest to be seated.

That meal was one of the most appetising of which Clive had ever partaken. There was not a great deal of food on the table, but what there was was exceptionally rich and palatable, and the middy, more hungry than he had believed himself to be till that moment, did ample justice to it.

Then, as Sing entered to clear the table, Fu Wan sank down upon a soft divan, drawing a gold-mounted cigar case from the pocket of his robe.

" One of your Western vices," he smiled, as he selected a weed. " In fact, I still have these sent me from London."

He struck a match, lighted the cigar and, after a few luxurious puffs, turned again towards his guest. Clive noticed that the mandarin's face had assumed an expression of the utmost gravity.

" I am expecting other visitors," he began, " but they need not disturb you, since your presence will not interfere with our meeting. As a matter of fact, I expect you will be in sympathy with our object, and therefore interested in what takes place here presently. Do you understand any of the Chinese tongues ? "

Clive nodded.

" Yes, I've something more than a smattering," he said. " I've been over two years out here, and I did not spend all my time fooling about."

" You English seldom do," the other remarked. " You learn a good deal wherever you go, and that is one of the secrets of your world-power. However, I may as well explain something before we are interrupted, because I feel sure you will prove a sympathetic listener. I am a good reader of faces, and I liked yours from the moment I saw you seated on that rope by the water-front."

Clive leaned forward expectantly. Something about this strange mandarin fascinated him. He guessed he was a straight individual, and he certainly possessed a most magnetic personality.

A sudden shattering explosion made Clive turn his head in amazement. He was just in time to see the torpedo-boat open like a paper bag and, with flames shooting from her, plunge downwards into the depths!

" In a few minutes, young man," Fu Wan pursued, " there will assemble in this room the principal members of the Order of the Green Cat. I have the honour to be chief of the Canton district, and therefore hold the high office of the order. Look! There is the emblem of my strength." He pointed to a small ornament standing in an alcove on the far side of the room. " He who has the Green Cat can count on possessing incalculable influence with the teeming population of this ancient city. My minions are all true men—the real honest workers of this great hive—but we have opposed to us the insidious Order of the Lotus, and at this moment that nefarious society seeks to exterminate the leaders of the Green Cat throughout Southern China.

" My emissaries have shadowed certain miscreants hovering around the true leaders these past five nights, so I know that underhand movements are afoot.

" A white man in these moments of disruption, when *anything* may happen, is not safe abroad ; so, observing you and hearing of the plight you were in, I took compassion upon you. I admire the Westerner and his ways——"

" I am greatly obliged to you, sir, and I trust I shall be able to repay you some day," Clive interrupted, with a smile. " To-morrow I expect some of our fellows will arrive from Hong Kong, for they are bound to have received news of the disaster by now. You may be sure I shall tell them what a friend in need you have been to me."

At that moment Sing reappeared, ushering in half a dozen Chinese gentlemen, who exchanged words of greeting with their host and took up positions round a larger table.

Clive leaned back, studying the group with interest; then he prepared to listen to what passed—or at least, to as much of it as he could catch.

THE SECOND CHAPTER

A MIDNIGHT VISITOR

"MY friends," said Mandarin Fu Wan, speaking very gravely and deliberately, " we are faced with a very determined attempt to overthrow our ancient organisation, and it is necessary that we be quite prepared for all eventualities. Two years ago we were threatened in a similar manner, and then we stood firm—as firmly as we shall stand now. But since that last attempt, our enemies have been considerably strengthened ; therefore, the present move on their part is all the more dangerous.

" Our main power, as you know, lies in the possession of the emblem of the Green Cat yonder." The mandarin pointed to the small ornament which he had already indicated to Clive. " I, as the chief of the Canton district, hold it at present. Should I die, it will pass to you, Most Illustrious Brother Kung Lu, as next in succession, and so on until each of the Six Sons of Wisdom possesses it on the demise of the reigning chief. This is all clear and straightforward ; but in that Cat lies at once our strength and our weakness. Should it be stolen or otherwise pass into the hands of the Lotus people, then it will mean the undoing of years of effort for good on the part of our honoured society ; for that which the emblem contains would prove a weapon which we could hardly fight against."

The others nodded in grave agreement with the words of Mandarin Fu Wan. Presently the latter pursued:

" For this reason, from this night onwards I intend to guard the Green Cat even more closely than before. I shall remove it to my sleeping apartment, safely though it has rested here for so long, and it shall never leave my sight until the time may come for Brother Kung Lu to take it over. That, I think, is a good plan."

Again the six nodded their heads, and the meeting progressed for some little while, various matters being discussed ere the Sons of Wisdom rose and took their leave.

After the last had passed through the door to the corridor without, the mandarin turned to his young guest, who had been trying to follow what was said, but had not succeeded in grasping all that passed. The others, it may be mentioned, had paid Clive no attention whatever, evidently taking his presence there as a matter of course, since Fu Wan had spoken openly before him.

" You have heard what was said, young man ? " the Celestial asked in English. " If so, you will understand that something very grave was under discussion."

" Yes, I gathered that," Clive replied, " but I do not pretend to fathom the whole thing yet. I learned that there was something hidden in the body of that ornament over there which must be guarded against theft, and that it is to pass from one to another of you as each assumes the chieftainship of your society. Isn't that so ? "

" Quite right, so far as it goes," Fu Wan replied, crossing the room and returning with the ornament in question in his hand. " Perhaps I should explain more fully."

Clive looked at the article with great interest. It was a beautiful example of ceramic work, jade in hue, and measuring some ten inches in length. It was a perfect model of a cat, the eyes consisting of two flawless emeralds, with tiny pigeon-blood rubies surrounding the larger stones. Fu Wan gave the head a peculiar twist, which caused it to part from the body, and from the hollow thus revealed he drew out a tightly rolled portion of silk secured with a rubber band. This he opened, displaying a chart or map so minutely executed that it was impossible to decipher much of the lettering with the naked eye.

Next the mandarin took up a large magnifying glass, which he handed to his companion, and with the aid of this Clive ascertained that the silk was really a most elaborate map of a city or town, drawn to an exceedingly small scale and containing a large number of tiny dots in gold, green, and red.

He looked up, his eyes asking many questions which Fu Wan was quite ready to answer.

"This is a map of the City of Canton," the latter explained. "It is absolutely accurate, giving every house, every street, and every alley. It was executed by the finest draughtsman in all China, and took some years to complete. The golden dots mark the houses of the district commissioners of our order, the green dots those of the sub-commissioners, and the red dots represent the dwellings of the rank and file of our supporters. You will notice that there are hundreds of the last-named compared with those of the other colours. This, then, constitutes the membership list of the Society of the Green Cat and would, of course, be a powerful weapon in the hands of our enemies, could they but obtain it. You see, Mr. Chester, all that would be required to strike at every loyal unit of our organisation would be a close study of this map, for it gives the residence of each one of us and is revised from time to time as members move from one part of the city to another. You see, it is always quite up to date."

"But to strike at all these people would be a long job, wouldn't it?"

"Yes," Fu Wan nodded, "but the organisation of the Lotus Order is very complete—and very ruthless. Also, their methods of extermination are sure and silent. Their emissaries—thousands of them—would steal abroad whilst Canton slept and deal death by means of the blowpipe and poisoned dart, after the manner of the savage of the woods. Indeed, some of our known members have already been killed in this way; but without this map, what you English term a 'clean sweep' could not be made. That is why we expect an attempt will be made to steal it, sooner or later, now that the Lotus Order has been strengthened sufficiently to become a real menace to our existence."

Clive shuddered. He had heard of this blowpipe and dart business before, and what he had heard was not very nice.

"The poison they use," Fu Wan continued, "is manufactured by a certain chemist in Nanking—a man suspected many times of evil work, but not convicted because he has a certain power which enables him to evade the law. But sufficient is known by us of his collusion in this matter to furnish ample proof that from him, and no one else, the Lotus Society gets its terrible supplies. Where the ingredients of the poison are first obtained is something of a mystery, but we have learnt that this chemist makes regular journeys to the Gobi Desert, taking with him several assistants, so that may explain matters.

"We have seen some victims of the dart during the past two years or so—isolated cases which, nevertheless, prove that our very life as a society for good stands in jeopardy. Now we learn that bigger things are about to be attempted—things which will require all our strength to combat. The squabbling you saw on the dockside is but a murmur of a breeze that may herald open rebellion among the lower orders, the majority of whom are supporters of the Lotus."

"I see," said Clive. "So that is why you announced your intention just now of never letting the Green Cat out of your sight?"

"Precisely." Fu Wan pointed to a door at the far end of the apartment. "My bedchamber is yonder. Yours is here"—he indicated another door at the opposite side—"until to-morrow, or until your Naval authorities need your services. I will inform the British consul of your present position. And now," the mandarin rose, replacing the map in its receptacle and putting the Cat's head back into position again, "I have had a tiring day, and so have you; therefore, let us retire. Sing should be within call if you require him."

Though it was not late, Clive was quite willing to get between the sheets, and having shaken hands with his kindly host, they parted in the middle of the long room, each leaving by an opposite door. Just once the middy looked back and saw Fu Wan disappearing into his private apartment with the precious Green Cat nursed to the folds of his robe.

Clive had no need to summon Sing, for that well-behaved servant had already done everything that was required of him. The comfortable bed was freshly made, a new robe and complete change of clothing were spread out on a settee close by, for wearing in the morning, and English pyjamas hung over the back of a chair.

"Jove! This is just like being at home," the middy thought, as he rapidly undressed himself and scrambled into bed. "I'd feel no end happy if it wasn't for the terrible happening that put me into this position to-day. Poor Simpson, and Watkins, and the rest! All wiped out in a flash, and this lucky individual only saved through chancing to have a swim before duty. Truly, Fate plays queer tricks!"

For a little while he lay awake, pondering upon this and upon the strange affair of the Green Cat. Then he dozed off, until the striking of the midnight gong aroused him again. He was conscious of a severe thirst, possibly owing to the rich food he had eaten, and, despite his efforts to sleep once more, he at length felt that he simply must have a drink.

This was, indeed, aggravated by the drip-drip of rain falling outside, for the weather had broken with sunset and a regular deluge was now pouring down.

He had noticed that a small bathroom adjoined his sleeping apartment, and, facing this, was another door leading to the garden outside—a door containing a large grid that was open for air.

Clive left his bed, thrust his feet into his felt slippers, and entered the bathroom, which was illuminated by the soft light of a paper lantern burning in the ceiling. He quenched his thirst and was about to return when a sudden sound caught his keen ears—a sound distinctive from the dripping rain, which made him start back in alarm.

Then, softly drawing aside the silken curtains which draped the bathroom entrance, he peeped out. His sleeping apartment was very dimly lighted by the reflected rays of the lantern, and by these he was just able to see the door containing the grid which now faced him.

And that door now stood slightly ajar! More, a shadow was moving away from it—moving towards the other door which led to the big apartment and to Fu Wan's room beyond it!

THE THIRD CHAPTER

A DANGEROUS MISSION

Clive's mind was made up in a flash. This nocturnal visitor meant no good to the occupants of that well-ordered abode. He might be a common thief, or worse—one of the dreaded emissaries whom Fu Wan had mentioned.

The shadow moved forward, the middy following step by step in his soft slippers. The pair entered the large chamber, which was still lighted by a single coloured gleam in one corner, and here the intruder paused, staring about him. Clive also halted, partly screened by those silken curtains which seemed to hang everywhere.

He heard the man's breath hiss through his clenched teeth—it sounded like a subdued exclamation of disappointment. Then the latter continued his way, softly opening the door of the mandarin's bed-room, and Clive noted with horror that something long and narrow was gripped in his hand.

Desperately the middy glanced round the room in search of a weapon. A small curved sword hung on the wall, and he swiftly drew it from its sheath. Then, seizing a wooden tray, he dashed forward with a shout, his makeshift shield held in front of him.

He burst into the bedchamber like a whirlwind. There was another lantern alight here, and by this Clive realised that his arrival had come too late by the fraction of a second; for even as he entered he saw the genial Fu Wan sink back on his couch with a dart embedded in his throat.

The murderer drew back with a snarl at this unexpected interruption,

The Chinaman drew back with a snarl at Clive's sudden entry and raised a blowpipe to his lips. Up shot Clive's tray, and a poison dart thudded upon it viciously.

and again raised the blowpipe to his lips. Up shot Clive's tray and something thudded upon it viciously. Before the man could make another attempt the sword had taken him fairly in the chest and he sank down with scarcely a cry, dead almost before he reached the floor.

Clive stooped over the stricken Fu Wan. The mandarin's face was already of a peculiar grey pallor, plainly telling that the poison had obtained a firm grip.

" Nothing can be done for me ! " he gasped. " Take the Cat—take it to the house of Kung Lu, in the Street of a Thousand Joys, and give it into his hands only. He is the next——"

" But where, sir, where *is* the Cat ?" the middy interrupted, gazing about him, and Fu Wan, summoning his last remaining strength, raised himself painfully on his couch.

" By Confucius ! " he gasped, " it is not here. It was there, beside my bed, when I lay down, yet—ah ! I know what happened. I woke and disturbed him. He had already taken the Cat and was going out, possibly by the window yonder, and—and he must have it on his person, boy ! "

" All right, sir ! I'll search him presently——"

" No, no ! Search him now—*now !* " Fu Wan gasped. " I must know that it is safe before—before—a-ah ! "

The end came with dramatic suddenness. The mandarin sank back again even as he was speaking, and his spirit fled to the Shades.

Clive summoned Sing and briefly told him what had occurred. The servant stared dumbly down at his late master's still form, but did not touch the corpse, for a Celestial has an inherent objection to doing so. Meanwhile, the middy was busily searching the person of the dead assassin, without result. Where *was* the Green Cat ?

" What can he have done with it, Sing ? " he asked in Chinese, waking the servant from what seemed to be a stupor of grief. " It is not here, and the illustrious Fu Wan commanded me, with his dying breath, to deliver it personally to the Mandarin Kung Lu, at his house in the Street of a Thousand Joys."

" Yes, I know the house," Sing nodded. " I can take you there——"

" Not without the Cat ! " Clive cut in. " We've got to find that. Ah ! What's this ? "

Suddenly crossing to the window, he pulled aside the curtains. The casement had been opened, whether by Fu Wan or his assassin it was impossible to say ; but more probably by the former, since the night was warm. And there, on a patch of lawn outside, lay the Green Cat of Canton.

Clive stepped out, returning with the precious object in his grasp. The head was still tightly fixed in its place, and a shaking betrayed a rattle of something inside, proving that the map was there intact.

" I see what happened," the middy said. " This ruffian took the Cat and threw it through the window when he saw signs of the mandarin awakening. He intended leaving by the window himself and picking it up as he went."

" Or," Sing suggested, " he had others waiting in the garden to recover the ornament when it was cast out. But, noting our presence here and possibly hearing some sounds, they feared to approach so close to the window."

" Phew ! " Clive whistled. " I never thought of that. What's to be done ? Can we leave here unobserved ? We must deliver the Cat to its new owner before doing anything else, Sing. It is most vital."

For answer the servant nodded

towards the dead mandarin on the couch.

" Round my master's neck, sir," he said, " is a golden key. It opens the door of the long passage which leads to the boat-house. We have a small launch there, and can make most of the journey by water. It will be the safest way."

" Good ! " said Clive, crossing over to the body and, sure enough, finding a small key hanging by a thin chain round the mandarin's neck.

He detached it and handed it to Sing, who swiftly led the way from the apartment.

They traversed numerous corridors, the servant instructing those he met to keep watch in the death chamber, and presently both paused at a small door of bronze hue. It was covered with numerous Chinese characters, and seemed, as well as Clive could gather from that brief examination, to be a list of Fu Wan's ancestors, with certain dates opposite each name.

" This door leads to the burying-place of my master's people, and through here he will be carried later," explained Sing. " But it is our best way to the boat-house, since we shall pass underground for a considerable distance ere coming up again."

He opened the door with the golden key and went on ahead, bearing a lantern of which he possessed himself en route. The passage wound like a snake between walls of dull-green marble, and half-way along its length the pair passed a massive ebony door showing still more hieroglyphics. Sing dumbly indicated this as he slowed down momentarily ; then he took a sharp branch to the left, and Clive felt the ground rising steadily beneath his feet.

Thus they came to the open air, and paused near the water's edge, in the drenching rain.

A few yards away stood a small boat-house, and the key of this Sing produced from his own person. He glanced round warily, as though fearing spies even here.

" I say," whispered Clive, noticing the action, " we have no arms in case we're attacked ! What's to be done ? "

Sing smiled to himself in the darkness, and again rummaged in the folds of his robe, bringing out a couple of short lengths of material which were heavily weighted at one end. He handed one of these to his companion.

" More silent than firearms ! " he replied. " One blow is generally sufficient. Now, come ! "

Clive swung the weapon in his hand. It was easy to use, and more deadly than a life-preserver. As Sing had said, one blow, properly delivered, would hardly require to be repeated.

" Is the launch ready ? " he asked. " Have you petrol ? "

" It is ready," the servant said. " My late master liked to journey on the water, and everything was kept prepared for his wishes. We shall travel down the river for about one mile ; then you can land at the Street of a Thousand Joys and deliver your burden."

In a very few minutes the launch was afloat. The pair got aboard and Clive himself started the engine. All seemed to be going particularly well—but it is just at such moments when surprises occur. And the surprise, in their case, took the form of two of the Lotus spies who, working with the dead thief, had since been watching the western end of Fu Wan's grounds.

These men caught sight of the escaping pair as the launch dipped into the river, and rushed forward just too late to attack their opponents on the bank. But, determined to avoid whatever punishment overhung them at the hands of their society in the event of failure, the spies plunged into the water, swimming strongly after the receding launch.

It was at this moment that the engine began to misfire, then to stop, and the little craft slowed down, drifting with the current. Sing bent over the mechanism, striving to put matters right, whilst Clive watched the progress of the two swimmers from the stern. Helped by the current, the latter were certainly creeping up mighty fast, and presently one of them grasped the gunwale with a yellow hand, his other arm shooting upwards as he cast a knife at the middy's form above.

But Clive had not been idle. As the pair approached, he drew the strange weighted weapon from the pocket of the jean blouse he had donned before leaving, and brought it down with all his strength on the man's upturned face, even as the knife sailed through the air and missed him by the fraction of an inch. The fellow grunted, and disappeared in the flood ; but the other was still coming on hand over hand.

At that moment Sing got the rebellious engine going again, and the little launch forged ahead ; but the swimmer was almost within arm's-length by now. Up went his hand, snatching the knife from his teeth and throwing it straight at Clive. Even as the steel whizzed towards him, the middy lurched forward and dealt a sure stroke at the thrower. Yet he only escaped by a hair's-breadth, for the knife ripped through the jean blouse at his left shoulder, cutting the flesh beneath.

But Clive's second stroke was as sure as his first. The weighted thong took the spy fairly on the temple, and he followed his confederate beneath the surface. As Sing had wisely said—there was seldom need for a second blow with such a weapon.

By now the launch was roaring downstream, and the rain had ceased suddenly. A watery moon peeped through the clouds overhead, and a few equally watery stars made their appearance. Surroundings grew clearer, and presently Sing, who had been scanning the left bank closely, motioned Clive to steer in that direction.

" Yonder begins the Street of a Thousand Joys," he said. " Shall I remain with the boat, or would you wish me to accompany you ? "

" Better come along, too—you say you know Kung Lu's house," Clive replied. " They may have other spies about here, in case that thief might have blundered. These fellows are cunning, and will very likely have taken every precaution. We can moor the boat to the bank."

" Assuredly, Young Son of Wisdom ! " the Chinese nodded. " You have a level head firmly placed upon strong shoulders. So be it ! "

THE FOURTH CHAPTER

THE SPY

SWIFTLY the middy and his companion passed along the narrow thoroughfare, Sing slightly in advance.

" The house you seek is some little distance down on the left-hand side," he explained as they progressed. " We shall reach it very soon."

They padded along, meeting not a soul. It was now very late and scarcely a light showed in any of the houses they passed. The moon was now shining brightly, and the sky had quite cleared of rain-clouds, but the shadows beneath the buildings were deep and sinister, causing Clive to give many a sidelong, anxious glance as he hurried onwards in the wake of his soft-footed companion.

Suddenly Sing paused, indicating a large building on the left.

No sooner had Clive and Sing reached the house of Kung Lu than a large piece of rock whizzed past the middy's face and struck the door.

" It is here, the illustrious Kung Lu's dwelling," he said. " And it seems that your fears were groundless, Wise One. There is nobody about."

Clive crossed over, seizing the heavy bronze knocker and giving a loud summons on the massive door. And then it was proved that his fears, instead of being groundless, were only too well-founded.

A head appeared round the corner of a neighbouring alley ; then something heavy whizzed through the air, striking the door a few inches from Clive's face and bursting with a discharge of white-powdered stone. It was a big lump of gritty rock, which would assuredly have brained him had it not missed its target.

Quickly the head withdrew, but Clive's blood was up. He thrust the Cat into Sing's hands.

" Take this and get inside as soon as they open the door ! " he snapped. " I saw that fellow's face, and I wish to make sure that my suspicions are correct. I'm going after him ! "

Ere Sing could restrain him he had hurried away, sprinting round the corner of the wall. He was soon overhauling the man, who was not a good runner and was panting along some yards ahead.

Clive increased his pace, drawing level. Then his arm went back, and down came that deadly weighted sling, the business end of it catching the fellow on the base of the skull. He pitched forward like a pole-axed ox, then rolled over with his face upturned towards the moon.

" Yes, I guessed as much," Clive muttered, gazing down. " I saw you working in the garden of poor Fu Wan's house when I arrived there, and I took a most strong dislike to you. I wondered how that other chap got in, but it's all clear now. You had the key of the door, so you deserve all you got ! "

A rush of feet from the darker depths of the alley sounded at that moment, and Clive bolted like a hare back the way he had come. He now realised that it was madness to have followed this fellow, who would surely not be alone, but he had felt incensed at being so nearly struck down by that huge lump of stone, and he was ever impetuous.

He should never have left Sing. Indeed, he had been told to deliver the Cat to Kung Lu personally and, in the excitement of the moment, he had disregarded the dead mandarin's express wishes. What if Sing had been attacked in the meantime, before the door was opened to their summons, and the Cat again stolen ?

But Clive, as it turned out, was worrying himself without cause. As a matter of fact, more than one spy had been watching Kung Lu's house for some hours, but as no one came, they had concluded that the man who entered Fu Wan's abode had succeeded in his task and that the Cat had now been handed over to the heads of the Lotus Order.

Consequently, with the exception of the fellow who had cast the stone, they had withdrawn into the network of alleys close by, and had only awakened to life again when their confederate had rushed towards them with the Britisher in hot pursuit.

When the middy again reached the Street of a Thousand Joys, it was to find Sing still rapping on the portals of the new chief's house. The hour being so very late, all the servants were in bed ; hence the delay in answering the summons.

And hard upon the sprinting lad's heels came half a score of ruffians armed with knives and sticks. They poured from the alley-mouth like an evil wave, but Clive was running as he had never run before, and joined his companion just as bolts were drawn on the inside of the door.

The pair tumbled through even as the vanguard of the enemy approached and, springing upright, Clive thrust the massive door to with his shoulder, shooting the central bolt.

" Jiminy ! That was a near squeak ! " he gasped, dashing the sweat from his forehead. " Another second, and——" He paused as he found himself confronted by the Mandarin Kung Lu in person. The latter looked at his unexpected callers strangely.

" What does this mean ? " he asked. " Surely you are the white youth who was with my friend, Fu Wan, during our conference ? I recognise your face."

" I am, sir," Clive nodded, speaking in English, for that was the language the other had used. " Your friend asked me to bring you something. Here it is ! "

He took the ornament from Sing and handed it over. Kung Lu's visage grew very grave and strained.

" The Cat ! " he ejaculated. " Why, what has happened ? Is my friend, Fu Wan——"

" I have bad news for you, sir," Clive cut in quietly. " The illustrious Fu Wan is dead—murdered by those fiends who support the Lotus. I was just too late to save him, and—and, with his last breath almost, he commanded me to bring the Cat to you. I have done so ! "

For a few moments Kung Lu was

silent. He unscrewed the head of the ornament, examined the map carefully, and replaced it. Then he held out his hand to Clive.

" You English can always be relied upon to act well under difficulties," he said gratefully. " You have done more this night than you perhaps realise. Had this thing fallen into other hands, it would have meant chaos ! "

Clive nodded.

" I know that. The lamented Fu Wan explained matters to me fully and I quite understand how important my mission was. But now, what is to be done ? Those others saw where we came, and may make a further attempt——"

" They may," Kung Lu said quickly, " but they will fail. I have the Cat, thanks to you and this loyal servant of my great friend, and I have means of hiding it which none knows of but myself. Rest assured, young sir, that our society shall live to flourish triumphant over its enemies ! "

At that Clive and Sing were content to leave matters. The mandarin, beckoning them to follow, passed along the corridor and into a small apartment, beautifully furnished, where he bade them remain for a short while.

When he returned, it was without the Green Cat of Canton, and a slight smile on his otherwise grave face suggested that it had been safely disposed of, as he had said.

" How did you come to be at the house of my friend ? " he asked Clive. " It was opportune—evidently."

Clive briefly related what had occurred, telling of the explosion which had sent his vessel to the bottom and stranded him on the quay in his unenviable plight, and how Mandarin Fu Wan had brought him home to remain with him until his position had been decided upon by the Naval authorities.

" Well," said Kung Lu, as the middy finished his story. " Pray look upon me as a successor to the illustrious Fu Wan. You will honour my house with your presence while I have a message sent to Hong Kong concerning your present whereabouts. As for this good fellow "—he glanced at Sing—" he will return to his late master's villa, for he will doubtless be needed there."

"The Finger of Fate"

By WILLIAM WIBLEY

(the actor genius of the Remove)

I'VE written a play that is sure to attract,
A drama of thrills and of vigour;
A play I intend the Removites to act,
Although I admit, as a matter of fact,
Their acting makes everyone snigger.

I know that the various plays in the past
Perhaps might have been a bit brighter;
But now we've got hold of a corker at last—
At least, there's ONE jolly good man in the cast,
Who, as you may guess, is the writer.

The play is entitled "The Finger of Fate,"
Or, "Death in the Temple of Twilight";
And I play the part of Sebastian Skate,
Who breaks into houses and pinches their plate
And finally falls through a skylight.

Then Wharton is cast as Professor de Breeze,
A potty old Indian scholar,
Who lives in a house full of poisonous bees
And cuts off the nose of each person he sees
For the pleasure of hearing him holler.

To Smithy is given the part of Wung Foo,
The Prince of Celestial wizards,
And he, with the help of his villainous crew,
Contrives to get rid of a victim or two
Before he is eaten by lizards.

Frank Nugent is clutched in the grip of a Tong
Who tickle his feet with a fescue;
And when he sees numerous bodies along
The floor of his room, he thinks something is wrong,
And so he bawls loudly for rescue.

This play would do credit to any large stage;
That's one thing of which I am certain.
Can any play beat it by one of my age?
A violent death upon every page,
An earthquake at every curtain.

And yet, though the play is so good, I must state,
In case you've decided to praise it,
That all the success of "The Finger of Fate"
Is due to the part of Sebastian Skate,
As played by—the actor who plays it!

The Hero of Tuckminster!

By

BILLY BUNTER

This is not the first time that William George Bunter, of Greyfriars, has burst into print, but we hasten to add that his style of spelling is, as usual, all his own; and we strongly suspect that, in his modest way, Bunter has modelled his hero on his own fat self!—Ed.

THE FIRST CHAPTER

THE FEED

THE name of the hero of this thrilling skool story is Billy Buster.

Billy Buster was in his study enjoying a whacking grate feed, when his loyle chums, Feeder and Gorge, rolled in.

"Help yourselves, chaps!" said Billy Buster, his handsum face beeming hospitably. "My treat, you know!"

"Thanks awfully, Buster, old chap!" corussed Feeder and Gorge gratefully, as they sat down and attacked the grub with rellish. "It's very jennerous of you, we must say."

"Of corse it is. It's my nature to be jennerous and kind-harted," was Buster's answer, as he pollished off a cupple of pork pies.

For the next five minnits or so, no sound was heard in the study save the steddy munching of tuck. Let us take advantage of the interval, deer reeder, to learn a little about the central figger of this enthrawling romance of public skool life.

Billy Buster was the handsumest, clevverest fellow in the Fourth Form at Tuckminster. He was far and away the best skoller in the Fourth, and but for the ignorance of his Form-master, Mr. Littlegrub, who didn't know a jeenius when he saw one, Buster would have been at the top of the Form. As it was, however, he was at the bottom.

At games, our hero was brilliant. He could score goals by the duzzen at kricket and runs by the hundred at football; in fact, Buster was the best all-round sportsman that had ever been seen at Tuckminster. Sad to relait, his amazing jeenius at games was rarely if ever displayed. Solely owing to the jellusy of Skelleton, the skipper of the Fourth, Buster was barred from the Form team. It's rotten to think of the lengths to which jellusy will carry some fellows, but the sad trooth must be told.

In appearance, Buster was strikingly good-looking. He had a boolet head and a perfectly-rounded snub nose of a dellicate shade of pink; his cheeks and chin had the graceful lines of a half-filled balloon and his eyes, though small, were intelligent. Skelleton called them piggy and cunning, but that was sheer prejudice. The ongsomble (French) was very striking, and Buster's face might well have eggsited envy in the brest of many a famous film star.

But Billy Buster's crowning glory was his figger. If you imajine it bore any resemblance to the lean and hungry-looking figgers of Skelleton, Bones, Broomstick and Waystead, the so-called leaders of the Fourth, you're jolly well mistaken. As a matter of fact, it resembled more closely than anything I can think of at the moment, a barrel. To get down to brass tax, Buster was well covered. He was not tall; but what he lacked in height, he made up for in width. Many Fourth-Formers compared him with a porpuss or a hippopotomuss, but, needless to say, that was only another eggsample of the jellusy of the beasts.

Now let us get back to the eggsiting events of this thrilling narrative. Buster and Feeder and Gorge were just coming to the end of the whacking grate feed which Buster had so jennerously provided, when there was a thunderous crash on the door, and three skinny-looking rotters looked in. They were Skelleton, the Fourth kaptin, and his pals, Broomstick and Bones.

Skelleton & Co. looked awfully eggsited.

"Where's our grub, you fat brigand?" roared Skelleton feercely. (That was the pleasant way the beast had of addressing the brilliant jeenius.)

Most fellows would have been fearfully scared at being spoken to in this way by the kaptin of the Fourth, for Skelleton had a bit of a reputation as a boxer. But Billy Buster feared no foe in shining armour. He simply eyed the enrajed kaptin with a skornful glarnse.

"How the dickens should I know?" he retorted calmly.

That reply seemed to enrage Skelleton still more. He pointed a trembling finger at the remains of Billy Buster's feast.

"By the look of things, you've skoffed it all, you fat scoundrell!" he hooted.

Billy Buster recoiled, as from a blow.

"Does that mean you accuse me of pinching your grub?" he asked, his handsum face a study in outraged innersense.

"It jolly well does!"

"Well, if that's not the limit!" breethed Buster, as the full meaning of the accusation pennytrated his branebox. "Chap can't have a feed in the privvacy of his own study now without being accused of pinching the grub! What next, I wonder?"

"Shame!" cride Feeder and Gorge,

"I can manage this myself, you fellows!" exclaimed Buster, hitting out at Skelleton & Co. Biff! Skelleton was laid out with one mighty swipe. Thud! Broomstick collapsed in a limp heap. Crash! Bones fell like a log.

their handsum, well-fed faces dark with anger.

Skelleton, however, was not to be put off.

"That grub was mine!" he roared.

"It jolly well wasn't!" yelled Buster indignantly. "I bought it at the tuckshop!"

"Pinched it from my study, you mean!" howled Skelleton.

Buster farely gasped with indignation. It really was a bit thick to have his word doubted like this. All the grub that had just been consumed—or nearly all of it—had been bought at the skool shop that afternoon. Billy Buster had receeved sevveral postal-orders for large sums of munny from some of his numerous titled relations and had eggspended it freely. And if, by any chance, some of the grub had been taken from Skelleton's study, Buster had meerly borrowed it, fully intending to pay it back afterwards, so there was no need to make a song about it.

"Now look here, Skelleton," said Billy Buster, patiently.

"Hand over our grub!" bawled Skelleton.

"If you're going to adopt this manner, I shall decline to discuss the matter any further," said Buster, with quiet dignity.

"The grub or a licking—which?" roared Skelleton, in boolying tones.

Billy Buster smiled. If there was any question of a licking, he was quite prepared to take all the lickings Skelleton could give him !

" Spare me, old chap ! " he cride, sarkastically

Skelleton attacked him instead.

Crash ! Bang ! Wallop !

The skipper's bony fists crashed into Buster's handsum face with terrific force. They were fearful blows—blows that would hastily have felled an ox—but Buster meerly larfed at them.

" I wish you'd stop tickling me, Skelleton ! " was all he said.

Skelleton turned to his followers.

" Come and help me, you fellows ! We'll lick him by fare means or fowl !" he cride fewriously.

Broomstick and Bones, with horse cries, rushed to the help of their leader and the three skinny beasts made a tremenjous onslawt on Buster.

Our hero, however, was more than a match for Skelleton & Co. He calmly waved back Feeder and Gorge, who jumped to their feet with the idea of assisting him.

" I can manage this myself, you fellows ! " he said.

Biff !

Skelleton was laid out with one mitey swipe.

Thud !

Broomstick collapsed in a limp heap.

Crash !

Bones fell like a log.

" Now chuck them out, you fellows, and perhaps we can finish our feed in piece ! " yawned Buster, flicking a speck of dust from his Eton jacket.

Feeder and Gorge grinned and carried out the limp bodies of Skelleton & Co. After which, the interrupted feed was finished amid much rejoicing.

THE SECOND CHAPTER

BUSTER THE BRAVE !

UNFORCHUNITLY, that wasn't the end of the incident of the missing tuck. Shortly afterwards. Meager minor of the Third poked his lantern jaws round the study door.

" Billy Buster wanted in the Head's study ! " he announced breefly, then buzzed off.

Feeder and Gorge looked awfully serious. A summons to the Head's study was no joke. Usually it ended up in a weeping and wailing and nashing of teeth. Dr. Scarecrow, the vennerable headmaster of Tuckminster, was a brute and a booly, who tempered injustiss with no mersy. A savvidge tiger, thirsting for gore, was quite a meek kind of creature compared with Dr. Scarecrow.

" Been up to more of your reckless pranx, Buster ? " asked Feeder, simperthetically. " Better stuff your baggs with exercise-books if you have. You know what a terror the Head is when he gets going ! "

But Buster's conscience was quite clear, though it must be admitted that he looked a trifle uneasy.

" Don't worry, chaps ! " he cride, reassuringly. " I am innersent of wrongdoing. If the Head thinks I pinched his feed, he's jolly well mistaken."

" Has the Head's feed been pinched, then ? " asked Gorge.

Buster grinned.

" I fansy Skelleton & Co. could tell you," he answered. " Matter of fact, I happened to overhear them planning to pinch it."

The orther would like to eggsplain here that Billy Buster was a remarkably intellijent youth who was quick to find out what was going on around him. Even at odd moments, such as when he was tying up his shoelaces,

" Yaroooo ! Yow-ow-ow ! Woooop ! " yelled Buster as Dr. Scarecrow wielded his birch with deadly effect. Suddenly the door was flung open and the terrified voice of Mr. Littlegrub bawled out : " Run for your lives ! The school is on fire ! "

his sensative ears would occasionally catch little items of interest—a gift that very few other chaps at Tuckminster possessed.

Leaving his loyle chums shaking their heads dewbiously, Billy Buster strolled cheerfully out of the study and made his way to the most dredded apartment at Tuckminster—the study of Dr. Scarecrow.

Reaching his destination, he kicked open the door and entered.

It was immejately obvious to Buster's practissed eye that the Head was in a dickens of a rage. His lean, haggard face was distorted with fury, his green, glittering eyes were almost bolting out of their sockits and his grate hawk-like nose twitched spasmodically. A less intellijent fellow than Billy Buster would not have perseeved these little signs, but Buster took in everything at a glarnse and knew at once that he was " for it."

Dr. Scarecrow showed his fangs in a snarl as Buster entered.

" You gormandising rotter ! " he hissed. " You have pinched my tuck ! "

Any other fellow in Buster's place would have coward and whimpered for mersy in the aw-inspiring presence of the Head at that moment. But Billy Buster was made of sterner stuff than that.

Drawing himself up to his full height, he regarded the Head with calm and skornful eyes.

" I never done it ! " he said quietly.

" I tell you you did ! " hooted the Head.

" And I tell you I didn't ! "

" You're gilty ! "

" I'm jolly well not ! "

" You jolly well are ! "

Lack of space prevents the orther rendering this eggsiting conversation in full. Anyway, after about half-an-hour of it, the Head suddenly roared :

" Well, if you didn't take it, who did ? "

Billy Buster's lipps set in a firm line.

" I'm sorry, sir, but I cannot sneak," he said with quiet determination. " My skoolboy code of honner makes it impossibul for me to answer your question. But if I could bring myself to do it, I should say that the gilty parties were Skelleton & Co. of the Fourth."

The Head picked up his birch.

" I'll go and see the rotters at once," he muttered. " Woe betide them if they've wolfed the lot ! "

Billy Buster laid a restraining hand on Dr. Scarecrow's arm.

" Eggscuse me, sir—— " he began.

" Well ? " snarled the Head.

" If they tell you I pinched the tuck from them, I hope you won't beleeve them. You can take it from me, sir, that particular feed was bought with the remittances sent me this morning by my titled relations ! "

For some eggstraordinary reason, Dr. Scarecrow seemed fearfully annoyed at that. Any reasonable headmaster would have felt nothing but grattitude to Buster for putting him wise. But there was no grattitude in Dr. Scarecrow's hart.

Instead of going out on the warpath against Skelleton & Co., he turned back into the study, skowling savvidgely.

" You admit, then, that you had my tuck ? " he said harshly.

" Nothing of the kind, sir ! " answered Billy Buster, in surprise.

Buster was continually being surprised by the density of the masters at Tuckminster. Somehow or other, they always misunderstood what he said.

On this occasion, the Head didn't wait for Buster to go into further eggsplanation. Without waiting to consider the possibility that he mite be chastising an innersent viktim, whose record was white and unblemished as the drivven snow, Dr. Scarecrow waded in, weelding his birch on Billy Buster with deadly effect.

" Yaroooo ! Yow-ow-ow ! Woooop ! " yelled Buster, biting his lips till they bled so that he should utter no cry of pain.

How long he mite have had to endure that terribul punishment is a matter for conjecture. Forchunitly, before the Head had really got into his stride, the door of the study was flung open and the terrified voice of Mr. Littlegrub bawled out :

" Run for your lives ! The skool is on fire ! "

Instantly Dr. Scarecrow dropped his birch and, with a yell of fear, raced out of the room, Mr. Littlegrub following close on his heels.

Billy Buster, calm and undawnted in the face of danjer, strolled out at a more leisurely pace, to find that the whole skool was assembulled in the old quad, watching the feerce flames roaring up from the roof of the Skool House.

Suddenly, a cry of horror rang out.

" Grate pip ! The Head's dawter ! "

Billy Buster was startled to see the Head's bewtiful dawter, Gertie Scarecrow, leening out of a window at the top of the building, ringing her hands pitteously.

Dr. Scarecrow tore his hair, almost fermented.

" Who will save her ? " he cride, in a strangled voice.

Nobody answered. Strong men turned pail and brave boys blarnched as they glarnsed at the consewming flames. Skelleton & Co., of the Fourth, slunk out of the way, their neeze nocking at the meer thought of it.

Then a calm voice spoke up.

" Don't worry your fat, sir. I'll bring Miss Gertie down in half a jiffy ! "

It was Billy Buster ! No sooner had he spoken than he was climbing up the old ivy with the ajillity of a monkey. In about three seconds he had shinned up the hundred-odd feet that separated Miss Gertie from the ground, heedless of the roaring flames that raged around him. Pawsing only to fling the helpless girl over his shoulder, he then dessended, and a few seconds later had restored Gertie Scarecrow to her doating father, while the skool cheered itself horse.

" Buster ! " sobbed Dr. Scarecrow. " My brave Buster ! You have returned good for evil ! "

" That's all right, sir ! " grinned our hero. " I'm used to doing things like that ! "

" Only to think that I was licking you a short time ago ! " muttered the Head. " The thought makes me feel awfully greeved. Is there anything I can do to repay you, Buster ? Meerly name it, and I will do it ! "

" Well, there is something, as a matter of fact ! " grinned Buster. " Just at the moment I'm feeling awfully peckish. If you could see your way clear to standing me a feed in the tuckshop, sir——"

" The plezzure is mine ! " said the Head immejately, and, without further ado, he led the way to the tuckshop.

And the orther is glad to be able to add that the feed was one that could be called really worthy of the suspicious occasion. The Head did himself proud, so to speak, in standing treat to the Hero of Tuckminster !

Tr-r-ring!—tr-r-ring! Hallo! "Holiday Annual" Phone Exchange? You want to speak to fellows of Greyfriars, St. Jim's, and Rookwood? Just look up their numbers and given questions and you are through!

RING up any fellow or master at Greyfriars, St. Jim's, Rookwood, Highcliffe or Rylcombe Grammar School whose phone number is in the list, and ask a given question. You will get an answer!

First select your question from the list which follows. *E.g.* Do you believe in corporal punishment?

By each question you will see a letter code—in this case "AK." You next look up the phone number of your "victim"—suppose we say Mr. Quelch? His number, as you will see, is Q 0333. Now add the question code ("AK") to the "Q," making QAK 0333—and under that alphabetical heading in the reply section you will find the answer to your question.

LIST OF QUESTIONS
With Code Letters

	Code
Which of your friends do you admire most?	AX
(Ring up boys only; masters will not answer.)	
Do you believe in corporal punishment?	AK
(Ring up masters, prefects, and leading characters.)	
What is your favourite pastime?	EP
(Ring up boys only.)	
If you were Form captain, what would you do with the present Football XI? ..	EX
(Ring up leading characters only.)	
What is your secret ambition?	IL
(Most fellows will answer.)	

As a member of the Junior Dramatic Society, what rôle would you most like to play? IX
(Ring up leading characters only.)

What is your pet superstition? OL
(Ring up leading characters only.)

Do you find juniors difficult to keep in order? .. .. OG
(Ring up masters, prefects, and Coker.)

Do you think the school curriculum could be improved? UX
(Leading Greyfriars characters only.)

What is your advice to a fellow on facing the world? .. UL
(Ring up all masters.)

TELEPHONE DIRECTORY

Name	Number
Bolsover, Percy	B 1234
Bull, Johnny	B 1300
Bunter, William George	B 1414
Blake, Jack	B 5166
Bulkeley, George	B 6446
Coker, Horace	C 0666
Cherry, Bob	C 1511
Cardew, Ralph Reckness	C 5499
Clive, Sidney	C 5555
Chisholm, Dr.	C 6262
Desmond, Micky	D 1633
Dupont, Napoleon	D 1705
D'Arcy, Arthur Augustus	D 5277
D'Arcy, Wally	D 6111
Dalton, Mr.	D 6300
Dodd, Tommy	D 7117
Doyle, Tommy	D 7222
Field, S. Q. I.	F 1855
Fish, Fisher T.	F 1919
Figgins, George	F 5733
Gosling, William	G 1066
Glyn, Bernard	G 4511
Grundy, George Alfred	G 4994
Grace, "Putty"	G 6970
Gay, Gordon	G 7777
Hobson, James	H 0702
Hoskins, Claude	H 0888
Holmes, Dr.	H 3600
Herries, George	H 5388
Kipps, Oliver	K 2000
Kildare, Eric	K 3944
Knox, Gerald	K 4000
Kerr, George	K 5885
Locke, Dr.	L 0133
Loder, Gerald	L 0511
Linley, Mark	L 2111
Lowther, Monty	L 4333
Lovell, Arthur Edward	L 6700
Mauleverer, Lord	M 2222
Merry, Tom	M 4200
Manners, Harry	M 4444
Mornington, Val	M 6837
Muffin, Tubby	M 7000
Nugent, Frank	N 2388
Nugent, Dicky	N 3566
Noble, Harry	N 4622
Prout, Mr.	P 0233
Penfold, Dick	P 2442

Gerald Loder: Lines and lickings make no difference to Wharton and his pals. They even put glue in my slippers the other day!

Ponsonby, Cecil	P 7666
Quelch, Mr.	Q 0333
Redwing, Tom	R 2525
Russell, Dick	R 2626
Railton, Mr.	R 3737
Ratcliff, Mr.	R 3811
Redfern, Dick	R 6000
Singh, Hurree	S 2777
Skinner, Harold	S 2811
Skimpole, Herbert	S 5055
Silver, Jimmy	S 6666
Silver, Algy	S 7337
Temple, Cecil Reginald ..	T 0911
Todd, Alonzo	T 2922
Todd, Peter	T 3037
Talbot, Reginald	T 4844
Trimble, Baggy	T 5611
Vernon-Smith, Herbert ..	V 3113
Vivian, Sir Jimmy	V 3227
Wingate, George	W 0411
Wharton, Harry	W 1188
Wibley, William	W 3300
Wun Lung	W 3477
Wynn, David Llewellyn ..	W 5959

Dicky Nugent : Pea-shooting is the finest sport, take it from me !

REPLY SECTION

BAX 1234 I think I admire myself more than anybody.

BAX 1300 Bob Cherry is the sort of chum I like.

BAX 1414 I admire Toddy tremendously—when he's prepared to stand tea in the study. Otherwise, he's a beast !

BAX 5166 Gussy is no end of an ass, but I can't help admiring his taste in ties, though I can't bear waiting about while he dresses !

BAK 6446 Neville and I have always got on splendidly together.

BAK 1414 Jolly well NO !

BEP 1234 Twisting the ears of hapless fags !

BEP 1300 I've always had a penchant for weight-lifting. I've even lifted Bunter off the ground !

BEP 1414 I don't mind an eating contest with anybody !

BEP 5166 The sound of a football bouncing is like a clarion call to me !

BEP 6446 Football ; then cricket.

BEX 1234 I should drop Bull or Redwing to make room for myself. At present Wharton only plays me as a reserve—favouritism, I suppose ! The team isn't so bad apart from that !

BEX 1414 With me as Captain, the Junior XI would go from strength to strength. All it needs is a fellow of real weight, like myself, to crash the ball through the back of the net

BEX 5166 I should leave the XI much as it is under Merry ; but, of course, under a Yorkshireman's leadership it would do better !

BIL 1234 I'd like to be a prize-fighter.

BIL 1414 I really don't see why I should have to work. With all my titled relations, it would be rather infra dig. Still, I shouldn't mind running one of the big chocolate firms !

BIL 5166 I rather incline to a business career

BIX 1414 Only Wibley's rotten jealousy keeps me from playing Hamlet. I refused to appear as Julius Cæsar I know he gets killed half-way through !

BOL 1414 I hate to see another fellow eat more than I do at dinner. Fortunately that rarely—if ever—happens.

BUX 1234 Yes ; cut out classes altogether !

BUX 1414 A fellow shouldn't be stopped from eating in class. I frequently need a little pick-me-up in the middle of a lesson !

CAX 0666 I like Potter and Greene about equally, though I don't know what either of the silly asses would do without me !

CAX 1511 It's a job to choose between Johnny Bull and Mark Linley !

CAX 5499 Gad, admiration isn't in my line ! Clive's a good fellow.

CAX 5555 I guess I like Cardew as well as anybody, though he's very cynical at times !

CAK 0666 I think corporal punishment should only be administered by a responsible person—like me, for instance. Incidentally, I ought to have been made a prefect long ago !

CAK 6262 Yes, providing it is not administered in anger.

CEP 0666 I'm so gifted in every branch of sport that I haven't any favourite !

CEP 1511 Boxing, though footer and cricket come close after.

CEP 5499 Sport is a dreadful fag, anyway !

CEP 5555 Hiking and camping.

CEX 0666 If my talents were recognised and I were elected skipper, I'd soon make a clean sweep of Wingate's crowd ! Not that it would matter much who played, if I were in command !

CIL 0666 I should like to become a dictator, running the country on the right lines; but all Potter and Greene can do when I mention it is to cackle !

CIL 1511 Exploring, like Harry Wharton, attracts me.

CIL 5499 My ambition is just to go on slackin'—and observin' life.

CIX 0666 I'd be a "dab" at Hamlet, or equally good as Macbeth, Romeo, or King Lear.

COL 0666 Superstitious ? Rot !

COG 0666 Fags are frequently cheeky to me, but though I'm not a prefect, as I ought to be, I find a smart cuff does a lot of good !

COG 6262 I find Rookwooders most orderly, as a rule. There was once a barring-out, but it was provoked by a temporary master.

CUX 0666 Yes ! There should be more time for sport—under my personal instruction !

CUL 6262 Don't let anything deter you; that is the secret of success. Keep that thought always before you, and many difficulties will melt.

DAX 1633 Sure, I admire Harry Wharton immensely, though I'd make a better Form captain myself, begorrah !

DAX 5277 I have always admired Blake and, of course, Tom Mewwy—both fine fellows in every sense of the word.

DAX 6111 Any fellow who doesn't plump for my major is asking for a punch on the nose !

DAX 7117 There's nothing to choose between Cook and Doyle for stout pals.

DAX 7222 Tommy Dodd is leader of the Modern side, and he ought to be junior captain !

George Kerr : My crowning triumph was when I impersonated a new master and succeeded in caning several School House men !

DAK 5277 Bai Jove, I weally think it can be overdone, you know. The othah day Kildare gave me "six" on my new twousahs; he might easily have split them !

DAK 6111 Lickings are all in the day's march, but old Selby, our Form-master, often overdoes it !

DAK 6300 Yes, if tempered with mercy.

DEP 1705 I think fencing is the finest exercise, and teaches a fellow to take care of himself !

DEP 5277 Bai Jove, you know, I think a fellow looks most elegant at the battin' cwease, pwovidin' he has wemembahed to put his pads on stwaight.

DEP 6111 Cooking herrings before the Form-room fire is pretty good fun !

DEP 7117 Footer, especially beating the Classicals !

DEX 5277 Bai Jove, I should make one big change, deah boy ! That is, playin' myself at centre-forward and puttin' Tom Mewwy on the wing, where I play now. I feel suah it would wesult in yet more goals bein' scored for St. Jim's !

DIL 5277 I weally think I could show them a thing or two in the House of Commons, you know !

DIX 1705 I should like to represent Napoleon on the stage, though I am rather thin and I should have to pad myself !

DOL 5277 Superstitions are wot, I think. All the same, I dislike passin' fellows on the stairs, but that is because some silly ass usually manages to wumple my clothin'!

DOG 6300 Silver and his friends set a sound example in conduct which is followed by the rest of my Form.

DUL 6300 I always think an active life is the best for health, but every boy must follow his own bent. Follow yours with all the enthusiasm you possess!

FAX 1855 I think Harry Wharton is a first-class skipper and sportsman.

FAX 1919 I guess it's no use wasting admiration on the sort of guys one meets up with in this joint!

FAX 5733 You can't beat old Kerr, though I'm equally fond of Fatty Wynn!

FEP 1855 Cricket is my game. We make a speciality of it in Australia, you know!

FEP 1919 Say, baseball is the only game worth playing!

FEP 5733 A long, swinging walk is one of the most exhilarating things on earth.

FEX 1919 I guess I'd reorganise the XI on up-to-date American lines, if I didn't change the code and make them play baseball instead!

FEX 5733 A New House skipper for St. Jim's could guarantee to win every match, but the School House rabbits won't let me try!

Mr. Ratcliff: I never walk under ladders now. A pot of paint once fell on my head!

FIL 1919 Some day I'll be a famous financier; then you guys will hop!

FIL 5733 I'd like to take up something athletic and compete in the Olympic Games.

GAX 1066 Lord Mauleverer has my unstinted admiration, bein' the most generous gent at Greyfriars!

GAX 4511 I admire Noble as a sportsman, but he should take more interest in my inventions!

GAX 4994 I'm very fond of my pals, Wilkins and Gunn, but I'm afraid they're not worth admiring!

GAX 6970 Jimmy Silver is a good skipper, but I'd make a better!

GAX 7777 Frank Monk is my bosom pal, but Carboy, the Tadpole, and the Woottons are always up to the neck with us in whatever we do!

GAK 1066 Wot I says is this 'ere—most of the young rips ought to be tanned once a week reg'lar!

GEP 4511 Mechanics. My inventions are my sole interest.

GEP 4994 I'm good at everything, but best perhaps as a centre-forward or a batsman.

GEP 6970 Joking—all kinds!

GEP 7777 Footer—come over to Rylcombe and see us some time. We'll guarantee to give you a licking!

GEX 4994 The Junior XI needs one thing—me! I could carry any team to victory—but somehow Tom Merry is too dense to see it!

GIL 1066 I'd like to retire and live a life of ease—free from these young rascals for good!

GIL 4511 Great inventors are always laughed at at first. I'm getting my share now!

GIX 4994 I'd look well as Alexander the Great, or Julius Cæsar, or any of the great heroes. Greatness calls for a great actor—though Lowther says I only act the goat!

GIX 6970 I'm the best actor in the junior school. Even Jimmy Silver admits it, though he says I'm conceited. I want eventually to play in modern farce.

GOL 1066 I 'ates to see a good glass o' liquor spilt—that worries me more than spilling the salt!

GOG 1066 Difficult? I 'ave nothing but cheek and impudence from 'em from mornin' till night!

GUL 1066 Thank you kindly, sir! I 'opes you 'ave good luck!

HAX 0702 I rather admire Hoskins, though he is a bit of an ass.

HAX 0888 I have a great admiration for my rather heavy-handed friend, Hobson.

HAX 5388 You can't go far wrong with Gussy

—though it's fun to pull his elegant leg!

HAK 3600 I agree with corporal punishment so long as it is not carried to extremes.

HEP 0702 I think Rugger ought to be introduced at Greyfriars. I have a very strong tackle myself!

HEP 5388 A ramble with my dog Towser is my idea of good sport.

HIL 0888 I hope some day to become a world-famous violinist, like Kubelik.

HOG 3600 Boys will be boys—but there is very little real trouble.

HUX 0888. Music should certainly play a great part in the curriculum. Every boy should learn to play something.

HUL 3600 Boys are always asking me to help them choose a career. I cannot do that for you. You must do it for yourself. But whatever you choose, do your job with all your might and main!

KAX 3944 Darrel is the best fellow I've met.

KAX 4000 Can't say I admire anybody. I think Kildare is a washout as Captain.

KAX 5885 Figgy or Fatty—I can't possibly choose!

KAK 3944 A light but firm hand at the rein is best.

KAK 4000 Certainly! Lick 'em till they can't stand!

KEP 2000 I like outdoor sports, but I'm most fond of practising my conjuring tricks—at which I'm said to be a "dab"!

KEP 3944 Cricket and football rank equally with me.

KEP 5885 Footer first, chess second, theatricals third.

KIL 2000 I intend to rival the great stage illusionists—like the Maskelynes.

KIL 5885 Business for me!

KIX 5885 My crowning triumph was when I impersonated a new master and succeeded in caning several School House men! They haven't forgotten it yet!

LAX 0511 I don't admire anybody particularly.

LAX 2111 I'd rather not choose; but I think of Bob Cherry as the best pal a fellow could have.

LAX 4333 I admire Tom Merry. He has just that little something the others haven't got!

LAX 6700 Jimmy Silver always thinks he should take the lead, but otherwise I think he's a great scout!

LAK 0133 The modern tendency is to dispense with it, though I cannot think that this is altogether a move in the right direction.

LAK 0511 Certainly! You can't lick the little beasts often enough!

LEP 2111 I like rowing best of all—preferably sculling on my own.

Wun Lung: Little Chinee plactise the art of ju-jitsu—velly useful against big bully Bolsover, when I throw him over my head!

LEP 4333 I enjoy all sport—if I can make a joke about it!

LEP 6700 Footer—playing at inside-right for preference.

LIL 4333 I'm going to be a comedian on the stage and films, if they'll have me!

LIL 6700 I'll go wherever Jimmy goes!

LIX 4333 Impersonating great heroes of the past is good fun. But I think my impersonation of Mr. Lathom was the best thing I ever did. It completely fooled the New House fatheads!

LOG 0133 I am fortunate in having a sound staff. There is very little trouble.

LOG 0511 Lines and lickings make no difference to Wharton and his pals. They even put gum in my slippers the other day!

LUL 0133 Work hard: don't despair, though the first years may be difficult. Knowledge and staying power will help you to win through.

MAX 2222 Begad, I admire Bob Cherry tremendously. His energy astounds a sleepy fellow like me!

MAX 4200 Monty or Manners—I really can't choose—

MAX 4444 Tom or Monty—perhaps Tom just gets it.

MAX 6837 By gad, Erroll's the only fellow I can stick for long!

MAX 7000 Jimmy Silver is a sportsman—

Johnny Bull : I've always had a penchant for weight-lifting. I've even lifted Bunter off the ground !

sometimes. He stood me some doughnuts yesterday !

MAK 4200 Give me a licking any time rather than a "gating"—but bullies like Knox should be restrained.

MAK 7000 Lickings should be abolished. I hate 'em !

MEP 2222 Sleeping, begad !

MEP 4200 Footer just beats cricket with me.

MEP 4444 Outdoor photography is my real hobby.

MEP 6837 Running is my favourite. I've a useful turn of speed.

MEP 7000 A sprint—to the tuckshop !

MEX 2222 Begad, I should leave it all to Wharton. He knows far more about it than I ever could !

MIL 2222 Ambition ? Begad, I suppose it would be as comfy as anywhere to sleep in the House of Lords !

MIL 4200 I'd like to take up flying—if I don't join the Army, like my father, the late General Merry.

MIL 4444 The International Chess Championship attracts me.

MIL 6837 Hadn't thought about it. What about a job as an ambassador ?

MOL 2222 I don't believe in unlucky numbers or anything of that sort. They make me feel sleepy, begad. Yaw-aw-aw !

MUX 2222 Begad, why start classes so early and keep them on so late ?

NAX 2388 I think Harry Wharton is an ideal chum and leader.

NAX 3566 Oh, I guess I admire my major—Franky—he's a good old sport, though rather prim.

NAX 4622 I think a lot of Glyn. He'll invent something worth while some day !

NAK 3566 No fag can honestly agree with corporal punishment !

NEP 2388 Football every time.

NEP 3566 Pea-shooting is the finest sport, take it from me !

NEP 4622 Give an Australian cricket every time!

NIL 4622 I'd like to play Test cricket for Australia.

NUX 3566 Classes are a necessary evil, but why not make them optional ?

PAX 2442 " When called to admire, my pen is on fire.
To praise one is folly, to praise all is jolly ! "

PAK 0233 For juniors, by all means ! I sometimes wish I could deal with seniors like Coker in a summary manner, too !

PEX 2442 " As Captain of the junior team
I'd jolly soon make it supreme;
Though I admit, 'tis only fair,
That Wharton's a captain without compare ! "

PEX 7666 Before Courtenay came to Highcliffe I used to run the Junior XI. If we didn't win so many matches, at least we had class !

PIL 2442 I've always yearned to become Poet Laureate.

POG 0233 The only boy I despair of training is Coker !

PUL 0233 I suppose every boy does not want to go abroad, but I think that is the way adventure lies.

QAK 0333 In moderation, I think it does more good than harm.

QOL 0333 I have no superstitions.

QOG 0333 I invariably find my boys amenable to reason. Firm treatment is occasionally necessary, of course.

QUX 0333 In some ways it could undoubtedly be modernised, but that would mean the omission of much valuable instruction in the Classics now given.

QUL 0333 Remember the world will be more severe than I have been; it will not always be just, but if you keep a good heart and hold your head high you will be a credit to Greyfriars.

RAX 2525 I think Smithy is a real sportsman—in spite of his "awkward" moods.

RAX 6000 Figgins is the best man to lead the New House—failing myself.

RAK 3737 I rarely have to "lick" a junior, but when I am forced to, I don't believe in sparing the rod.

RAK 3811 Juniors should be punished much more frequently and severely than they are at present. I do my best to make up for the deficiencies of my colleagues in this respect.

REP 2525 Footer takes pride of place with me.

REP 2626 I prefer boxing to anything—possibly because I'm pretty good at it.

REP 6000 Footer—and I aim to show Figgy that he isn't the only pebble on the beach!

RIL 2525 Captaining a big Atlantic liner would suit me.

RIL 6000 I hope to become a distinguished journalist.

ROL 3811 I never walk under ladders. A pot of paint once fell on my head in front of a crowd of juniors.

ROG 3737 My boys are usually very well behaved.

ROG 3811 Junior boys at St. Jim's are nothing but lawless young rascals. I am frequently severe with them, but to no purpose.

RUL 3737 You can't all be winners, though I hope you will be. " Go in and win" is just as good a motto as ever it was. The harder you go in the more likely you are to win.

RUL 3811 Mr. Railton will be more likely to give you advice on this subject. I have some impositions to correct, and I really can't be bothered.

SAX 2777 The admirefulness of the esteemed and ludicrous Bob Cherry is reprehensibly terrific.

SAX 2811 Nothing much to admire in anybody, if you ask me.

SAX 5055 My dear friend, I have the most sincere admiration for Tom Merry, but as a student of Determinism he lags far behind the ideal.

SAX 6666 Old Lovell annoys me at times, but you couldn't have a better man at your side.

SAX 7337 My major Jimmy isn't a bad old stick—though a bit cocky, like all majors.

SAK 6666 Dicky Dalton often licks us, but we don't grumble. He keeps within bounds.

SEP 2777 Football. It keeps out the coldfulness of the marvellous British winter.

SEP 2811 Why do you keep ringing up to ask silly questions. Sport's a waste of time.

SEP 5055 Sport, my dear friend, is much too dangerous a pastime for me. I prefer the study of the various " ologies " and " isms."

SEP 6666 Cricket—and I prefer bowling, being the champion bowler of the junior school. Excuse my modesty.

SEP 7337 Footer. I'm good enough for the junior XI—but my major can't see it.

SEX 2811 I'd soon get rid of Wharton's crowd and have a real team—unless I felt like cards in the study, when footer would be " off " !

SIL 2777 I hope eventually to rule my State of Bhanipur in India. When I do so the justice will be terrific!

SIL 2811 I wouldn't mind being a " bookie " —a successful one!

SIL 6666 Your " Uncle James " leans towards discovery by land, sea and air!

SIX 2811 I could play any of Shakespeare's heroes on my head—if I cared. But it's too much trouble.

SIX 6666 I like all Shakespeare's stuff—and I enjoyed playing Hamlet in the Common-room. I hope the audience enjoyed it, too!

SOL 6666 I believe your fate is in your hands, to make or mar as you will.

TAX 0911 Oh, gad! Does a fellow have to admire his friends?

TAX 2922 My brother Peter is in many respects an ideal comrade, though rather apt to be thoughtless.

TAX 3037 I have a sneaking regard for " Lonzy." He's the most sincere ass I know.

TAX 4844 I admire Tom Merry most of all.

TAX 5611 If you'll lend me five bob, old chap, I'll admire you immensely!

TEP 0911 I think the most beneficial form of sport is a gentle stroll, with due regard for your appearance.

Billy Bunter: A fellow shouldn't be barred from eating in class. I frequently need a little pick-me-up in the middle of a lesson!

TEP 2922 I am afraid I do not take much interest in sport, though I do not think it does very much harm.

TEP 3037 A bracing game of footer for me. I play at centre-half.

TEP 4844 Football or cricket in season—I love them both!

TEP 5611 Eating and/or sleeping.

TIL 2922 My ambition is to lecture on humanitarianism and kindred subjects.

TIL 3037 To become a great counsel-at-law is my aim. I practise now at the Rag debates!

TIL 5611 Why worry about the future? The present's enough for me to go on with—providing I've got plenty to eat!

TUX 0911 More time should be allowed for a fellow to make himself look natty in the morning.

VAX 3113 Redwing is a great pal. How he puts up with my savage temper I don't know!

VAX 3227 I think of Mauly as my best pal—though I admire Wharton.

VAK 3113 What's all the fuss over a lickin', anyway?

VEP 3113 Anything energetic — football, cricket or boxing!

VIL 3113 I wouldn't mind a stab at the Stock Exchange, where my father operates.

WAX 0411 You couldn't desire a better pal than Patrick Gwynne, Irish and staunch!

WAX 1188 I think Frank Nugent is the best pal a fellow could have. He stood by me when I came to Greyfriars.

WAX 3300 I admire Dick Rake, though he's a rotten actor!

WAX 3477 Me likee handsome Bob Chellee velly much—he velly kind, keep bullies off little Chinee!

WAX 5959 I think Figgins is a great scout. What he says "goes" in the New House!

WAK 0411 I have occasionally to ask juniors to "bend over," but I don't believe in overdoing it.

WAK 1188 I'm not averse to a licking, rather than sit in the study all the afternoon writing out lines.

WEP 0411 Association Football.

WEP 1188 Football or cricket in season; I ask no more!

WEP 3300 I prefer acting to any other form of activity—and, believe me, acting properly done is hard work!

WEP 3477 Little Chinee plactise the ancient art of ju-jitsu—velly useful against big bully Bolsover, when I thlow him over my head!

WEP 5959 I enjoy keeping goal or bowling "googlies" equally well.

WIL 0411 Long-distance flying attracts me immensely.

WIL 1188 Exploring in unknown parts takes my fancy.

WIL 3300 I shall never rest till I've equalled the great tragedians—like Irving.

WIL 5959 I wouldn't mind running an hotel!

WIX 3300 Every actor's dream is to take his audience by storm. I think I should do best as the immortal Shylock in "The Merchant of Venice."

WOL 3477 Vellee sad if I dlop chopstick while eating mice, which I cook in my study!

WOG 0411 The kids are pretty good as a rule. Now and again I have to use the ashplant, just as a reminder!

WUX 1188 It's quite good as it stands. We have a wide choice of alternative subjects.

The LOST HERDS!

By PERCY A. CLARKE

Where do the Double-H herds disappear to? And who are the rustlers? These are mysteries that two stalwart cowboy pals have got to solve to save themselves from the "calaboose"!

THE FIRST CHAPTER

THE TRAIL TO NOWHERE

The cattle stood or lay huddled together in the moonlight out on the wide mesquite plain. Now and again a plaintive lowing would answer the shrill yapping of a coyote away in the distance. A camp fire glowed dully near by, revealing one figure lying shrouded in a horse blanket, while the glowing end of a cigarette showed where another man kept watch over the Double-H herd.

It was a peaceful scene—but the peace didn't last. Suddenly, away to the westward, a flaming flare shot hissing into the sky. It was followed by another—and a third.

"Suffering snakes!" howled Bill Parker, starting to his feet.

The cattle, bellowing with fear, milled together, jostling, rearing, terror in their eyes.

"Stampede!" cried Bill, grabbing his buddy by the shoulder to arouse him. "Dirk! Quick! Stampede!"

The cattle broke and fled as another flare went up. The thunder of their hoofs was enough to drag Dirk Robbins from sleep.

"What'n heck——" he blurted out.

Bill was seizing the halter of his horse. Dirk cast the blanket from him. His own cayuse was rearing and snorting with terror, and jerked the tethering pin clean out of the ground. Another second and he would have bolted, but with a frantic dive Dirk flung himself forward and grabbed the dangling rope. The next moment he was in the saddle of the bucking pony and galloping away over the mesquite in the rear of the stampeding herd.

He came level with Bill, who was riding like a demon.

"What's it mean, Bill?" he panted.

"I'll be gol-darned if I know!" grunted Bill. "Three flares I saw. Guess it was enough to scatter the beefs, and we've gotta catch 'em. Look! There goes another!"

To the north, this time, the flame shot up in the darkness, and vanished. Brief though its appearance had been, it was enough to swing the terrified steers towards the south.

"Heck!" exclaimed Dirk, as yet another flare hissed up to the southward. "Rustlers!"

"Ride, buddy!" snapped Bill. "Mebbe we'll turn 'em."

They rode for all they were worth, but the herd kept well ahead of them. Their cayuses gave of their best, but with streaming tails the terrified steers headed east at a speed that was amazing.

The dust flew up in dense, choking clouds that at times completely hid the cattle from the two pursuing cow-punchers. Dirk and Bill said no more—they couldn't. The dust was in their eyes and nostrils as they crouched over their horses' heads.

The pace was terrific, and the ground fairly shook beneath the thunder of the stampeding hoofs. The buddies' horses were the best the Double-H ranch could produce, but they couldn't catch up with the terrified cattle that pelted eastward in a panic.

"We'll never turn 'em," panted Bill.

"Know this country?" queried Dirk.

"Not much."

"I do—a bit. Guess there's cliffs where we're heading. The brutes'll sure hev to turn mighty soon now. Keep going."

"Hi—yip!" yelled Bill. But he might have been crooning a love song for all the notice the herd took of him.

But sure enough mountains appeared away beyond the tossing horns of the cattle. The mesquite plain seemed to end in precipitous cliffs.

"Got 'em!" grunted Bill.

They wanted a chance to turn the terrified beasts, to get them milling round and round in circles until they stopped from sheer exhaustion, which is the only way of dealing with stampeding cattle.

But suddenly flares went hissing up into the darkness to north and south.

"Heck!" growled Bill.

The cattle seemed to shoot ahead faster than ever, straight for the towering cliffs. The two buddies followed and the thunder of hoofs echoed in the confines of a gorge, barely twenty yards wide.

The cattle blocked it completely from side to side, but they kept travelling. The dust was like a dense fog, only worse, on account of the grit. Bill and Dirk, racing on, urging their horses to fresh endeavours, could see nothing except the swirling dust.

But they held on grimly, the perspiration streaming down their faces, their horses in a lather—on, on, down the echoing gorge.

Suddenly Bill stooped and pointed to the floor of the sheriff's office. "Look!" he exclaimed. Dirk started—for clearly to be seen were the imprints of moccasined feet! "Indians!" he gasped.

The dawn began to show over the mountain peaks and the shadows faded. The ponies were showing signs of flagging, and the herd, lost to view in the wreathing clouds of dust, had drawn ahead of the pals. Try as they might they could not gain on the runaways.

There were no more flares—no need for them. The terrified cattle were not likely to stop for another hour or more.

Then the gorge ended, so suddenly that it took the pals by surprise. They found themselves riding over a treeless, grassless plain—a desert, in fact—where the air, even at dawn, was hot and stifling.

Away ahead rose a cloud of dust to show where the herd still stampeded, and the cowboys followed, grimly, remorselessly, but at a slower speed as their horses slackened in distress.

"What's it mean?" queried Bill hoarsely.

"Rustlers, I guess," returned Dirk. "But—look! The dust's clearing, and——"

His voice trailed away into a gasp of utter amazement. A gentle breeze from the mountains flung the dust up into the air in spirals. It rose, thinned out, faded, and vanished.

So had the herd! Away to the misty horizon stretched the arid desert—miles and miles of reddish dust with boulders here and there, but not a sign of a single steer. The earth might have opened and swallowed them up for all the pals could tell.

" Now what d'you know 'bout that ? " gasped Bill.

" Guess they were moving faster'n we thought, an' we couldn't see 'em for dust."

" You're telling me ! " grunted Bill. " But we kin see fer miles right now on this blamed desert, and steers don't go up in steam, no-how. Where'n heck hev they gone, an' what do we do now ? "

" There's the trail, I guess," said Dirk. " Got'ny water ? "

" Not a drop."

" No more have I, and this is the Salt Pan desert, the hottest spot on this blamed continent—below sea-level, if you know what that means. The sun is rising."

" Let's be moving," growled Bill.

He wasn't troubling about the risks just then. Nor was Dirk. They followed the trail left by the stampeding herd, but it didn't take them far. It suddenly ceased.

The sandy dust gave place to bare rock—as bare as the back of a man's hand—on which no boot or hoof could leave a mark. It stretched for miles before them. It was hopeless to attempt to find the vanished herd. The trail just led nowhere.

They parted and tried different directions, but hours of arduous search found them beaten and baffled. To make matters worse the sun rose above the mountain peaks and scorched down in fury.

And they had no water ! The Salt Pan was known to them by reputation as a spot that had never been explored —a grilling desert where men went mad and died. And the herd—it had gone—vanished.

" Better get back hot-foot and report," said Dirk.

He spoke scarcely above a whisper and his voice was only a croak, for his lips were blackened and cracking and his tongue was swollen for want of water. Bill was in no better plight, and their horses were drooping pitifully.

Bill turned his pony, and they rode back slowly through the gorge, back the way they had come, and out on to the mesquite plain until they came to their hurriedly deserted camp. They pounced on the water flasks, but before they attended to their own wants the horses were cared for and given water.

" Waal," drawled Bill eventually. " A fine pair of goofs we're goin' ter be. ' Where'n heck's the herd ? ' the boss'll ask. ' Turned into nothing and gorn to be ghosts,' we'll say. ' Vanished into thin air afore our very eyes.' And he'll sure clap us in an asylum or something. And, further, buddy—what's that ? "

He stepped away from the dead fire and, stooping, picked up something that glittered from the ground. He held it in the palm of his gnarled hand. It was a sheriff's badge of office.

" Jake Morton's, for a million," he said harshly. " And Jake allus was a crook, to my way o' thinkin'."

" Steady, buddy," put in Dirk. " I know you never cottoned on to the sheriff o' Canyon Gulch. Come to that, he ain't the sort I'd make a pal of. But that don't connect him with the loss of the herd. There ain't no reason why he couldn't ha' come riding this way any time in the past week and lost that by accident. We're goin' to look fools enough when we tell our tale to the boss, wi'out makin' things worse by accusing the sheriff wi' no proof to back us up."

" H'm, mebbe you're right, Dirk,"

agreed Bill reluctantly. " Guess I'll keep the badge, all the same. There's been dirty work, anyway. Solid steers don't go fading into nothing—but, heck, those did, Dirk. What d'you make of it ? "

" I can't make a thing ! " snapped Dirk irritably. " That herd vanished. Guess somebody helped 'em vanish. It's a mystery—and not the first that's happened in the Salt Pan. I'm goin' back to tell the boss, then I'll stock up wi' grub and water, and I'll ride that Salt Pan from end to end. I'll turn over every darned rock there till I solve the blamed mystery ! See ? Come on ! Ride ! "

It was a puzzled and disconsolate pair that took the trail back to the Double-H Ranch. Sam May, the boss, met them with utter consternation.

" You ain't been to Dallas City and back. Where's the herd ? " he rapped out.

" Guess they're ghosts be now," said Bill.

" Ghosts ? Is this rustling, or crooked stuff, you're handing me ? " roared the boss. " Where's my herd ? "

" Steady, boss," said Dirk. " It's a mystery. I'll tell you."

He explained all that had happened, just as he had seen it happen, and Sam May's face grew darker and darker.

" Vanished, eh ? " he snapped, when Dirk had finished. " D'you boys happen to know that if I don't meet that contract at Dallas City I'll be ruined and hev to sell out ? "

" Sure, boss, I knew things wasn't too good," said Bill. " But I never guessed they was that bad."

" Well, they are. Thought I'd pull through, but now—the herd's gone—vanished." His face was ashen as he saw plain ruin confronting him.

Suddenly a hard glitter came to his eyes as if an idea had occurred to him. With lightning speed he drew a bead on the pals, a six-shooter in each hand.

" Reach for it, you coyotes ! " he snapped. " Lively, now. You don't pull this stuff——"

" Boss ! " cried Dirk, raising his hands, as Bill did the same. " We're not double-crossing you. Honest to——"

" Cut it out. Yew c'n talk to the judge ! " retorted Sam May.

He fired one shot in the air, and men came running to his assistance.

" Take their hardware, boys. Tie 'em up and ride 'em into Canyon Gulch. Guess I'll tote along with 'em and see 'em stowed in the calaboose. I ain't having fifty head o' cattle rustled under me very nose. Vanished in thin air, eh ? Expect me to believe that sort o' yarn ? Heck ! I wasn't born yesterday. If you didn't rustle 'em yourselves you was bribed to let it happen."

Bill burst into a torrent of indignation, but Dirk stopped him.

" I'll talk, Bill," he said. " Listen, boss. You're making a terrible mistake. I tell you——"

" Can it ! " interrupted Sam May. " Another crack from either of you and I'll gag you. Git going, boys."

Three hours later Bill and Dirk, disarmed, were in the lock-up at Canyon Gulch. Sam May was in the office talking to Jake Morton, the sheriff.

" And I'd ha' gone bail on them two being straight," he was saying.

" Money'll tempt any man, boss," said the sheriff. " Mebbe Black Burgis of the Three Bees' outfit bribed 'em. You know how Burgis has hated you ever since you beat him in the Dallas City contract ? "

" Sure ! " cried Sam May. " Never thought o' that, Jake. But I'm not whacked yet. I'll send another herd to Dallas City right away. I'll have men riding the range along Burgis' borders so's he can't steal out on my herd wi'out someone seeing him. What's more, the cattle kin leave home at midnight so's they'll be crossing the mesquite at sun-up. Guess Black Burgis'll hev to be slick to horn in this time."

THE SECOND CHAPTER

THE MOCCASIN MARK !

" WHAT'N heck d'you think you're doing ? " queried Dirk.

Bill was squatting on the floor of the cell over by the door, using his drinking water to wet the stone step that protruded from the bottom of the door, and industriously chafing one of his spurs, sharpening it until it was worn down to a point, with the appearance of a stout stiletto.

He glanced up with a queer grin on his bronzed face.

" If solid steers kin fade into nothing in the middle of the Salt Pan, guess we kin fade out o' this lock-up," he said.

Dirk stooped so that he could whisper to his pal.

" How's that going to help us ? " he asked. " The boss was hasty. Mebbe he was rattled some, Bill. He can't prove a thing against us."

" That won't stop him losin' the second herd he sends to Dallas City, bo ! " retorted Bill grimly. " He told the sheriff, and I've got a hunch Jake Morton's at the bottom of this."

" Hunches won't help ! " snapped Dirk. Then he straightened, a gleam in his eyes. " But, Bill, old pard, if we kin get out o' here to-night we kin ride scout on that herd, watch that gorge, and——"

" Nix on the plans for a bit, chum, " said Bill. " Let's win clear first."

He worked on his spur diligently, and the hours dragged by. After dark the sheriff went the rounds of his lock-up, then vanished. For a time the pals heard the rumble of voices in the office, then a door slammed, someone galloped away, and all was silence.

" Time we went," said Bill. He tried to speak calmly, but his voice was tremulous with excitement.

He was working away at the lock on the door with his specially prepared spur. It seemed like ages before the thing clicked sharply and the door opened.

Stealthily they crept out into the passage and along to the sheriff's office. There was not a sound. The shades were drawn over the window. Dirk found matches and lit a candle, setting it on the desk.

He was going about things deftly, calmly, and with a fixed purpose. He opened a drawer in the desk and took out two six-shooters and a supply of ammunition.

But Bill was studying the office suspiciously, as if he expected to find proof of the sheriff's guilt before his eyes.

Suddenly he stooped to the floor, pointing.

" Look ! " he exclaimed, in a husky whisper.

Dirk stared too, for on the boards were the clear imprints of feet. Mostly they were made by boots—the sheriff's boots, maybe. But clearly to be seen were marks made by moccasined feet.

" Indians ! " he gasped.

" One Injun," said Bill. " And there ain't been Injuns in these parts for the past ten years. That I do know What's it mean, Dirk ! How

Here are water flasks. Fill 'em and let's go! Snatch that loaf and some tinned grub. Mebbe it's near stealing, but we can't be particular."

"You've said it," growled Bill. "C'mon! All the same—the moccasin marks git me guessing, Dirk."

"Aw, beat it!"

Dirk led the way out into the night. Canyon Gulch seemed deserted. They had no difficulty in finding horses. Half a dozen were in the compound, and they selected the best two. Leaping into the saddles they galloped away into the night, heading for the mesquite plain.

"Listen!" hissed Dirk. From above came a scraping sound. Then the two cowboys saw a figure come dangling down on the end of a rope. It was an Indian!

There was neither sight nor sound of pursuit. Canyon Gulch was not a big place, and the townsfolk expected the sheriff to look after his own prisoners. But the sheriff wasn't at home that night—which was peculiar, to say the least.

"Mebbe he's out helping Sam May keep a watch on Black Burgis," suggested Dirk.

"And mebbe not," retorted Bill. "Jake Morton's a snake, Dirk. Guess he's more likely to be fixing up how to stampede the second herd into the gorge."

"I wonder," mused Dirk.

He said no more. But his brain

come we never knew there was Injuns hereabouts?"

"Does that matter now?" retorted Dirk impatiently. "Here—hang on to this gun—and these shells.

was busy as he rode. They kept on at a fair lick along the mesquite and came to where the plain ended abruptly in a steep cliff that rose high above them.

They rode in close under the cliff and about ten yards from the mouth of the gorge Dirk called a halt. The night was dark, but he had seen a cave in the cliff, with a boulder at the mouth.

" What now? " asked Bill, dismounting.

" Guess this is where we wait and watch," replied Dirk. " Put the cayuses in the cave and we'll lie doggo behind this rock."

" Okay," grunted Bill. " But don't it strike you, Dirk, that us breaking out o' the calaboose makes it look like we are guilty? "

" Too late to worry about that," said Dirk. " We were framed, Bill, and I don't sit down under it."

" Nor me."

" Besides," Dirk went on grimly. " You got a hunch the sheriff's a crook and I've got a hunch the second herd will be stampeded just like the first. Some crook, or crooks, has got a cute stunt on in the Salt Pan desert. It's succeeded once and he'll try it again. But mind, Bill. When I yells for action, don't stop to argue. Jump to it."

" I'm with you, pard," growled Bill.

They stabled the horses in the cave, ready to hand, and out of sight, while they crouched behind the boulder and waited for dawn. The cliff bulged out above their heads and hid them from view of anyone who chanced to be up on the mountains. Not that they expected any sort of danger from that direction.

The hours went by slowly, and it was cold out on the mesquite. Just before dawn the darkness was more intense than ever, and it was then that Dirk's hand clamped hard on Bill's arm.

" Listen! " he hissed. " Injuns! "

From above them came a strange scraping, shuffling noise. Then through the gloom they saw a figure dangling on the end of a rope. It was an Indian, but what tribe he belonged to it was too dark to see. But both the cowpunchers observed that a bundle of some sort dangled from his belt.

He dropped from the rope, landing without a sound, and slunk off into the darkness and vanished. He was followed by another—and another—half a dozen in all. They went off in different directions—two out due west, two to the north and two to the south.

" What's in them bundles? " whispered Bill.

" Quiet! " hissed Dirk. " Dawn's coming, I guess. Hear anything? "

Somewhere out on the mesquite a stock whip cracked and the breeze carried the shrill " Hi-yip " of a cowpuncher.

" I kin smell 'em," whispered Bill, sniffling the wind. " The boss is driving 'em fast, I reckon."

" If anything's to happen it'll happen right now, before the light's too good," suggested Dirk.

He peered through the gloom. The sun was rising, but the mountains to the east prevented the rays reaching the mesquite as yet. Over the surface of the plain hung a dense mist that even the morning breeze could not, as yet, disperse.

And suddenly it happened. Away to the west a huge tongue of flame shot up into the sky, hissing like a thousand serpents. But there was a difference from the night before, for the fire travelled along towards the herd that broke in terror and bolted for it.

To the south and north more flares appeared. They too seemed to move along the ground, hissing and crackling in a way that sounded terrifying in the stillness of the dawn.

Out of the mist appeared the herd, with tossing horns and streaming tails, the thunder of their hoofs making the earth tremble. Behind them sounded the cracking of whips and the startled yells of the cow-punchers. But Dirk and Bill knew from experience that nothing short of exhaustion would stop that stampede, and the fire was travelling all the time, keeping level with the startled beasts, to the north and the south, heading them towards the gorge where the pals waited and watched.

" The horses ! " snapped Dirk. " Ride for it ! "

Bill didn't argue or question. He was in the saddle as quickly as Dirk, and knee to knee they rode out on to the mesquite, and into the gorge, barely thirty yards ahead of the stampeding cattle.

" Say ! " panted Bill, as he rode like a man possessed. " What's the idea ? Them cattle hev got to vanish in the Salt Pan."

" Sure," snapped back Dirk. " This is where we solve the mystery. Keep ahead of 'em, Bill. When they vanish, guess we'll hev to vanish, too ! "

Bill guffawed as he urged his horse onward beside Dirk's.

" I git you, Pard ! Ride for it ! Hi-yip ! "

THE THIRD CHAPTER

THE VANISHING TRICK !

THE sun was sucking up the mist and scorching down as they rode madly along the gorge with a herd of terrified cattle thundering behind them. The dust rose in dense, suffocating clouds, but this time the pals were ahead of it. But if anything happened—the slightest mischance—a loose stone to turn a horse's foot—it would mean certain death beneath those stampeding hoofs.

The speed was terrific, and it was all the horses could do to keep ahead of the herd. The pals crouched over their ponies' manes, urging them on, helping them over the rocks that strewed the floor of the gorge.

The din echoed and re-echoed amongst the crannies of the cliffs on either side, but suddenly another sound startled the pals—a shrill whooping and yelling, and the rattle of rifle fire, while bullets hummed around their heads.

They had been seen, and their presence ahead of the herd that was to vanish was obviously resented.

Bill turned his head, gazing over his shoulder up at the cliffs that bordered the gorge. On the plateau at the top rode a number of Indians in full war-paint !

" Piyutes ! " he roared. " How about the moccasin mark in the sheriff's——"

He got no further. Half-way up the cliff more Indians appeared from behind the boulders. They were on foot. One warrior took careful aim and fired, and Bill's horse stumbled and fell, shot through the head, while Bill took a header in the dust, full in the path of the stampeding cattle.

Bill was on his feet as Dirk rode alongside him, freeing one stirrup.

" Leave me ! " panted Bill.

" Git up, you tarnation fool ! " snapped Dirk.

He grabbed Bill's shoulder and helped him up into the stirrup. By that time the snorting, plunging, speeding cattle were almost on top of them.

Dirk flogged his horse, but the animal couldn't make the speed with a double load. The terrified herd was gaining on them.

Dirk reined his horse round, riding close in under the cliff behind a spur of rock. Dismounting, he and Bill drew the horse close in, and the men and the cayuse crouched there as the thundering herd floundered past, snorting, bellowing with fear, rushing ahead blindly towards the Salt Pan desert.

" The boys'll be riding on the tail of the herd," said Bill.

He spoke huskily, for he couldn't be sure what sort of reception he and Dirk would receive at the hands of the Double-H outfit, now.

But no cowpunchers appeared. The last of the herd went by, the choking dust settled down, and silence descended in the gorge.

" Funny," muttered Dirk.

" Hev they funked it ? " queried Bill. " Mebbe they went back for help."

" Anyway," said Dirk. " I'm going to follow the herd. Guess my plan went wrong. I never calculated on them Piyutes showing up like that. Let's go."

But the one remaining horse was crippled, and limped badly. Dirk tethered it close to the rock out of harm's way, and they proceeded on foot.

The Indians had vanished, maybe thinking that the pals had perished under the hoofs of the herd. The cattle had gone out into the desert, but they had left a trail which the pals followed.

On and on they plodded, as the sun rose higher and hotter. They came out of the gorge and proceeded on along the trail across the terrible Salt Pan desert. It was slow work on foot, but they stuck to it grimly until the trail ended abruptly, as it had done before, where the bare rock began.

" Listen, Bill," said Dirk. " Maybe we'll peg out in this desert. You don't have to come with me if you don't want to, but I'm aiming to find the truth or leave my bones here."

" Aw, don't talk so much, buddy," growled Bill. " Which way do we go ? "

" Straight on, I guess," returned Dirk. " Cattle usually run like that. We keep straight on."

They continued, keeping a course in line with a distant mountain peak, to prevent them walking in circles. They were two insignificant specks in a vast desolate expanse, and the sun beat down upon them mercilessly.

Sipping at their water sparingly, they held on their way for a couple of hours.

" Notice anything ? " asked Dirk eventually.

" Sure," said Bill. " The ground's rising all the way."

" Here's the ridge, though."

They crossed it and found that the bare rock surface of the desert went down in a long, gentle gradient on the other side. After plodding down this slope for half an hour they glanced back to discover that the mountains and the gorge through which they had come were completely hidden.

" Shucks ! " exclaimed Bill. " That's how the cattle vanished. The dust hid 'em, and by the time it had cleared they was over the ridge and out o' sight. And a thousand cattle couldn't rise dust off this rock. We're on the right trail, buddy."

The slope became steeper the farther they went, and suddenly it

" Look out ! " roared Dirk, and he spun round, his revolver spitting fire. Bill was at his back as a party of savage warriors rushed at them. But above the din of fighting rose another roar—as Sam May, at the head of his punchers, rode to the rescue !

swooped down to a gulch that ran southward like a long cleft in the earth. At the bottom of this gulch the dust was thick, and bore the imprints of hoofs.

" Heck ! We're gitting warm ! " exclaimed Bill. " And look here ! "

He picked up an Indian's feather from the trail.

" Stationed here to head the herd south," said Dirk, drawing his gun. " Guess we'll solve this mystery mighty slick."

But he spoke too soon. The gulch continued for five miles or more. It was like walking along a tremendous rut left by a cart-wheel.

As the pals plodded on, covered with dust, their clothes saturated with perspiration, the gulch dropped deeper and deeper, cut through a spur of the mountains, so that the peaks towered thousands of feet above their heads, then suddenly came out on the edge of a fertile valley !

" Suffering snakes ! " gasped Bill.

Green grass, trees, cattle browsing peacefully in the shade—who could have suspected the existence of such a place in the heart of a desert ? A stream trickled down from the hills and wound its course across the pasturage.

But Dirk saw other things away beyond the trees.

" Tepees ! " he cried. " The Piyutes' village. And, say—is that a white man ? "

" Jake Morton, for a million ! " snapped Bill.

They crept out into the valley, crawling from tree to tree until they were on the verge of the village, crouched behind a thorn bush, watching a white man who was obviously bargaining with the be-feathered chief of the Piyutes. It was Jake Morton, the sheriff of Canyon Gulch !

" The snake ! " hissed Bill. " If I could only——"

" Look out ! " roared Dirk.

He spun round, his revolver spitting fire. Bill was at his back as a party of warriors rushed at them. The savage bronzed and painted faces glowered all round them. Their guns empty, the two chums clubbed them and fought madly, dodging the whirling tomahawks until a rifle butt crashed on Bill's head and brought him down.

Dirk stood over his pal and fought. He didn't expect mercy and asked for none. He knew that Jake Morton wouldn't want any living witnesses to get back to Canyon Gulch.

But another roar rose high above the bedlam—a ringing cheer and the thunder of hoofs. Dirk stared as the Indians before him broke and fled, scuttling for safety.

Sam May, the boss of the Double-H, was riding in at the head of his punchers.

Dirk saw Jake Morton bend almost double and dive for the bushes, and he flung himself at the crook. The sheriff wheeled with a snarl of hate and brought up his six-shooter. Before he could let fly, however, Dirk smashed his fist full in his face, and the man dropped with scarcely a moan, out to the wide.

Dirk, dazed and bewildered, stood over him what time Bill rose groggily to his feet.

" Guess my hunch was right, pard," he said. " But here's the boss."

Sam May, astride his horse, was grinning down at them, a trifle awkwardly.

" Howdy, boys ? All sound, I hope ? Guess I treated you two kinder rough. I was sure rattled over the loss of the herd, you see. Might ha' known you two weren't crooked. I was out on the mesquite afore dawn watching for trouble, and saw you two go into hiding by the gorge. At first I thought you were crooked, but when I saw them Piyutes I tumbled to your game. I rode back for help and came along with every man I could rustle, and then—well, guess we followed your trail right here. Your yarn was correct all the time, and the crooks pulled the deal twice."

" But the fire which scared the cattle *travelled* the second time," said Bill. " How was that done ? "

" Simple," explained the boss. " The sheriff had given them Indians cans of oil and they laid trails from one flare to another."

" Cute," remarked Dirk. " But I guess there won't be any more vanishing herds round these parts."

He was right. The Piyutes were cleared out, and Jake Morton went to jail. Bill Parker is sheriff now at Canyon Gulch, and Sam May's range boss is Dirk Robbins.

The Double-H met the Dallas City contract and have prospered ever since. As for Black Burgis of the Three Bees, he never had anything to do with the business, which, but for Dirk and Bill, would have brought ruin to their boss.

THE END

THE BOY WHO WOULDN'T BUDGE!

By OWEN CONQUEST

THE FIRST CHAPTER

MR. BOOTLES IS WRATHY!

"MORNY! It's rotten!"

Kit Erroll, of the Classical Fourth at Rookwood, was speaking as Jimmy Silver & Co. came along the Form-room passage. It was close on time for afternoon classes, and the juniors were gathering round the doorway of the Fourth Form-room.

A great yarn of the lively adventures of Jimmy Silver & Co., the popular chums of Rookwood School, starring Valentine Mornington in the role of "The Boy Who Wouldn't Budge"

Mornington, with a stump of chalk in his hand, was scrawling on the big oak door, and some of the fellows were chuckling as they looked on. Only Erroll, Morny's best chum, was remonstrating, and Morny did not heed what his chum was saying.

"What's Morny up to?" asked Jimmy Silver, as he joined the group.

"Playing the giddy goat!" said Erroll tartly. "Chuck it, Morny, you silly ass! Mr. Bootles will be coming in a few minutes."

"Let him come!" answered Mornington, without turning his head.

"There'll be a row!"

"Rats!"

"And it's rotten, anyway!"

"Rot!"

Jimmy Silver pushed through the crowd of Fourth-Formers, and looked over Mornington's shoulder. Then he frowned.

It was a caricature of Mr. Bootles, the respected master of the Fourth Form, that Morny was chalking on the oaken door.

Morny could draw well when he chose to take the trouble, and he was putting all his skill into this work of art. Lately, Mornington had been called rather severely to account by Mr. Bootles, owing to one of his periodical fits of slackness, and Morny resented being called to account for anything. He was now drawing the head and shoulders of Mr. Bootles, much to the entertainment of his Form-fellows. Probably nobody but Morny would have had the nerve to do it, when Mr. Bootles might have walked along the passage at any moment; but Morny was recklessness itself.

"Rather a likeness, what?" remarked Morny, with a grin at Jimmy Silver, as the captain of the Fourth looked over his shoulder.

But Jimmy Silver did not grin.

He liked and respected Mr. Bootles, and he was quite well aware that the Form-master's recent severity to Mornington was well deserved.

"Bosh!" said Jimmy. "Rub it out! What do you want to rag old Bootles for?"

"Because he's such a dashed old fossil!" grunted Mornington. "This will let him know what we think of him."

"We don't think anything of the kind of him."

"Well, I do!"

"You're an ass, then!"

"Thanks!"

Jimmy Silver pushed open the Form-room door, and Morny had to suspend his artistic work for a moment. But he resumed it, with the door open. The Fistical Four went into the Form-room, and most of the juniors followed them. It was near time for Mr. Bootles to arrive, and they did not want to be on the spot when the Fourth Form-master discovered the caricature. Mild little gentleman as Mr. Bootles was, it was certain that he would be very angry.

Only Erroll remained with his wilful chum, watching him with great uneasiness.

There was no doubt that the caricature was comic, but it did not make Erroll smile. He was thinking of the wrath to come.

"There!" said Mornington, stepping back at last and surveying his handiwork with great satisfaction. "What do you think of that, old scout?"

"Rotten!"

"How complimentary you are!"

"You oughtn't to insult Mr. Bootles. He's a good sort."

"He caned me this morning."

"Well, you cheeked him."

"Erroll, old chap, you're a good boy, but you're too much given to preachin'!" yawned Mornington. "Let's go in before you get to seventhly."

"Let me rub that nonsense off the door first."

"Rot! Let it alone!"

Valentine Mornington took his chum's arm, and walked into the Form-room. The chalked caricature remained to greet Mr. Bootles' eyes when he arrived.

Mornington went to his place, but Erroll did not follow.

He took a duster from the blackboard easel and turned back to the door.

Morny called out to him sharply.

"What are you goin' to do, you ass?"

"Save you from a flogging, fathead!"

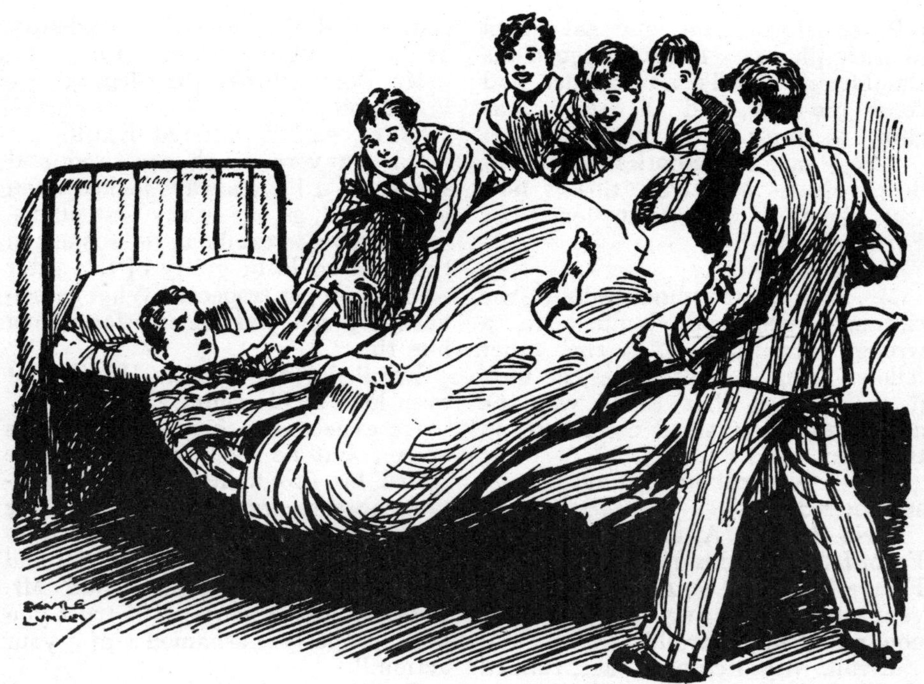

"Turn him out!" exclaimed Jimmy Silver. In a moment half a dozen fellows rushed to Mornington's bed and rolled him out upon the floor. Bump! There was a loud howl from Morny as he landed.

"Look here——"

Mornington jumped up angrily as Erroll went towards the door. Jimmy Silver made a sign to his chums, and at the same moment he grasped Morny by the arm, and Lovell, Raby, and Newcome grasped him also. In the grip of the Fistical Four, Morny was held in his place.

He struggled angrily.

"Let me go, you fools!"

"No fear!"

Mornington sat helpless, gritting his teeth, while Erroll went to the door and began to rub at the chalked figure. But he was a little too late.

He had given one rub with the duster, when Mr. Bootles loomed up in the doorway.

Mr. Bootles blinked at the junior over his spectacles, and then at the chalked caricature.

"Erroll!" he ejaculated.

"Oh! Yes, sir!" stammered Erroll.

"Stand back!"

The junior stood back, and Mr. Bootles approached the door more closely, peering at Morny's workmanship through his glasses.

His brow knitted.

Erroll had not had time with the duster, and Mr. Bootles had the pleasure—or otherwise—of surveying his own caricatured features. The likeness was quite near enough for recognition, though the features were comically exaggerated.

In the Form-room there was silence as of the tomb. Jimmy Silver & Co.

released Mornington, and sat down in their places. Morny shrugged his shoulders. Erroll's interference had come too late, and the storm was going to burst.

"So," said Mr. Bootles, in a very deep voice—" so, Erroll, this is how you show your respect for your Form-master!"

Erroll started.

Mr. Bootles, not unnaturally in the circumstances, had jumped to a wrong conclusion. All the other fellows being in their places, he took it for granted that Erroll was the author of the chalked caricature on the door.

"I—I was rubbing it out, sir!" stammered Erroll.

"No doubt. After amusing your Form-fellows in this disrespectful way, I have no doubt you wished to prevent me from seeing it. You may now rub it out, Erroll."

Erroll, with a crimson face, rubbed the chalk from the door. Mr. Bootles motioned him into the Form-room, and then followed him in.

THE SECOND CHAPTER

FOR ANOTHER'S FAULT!

The Fourth Form looked on in silence.

Mr. Bootles, standing by his desk, fixed his eyes upon Erroll, who stood before him with downcast, crimson face.

Jimmy Silver glanced very expressively at Mornington.

It was for Morny to speak and remove the Form-master's misapprehension before punishment fell upon his chum. It was certain that Erroll would not explain.

But Mornington did not speak.

He looked on with a grim, sardonic smile. He shrugged his shoulders as he met Jimmy Silver's glance, and that was all. Evidently he did not intend to own up.

Mr. Bootles broke the silence:

"Erroll!"

"Yes, sir?" faltered Erroll.

"I am very much surprised and shocked. I have always looked upon you, Erroll, as one of my best pupils, and I have certainly never suspected that you could be guilty of this utter want of proper respect. What reason have I given you, Erroll, for acting like this?"

Erroll did not speak. He did not even look at his chum.

He expected to hear Mornington's voice; but he did not hear it. He closed his lips a little. If Mornington chose to leave him to bear the blame, he would not speak.

"I am not surprised that you find nothing to say, Erroll," said Mr. Bootles, after a pause. "I trust you are properly ashamed of your action."

Erroll was still silent.

"I cannot allow this to pass," continued Mr. Bootles. "I do not wish to cane you, Erroll; but I cannot let this pass unpunished. You will be detained for your half-holiday tomorrow, and I shall set you a task in the Form-room. You may go to your place."

Without a word, Erroll went to his place.

He passed Mornington, and his eyes met his chum's for a moment. Morny smiled mockingly.

Erroll sat down quietly.

"Morny, you rotter!" breathed Lovell. "Get up on your hindlegs and own up, you cad!"

"Mind your own business!"

"Are you going to let Erroll——"

"Silence in the class!" rapped out Mr. Bootles.

And there was silence.

During lessons that afternoon there were a good many whispers in Mr. Bootles' class, and most of them reached Morny's ears.

The Fourth Form did not leave him in any doubt as to their opinion of his conduct.

For a fellow to sit silent, while another fellow took his punishment, was quite against all the unwritten laws of Rookwood.

It was surprising, too, in Valentine Mornington. Morny was too reckless to care much about punishment, and Erroll was his best chum. But the wilful and obstinate side of Morny's rather peculiar nature was uppermost now. Erroll had chosen to interfere with him, and Erroll could take the consequences. That was how Morny was looking at it; but it was a view with which nobody else in the Fourth was likely to sympathise.

After lessons, when Mr. Bootles dismissed the class, the juniors were surprised to see Erroll join his chum in the passage as usual. Perhaps Mornington was surprised, too, for he looked very curiously at Erroll's quiet face and compressed lips.

"You're in for it, old bird!" he remarked.

Erroll nodded.

"Latin conjugations to-morrow afternoon, instead of cricket," said Mornington.

"Yes."

"All your own fault, isn't it?"

"Yes."

"You don't mind?" grinned Mornington.

"No."

Mr. Bootles came along the passage, and passed the juniors, giving Erroll a rather grim glance as he passed. Poor Erroll was evidently in his Form-master's black books now.

When Mr. Bootles was gone, a good many of the juniors gathered round Mornington and Erroll. What had only been whispered in the Form-room could be said aloud in the passage, and it was said with emphasis.

"Morny, you rotter——"

"Morny, you sneak——"

"Morny——"

"Hallo!" said Mornington agreeably. "What a rush for my society all at once! Dear boys, is anythin' the matter?"

"You know what's the matter!" exclaimed Jimmy Silver. "Why didn't you own up when Bootles was ragging Erroll?"

"Is that a conundrum?"

"Are you going to let him be detained to-morrow afternoon in your place?" demanded Lovell hotly.

"Why not?"

"Why not?" repeated Lovell. "Why, if you do, you're a rotter—that's why not! And a cad! And a worm——"

"Don't run through the whole list, old top! You're eloquent, but you're rather a bore."

"Why, you—you——" stuttered Lovell.

"I suppose this is one of your queer jokes, Morny," said Jimmy Silver quietly. "But you can't let it go on. Erroll can't be detained to-morrow afternoon."

"Better tell Bootles so."

"You've got to tell Bootles the truth——"

"Rats!"

"You've got to own up, Morny," said Jimmy Silver. "Not only because it's decent, but Erroll's in the eleven for the Bagshot match to-morrow, and he's wanted to play."

"Dear me!" said Mornington nonchalantly. "I'm afraid I'd quite forgotten about the Bagshot match."

"You cheeky ass!" roared Lovell.

"Besides, I'm in the eleven, ain't I?" pursued Mornington. "If I'm detained instead, you lose a good man from the team."

"That's awkward!" said Jimmy. "It can't be helped, though. I'd rather lose you than Erroll."

"Thanks!"

"There's such a thing as justice, too, and fair play."

"Is there?" asked Mornington.

"To cut it short, are you going to Bootles to own up about that silly caricature?"

"No!"

With that, Valentine Mornington turned on his heel and walked out into the quadrangle.

A hiss followed him from the juniors.

Erroll, after some hesitation, went up the staircase to his study. The juniors remained in an excited group, discussing the situation. Jimmy Silver's brows were knitted in anger.

"He will have to own up, Jimmy," said Lovell. "We can't have Erroll left out of the game to-morrow."

Jimmy nodded.

"I can't understand Morny," he said. "He's never acted in this caddish way before. He's got his faults, and plenty of them; but a thing like this—it's rotten, mean!"

"Beastly!"

"Anyhow, he's got to own up, and get Erroll off. I'm not going to lose a good man out of the eleven to please him."

THE THIRD CHAPTER

A PECULIAR PAL

JIMMY SILVER left the end study after prep that evening and came along the passage towards the stairs. He stopped at the door of Study No. 4.

The door was half-open, and Mornington and Erroll could be seen, working at the study table.

There was no sign of trouble in the study.

Mornington's face wore its usual careless, nonchalant expression, and Erroll, though perhaps a little quieter than usual, did not look in any way resentful. Probably there was no other study at Rookwood where such an incident as that of the afternoon would not have caused a rift in the lute.

Both the juniors glanced up as Jimmy looked in.

"Hallo, old top!" said Mornington, pleasantly. "Done your prep?"

"Yes."

"Lucky bargee! You always get through before I do."

"I don't slack at it," said Jimmy drily.

Mornington smiled.

"A hit—a very palpable hit!" he remarked. "I stand corrected! If I could only follow your shining example——"

"Oh, don't rot! I looked in to speak to you——"

"Go ahead; no charge for admission."

"I'm putting Putty Grace into the eleven to-morrow, in your place."

"In Erroll's place, do you mean?"

"I mean what I say."

Mornington's brow darkened for a moment.

"Then I'm not playing?" he asked.

"You can't, when you will be detained."

"I'm not detained."

"You will be, when Mr. Bootles knows the facts."

"Are you goin' to tell him?" sneered Mornington.

"You are going to tell him," answered Jimmy Silver quietly.

" You've got the rest of the evening to do it in."

" And if I don't ? "

" I hope you will ! "

" Hope springs eternal in the human breast ! " grinned Mornington. " But supposin', for the sake of argument, that I don't ? "

" Then we shall talk to you in the dorm to-night."

" I understand. Go and eat coke ! " said Mornington, and he turned back to his work.

" You've filled my place, Jimmy ? " asked Erroll, as the captain of the Fourth was turning away.

" No ; that's not necessary ! "

" But I'm detained——"

" Mr. Bootles will let you off when he knows the facts of the case."

" But—but——"

" Morny's going to tell him," said Jimmy Silver.

And with that Jimmy walked away.

Erroll glanced at his chum for a moment, but Morny's eyes were bent on his books. He resumed his work, and for some time there was silence in Study No. 4.

Prep was over at last, however, and Mornington rose to his feet. He stood for some minutes leaning on the mantelpiece, regarding his chum with a curious glance.

A fat face grinned in at the doorway. It belonged to Reginald Muffin, of the Classical Fourth.

" I say, Morn——"

" Cut ! " snapped Mornington.

" You're going through it ! " said

" For the last time, Morny ! " said Jimmy Silver. " Will you own up to Mr. Bootles ? " " Go and eat coke! " gasped Mornington, spread-eagled upon the bed. " Very well. Go it, Newcome! " Whack! Whack ! Whack ! The slipper rose and fell with resounding thwacks upon Mornington.

Tubby Muffin, impressively, wagging a podgy forefinger at the dandy of the Fourth. " If you don't own up, we're going to give you a high old time in the dorm to-night. We've been holding a meeting on the subject in the common-room, I can tell you, and——"

Mornington made an angry stride towards the door, and Tubby Muffin promptly backed into the passage.

" You wait for dorm, Morny ! " he hooted. " You're going to be put through it. Yah ! You beast ! "

Tubby Muffin fled, just in time to escape a lunging boot. Mornington slammed the door of the study.

Erroll had risen from the table.

" Goin' down ? " asked Mornington.

" May as well."

" Shall I come ? "

" Of course ! "

Mornington burst into a laugh.

" You're a queer fish, Erroll. Most fellows would be scrapping with me now, for what happened this afternoon."

" Perhaps I'm not like most fellows, then," said Erroll, with a faint smile. " I'm certainly not going to scrap with you, Morny ! "

" You don't feel ratty ? "

" No."

" You're missing a cricket match to-morrow."

" I suppose it can't be helped."

" Everybody else in the Fourth has been calling me some pretty names," grinned Mornington. " Haven't you any to add to the list ? "

Erroll shook his head.

" I know you're only playing the goat," he said. " The fellows think you've acted meanly——"

" And you don't ? "

" I think you're playing the goat, as I said. It's only your silly obstinacy. You're not afraid of a licking or detention. You'd have gone to Bootles before this, but you've got your back up."

" They're goin' to rag me in the dorm to-night, if I don't go," remarked Mornington.

" Well, you can't blame them ; they don't understand you as I do, and don't make allowances."

Mornington laughed and left the study. Erroll followed him, and they came into the junior common-room together.

It was a surprise to the juniors to see them still together, and on evidently friendly terms. Dark looks were cast at Valentine Mornington on all sides. He did not seem to observe them. He strolled carelessly into the room, and chatted with Erroll, apparently regardless of the fact that no one else spoke a word to him.

Bulkeley of the Sixth looked in at half-past nine, and there was a general move.

Then Jimmy Silver came over to Mornington.

" Have you been to Mr. Bootles ? " he asked.

" Oh, no ! "

" Then there's just time to cut in before dorm."

" Go hon ! "

" Are you going ? "

" Not at all ! "

" Very well ! " Jimmy Silver compressed his lips and turned away

Mornington glanced at Erroll with a smile as the juniors crowded out of the common-room. Erroll's face was clouded. He knew what was going to happen in the dormitory, and he was deeply troubled, and Valentine Mornington sauntered into the Fourth Form dormitory with perfect coolness. Whatever was in store for him, there was no doubt that the dandy of the Fourth had nerve enough to go through with it.

THE FOURTH CHAPTER

BROUGHT TO BOOK

BULKELEY put out the light, and the door closed.

In the dormitory of the Classical Fourth all the juniors were in bed, and were supposed to be settled for the night.

But, though Bulkeley was not aware of the fact, they were very far from settled.

The prefect's footsteps had hardly died away down the passage, when Jimmy Silver sat up in bed.

" Ready, you fellows ? " he called out softly.

" You bet ! " came an emphatic grunt from the bed of Arthur Edward Lovell.

" Turn out ! "

" What-ho ! "

" Not too much row ! " remarked Putty Grace. " We don't want Bulkeley coming back."

" Anybody got a candle ? "

" Here you are ! "

Four or five candle-ends were lighted, and they shed a glimmering light in the long, lofty dormitory.

The Fourth-Formers were quickly out of bed, with the exceptions of Valentine Mornington and Tubby Muffin. Tubby preferred to watch the proceedings from his bed, and Mornington appeared to be quite unconscious that anything unusual was going on. Jimmy Silver glanced at Erroll.

" You needn't take a hand in this, Erroll, if you don't like," he said.

" It's a Form ragging ! " exclaimed Higgs. " Erroll ought to take a hand along with everybody else ! "

" Rats ! You can turn in now, Erroll."

Erroll shook his head, and sat on the edge of his bed. Certainly he was not likely to take a hand in ragging his chum ; and still more certainly he could not hope to be able to help him. Mornington had brought down his punishment upon himself, and there was no averting it.

Erroll's quiet face expressed only distress.

" Mornington ! "

Morny did not move or speak.

" Get up, Morny ! " rapped out Conroy.

No answer.

" Turn him out ! " said Jimmy Silver.

Morny's lofty indifference to their proceedings had a rather exasperating effect upon the juniors. They were not prepared to stand any of Morny's superb loftiness just then.

Half a dozen fellows rushed to his bed and rolled him out, bed-clothes and all, upon the floor.

Bump !

There was a howl from Valentine Mornington as he landed. It was rather a concussion upon the hard floor.

" He, he, he ! " chortled Tubby Muffin. " Give him beans ! "

" Stand up, Morny ! " said Jimmy Silver.

Mornington struggled in the bed-clothes. For a moment his face was like that of a demon. All the evil in his nature—and there was a good deal of it—was aroused just then.

He scrambled to his feet, and looked for a moment as if he would rush at the juniors, hitting out right and left.

But he controlled himself.

His indifferent manner returned, and he stood with his hands folded across his chest, an insolent smile on his face.

" Well, what's this kid's game ? " he inquired, with a sneer.

"Kid's game! I'll give you kid's game!" howled Lovell. "I'll——"

"Order!" rapped out Jimmy Silver. "This isn't a dog fight, old chap. Mornington, you know what the Form expects you to do."

"Blessed if I care."

"You chalked a silly picture of Mr. Bootles to-day, and he thought it was Erroll's work, and detained him for it," said Jimmy. "It was up to you to speak up at the time."

"Any decent fellow would have done it!" growled Lovell.

"You didn't do it, Morny," continued Jimmy Silver. "You've been given all the evening, and you haven't done it. If you choose to act rottenly towards your own chum it's your business; but, as it happens, Erroll's wanted in the cricket eleven to-morrow. That makes a difference. Erroll's got to be let off."

"I—I say, you could fill my place, Jimmy!" interrupted Erroll.

"I dare say I could, but I'm not going to," answered the captain of the Fourth. "I'm not going to leave one of the best bats out of the game because Mornington doesn't choose to do the right thing. I'm skipper of the eleven—not Morny, and Morny can't run the show at his own sweet will. Now, Morny, we don't want to take rough measures——"

"Oh, don't mind me!" yawned Mornington.

"Will you promise to go to Mr. Bootles in the morning and tell him the facts, and see Erroll clear?"

"No."

Morny's answer came short and sharp, and there was an angry buzz from the Fourth-Formers.

Several of the juniors made a movement towards Mornington, who stared at them with angry defiance. But Jimmy waved them back.

"Hold on! Give him a chance!" he said. "Morny, will you do the sensible thing? You don't want the whole Form to despise you as a sneaking cad——"

"Oh, I don't mind!"

"If you don't care what Rookwood thinks of you——"

"Not a bit!"

"Very well," said Jimmy, as there was another angry growl. "If that's so, we may as well get to business. You're going to be ragged till you promise to own up to Bootles in the morning."

"Rats!"

"'Nuff jaw!" howled Arthur Edward Lovell angrily. "Collar the cad, and put him through it!"

"Collar him!" said Jimmy Silver.

And there was a rush.

Mornington's hands went up like lightning, and he hit out furiously as the juniors closed round him.

Arthur Edward Lovell was the first to reach him, and he was met with a drive on the point of the jaw that sent him spinning. Lovell crashed into Jimmy Silver, and bowled him over, and they went to the floor together.

Raby was down, and Newcome staggered—but then a drive from Conroy flung Mornington across his bed.

The next moment five or six pairs of hands were upon him, and he was secured.

Jimmy Silver scrambled up.

"Ow! Ow! Ow!" came from Arthur Edward Lovell. He sat on the floor, nursing his chin. "Ow! Ow! Ow!"

Mornington was struggling furiously. Jimmy Silver ran to grasp him; but the dandy of the Fourth had no chance. Lovell staggered up, and, holding his chin with one hand, held Morny's neck with the other. The dandy of the Fourth gasped helplessly.

"Hang you! Let me go! Hang you!"

"Keep the cad pinned!" said Jimmy Silver. "Hallo! Keep off, Erroll, you ass! What do you want?"

Erroll, with pale, set face, shoved into the group.

With socks, towels and slippers raining on him from both sides, the hapless Mornington had to run. Panting savagely he staggered through the juniors, dazed by the many swipes. His caddish action was costing him dear.

"Let Morny alone!" he said. "He's my pal, and I'm standing by him. Let him go!"

"You silly ass! Stand back!"

"Sheer off!"

Erroll shoved on, and four or five fellows collared him, rushed him back to his bed, and hurled him upon it, breathless. Then they gathered round Valentine Mornington again.

THE FIFTH CHAPTER

A FORM RAGGING!

MORNINGTON stood in the midst of his captors, his face flushed crimson, and his eyes glittering. He was still feebly resisting, and the juniors had to keep a firm grasp on him. But no cry had left Morny's lips. One shout would have brought a prefect to the dormitory; but Morny did not think of uttering it. Wilful and wrong-headed as he was, he was "game" all through.

"Now, you silly, cheeky ass!" said Jimmy Silver grimly. "Now you're going to get your ragging! You'll get it till you give your word to own up to Bootles in the morning. Lay him across his bed, you fellows! Did you bring the slipper, Newcome?"

"Here it is!"

"Good! Lay it on while I count!"

"You bet!"

Mornington struggled desperately as he was laid face down on his bed. But resistance was vain with each arm and leg held in three or four hands. He was spread-eagled on the bed, and Newcome stood over him with the slipper.

"For the last time, Morny!" said Jimmy Silver.

Mornington gasped.

"Go and eat coke!"

"Very well. Go it, Newcome!"

Whack! Whack! Whack! Whack!

Newcome "went it" with a vim. The slipper rose and fell with sounding thwacks upon Mornington.

Whack! Whack! Whack!

Mornington set his teeth hard.

His pride would not allow him to utter a cry. But the castigation was not easy to endure in silence. "Slippering" was a severe form of punishment, very nearly as severe as a flogging from the Head.

With his teeth shut hard, Morny bore it in savage silence.

"Fifty!" counted Jimmy Silver. "Chuck it, Newcome. Now, will you do as the Form wants, Morny?"

"No!" choked Mornington.

"Give him another fifty!" said Higgs.

"He, he, he! Give him five hundred!" chuckled Tubby Muffin. "The cheeky rotter hasn't yelled yet. It's like his cheek not to yell!"

Jimmy Silver hesitated.

Fifty "whacks" with a slipper was a severe punishment, and he would have given a good deal for Morny to abandon his attitude of wrong-headed, obstinate defiance. But nothing, evidently, was further from Mornington's thoughts.

"Am I to go on?" asked Newcome.

"A dozen more," said Jimmy Silver at last.

The slipper rose and fell.

Still no sign from Mornington—no sign and no sound. Newcome gave the last strokes lightly, in spite of himself. He was as exasperated as anyone by the obstinacy of a fellow who was utterly in the wrong; but he could not help admiring Morny's grim pluck and endurance.

"That will do," said Jimmy uneasily. "Let the silly ass go!"

"But he hasn't promised——" began Lovell.

"If he doesn't, he shall run the gauntlet."

"Good!"

Mornington was released, and he rolled, panting, off the bed, and stood rather unsteadily. Erroll came quickly towards him.

"Morny——"

"Leave me alone!" muttered Mornington. "I won't promise, and I won't do anythin' I don't choose—not if I'm cut in pieces! So you can put that in your pipe and smoke it, Jimmy Silver!"

Jimmy knitted his brows.

"You'll run the gauntlet next, then," he said.

"I won't stir!"

"We'll see about that," said the captain of the Fourth curtly. "Form up, you fellows!"

"Jimmy——" began Erroll appealingly.

"Shut up! Stand back, Erroll!"

Erroll was pushed back, and the juniors formed up in a double row for the "run." Even Tubby Muffin turned out of bed, and stuffed a sock to have his "whack" at the victim. Mornington did not move as he was called upon to run.

"You hear, Morny?" exclaimed Jimmy Silver.

"Go and eat coke!"

"Start him!" said Jimmy.

Conroy and Pons collared the obstinate junior without ceremony, and flung him between the waiting rows.

The fellows nearest to Morny started lashing out with socks and towels and slippers, and the hapless dandy of the Fourth had to run. He panted along savagely, with swipes raining on him from both sides. Tubby Muffin, in his eagerness, overshot the mark, and missed Mornington, and caught Higgs of the Fourth upon the nose with his stuffed sock. There was a bellow from Higgs, and he rushed upon the fat Classical, who fled frantically among the beds.

Mornington staggered on, with raining blows descending on him, and as he reached the end of the lines he staggered and fell.

Erroll ran to his aid.

"Now——" began Lovell.

Arthur Edward was interrupted. The door of the dormitory opened, and Bulkeley of the Sixth appeared in the doorway. "Running the gauntlet" was rather a noisy form of ragging, and the commotion in the dormitory had reached other ears.

"What the thump——" exclaimed Bulkeley angrily, as he surveyed the startling scene in the glimmering candle-light.

"Cave!" howled Putty.

The juniors bolted to their beds, like rabbits to their burrows.

Tubby Muffin, thus providentially rescued from the vengeance of Alfred Higgs, plunged into bed, and drew the blankets over him, bursting into a snore as he did so. Tubby thought that that snore showed great presence of mind.

Bulkeley strode into the dormitory.

Only Erroll and Mornington remained out of bed. Erroll was helping his chum to his feet.

"Well, what do you mean by this row after lights out?" demanded the captain of Rookwood.

"Ahem! Only a—a—a little rag, Bulkeley," murmured Jimmy Silver.

"Do you know it's nearly ten o'clock?" snapped Bulkeley.

"Ahem!"

"Get into bed, Mornington, and Erroll."

"Certainly, old top!" answered Mornington, with all his old coolness, and he limped to his bed.

"Now, what is all this about?" demanded Bulkeley.

No reply.

Some of the fellows expected Morny to speak, but he did not. As in the Form-room that afternoon, he disappointed expectation, though in a different way.

"Well, turn in!" growled Bulkeley. "Every kid in this dormitory will take two hundred lines!"

"Oh!"

"And if there's another sound from this room to-night, I shall come back with a cane, and then——"

Bulkeley did not complete the sentence; he left the rest to the imagination of the juniors.

He collected up the candle-ends, blew them out, and quitted the dormitory.

Tubby Muffin ceased to snore.

"I say, who's going to do my lines?" Muffin inquired "Are you going to do them, Jimmy? I was only backing you up, you know."

"B-r-r-r!"

"I say, let's make Morny do the

lot," said Tubby. " It's all Morny's fault, you know ! "

" Are we going on, Jimmy ? " asked Lovell.

" No. Bulkeley will be keeping his ears open after this," answered Jimmy Silver. " Besides, Mornington's had enough."

" But he hasn't promised to own up to Bootles."

" I know. There's a limit, though," said Jimmy. " He's had a Form-ragging, and a jolly good one. I'm done with him ! "

And with that, Jimmy Silver turned his head on the pillow to sleep. The rest of the Fourth followed his example ; but it was a long time before sleep came to Valentine Mornington.

THE SIXTH CHAPTER

MORNY'S LITTLE WAY

JIMMY SILVER did not speak to Mornington, or look at him, when the Classical Fourth turned out the next day.

Some of the juniors were inclined to renew the ragging ; but Jimmy set his face against that, and he had his way.

Mornington had sinned against the laws and customs of the Rookwood Fourth, and he had had his punishment ; and there, so far as Jimmy Silver was concerned, the matter ended.

Mornington strolled elegantly out of the dormitory, his easy manner not betraying in the least that he was feeling severely the effects of the overnight's ragging.

Some dark glances were cast after him, and that was all.

" He ought to have another dose of the same medicine ! " muttered Arthur Edward Lovell gruffly.

Jimmy Silver shook his head.

" It wouldn't make any difference," he said. " Morny is as obstinate as a mule. He's had his medicine. The trouble is that I shall have to fill Erroll's place in the team. There isn't another man as good ! "

" What about little me ? " grinned Newcome.

" Next best ! " said Jimmy. " If Morny doesn't do the decent thing, you'll have to go in instead of Erroll, Newcome ! "

" Then I'll look for my bat ! "

Jimmy Silver had little hope now that Mornington would do the decent thing, as he termed it. He was almost inclined to explain to Mr. Bootles himself how the matter stood ; but that was not quite feasible. He gave Morny a grim look when they went into the Form-room for morning lessons, and the dandy of the Fourth came to him.

" You've decided not to play me to-day, Silver ? " Mornington asked.

" Quite ! " said Jimmy curtly.

" Why lose two men instead of only one ? "

" Grace can take your place pretty well ; and you know that you ought to be detained instead of Erroll. I'm leaving you free to do what is right."

" Oh, rats ! "

Jimmy Silver turned his back on him, and went to his place. He had had enough of Mornington just then.

Mr. Bootles came into the Form-room, and the buzz of talk among the juniors ceased. It was noticeable that Mr. Bootles had lost his usual urbanity in dealing with Erroll. He had not forgotten the incident of the previous day.

When lessons were over, and the Fourth Form were going out, Mr. Bootles called to the junior in disgrace.

" Erroll ! "

" Yes, sir."

" Erroll ! " Kit Erroll started to his feet as Mr. Bootles came into the room. " Yes, sir ? " " You foolish boy ! " exclaimed Mr. Bootles. " Why did you not tell me the facts yesterday ? I could not guess that you were shielding another. Mornington has confessed to me ! "

" You will come to the Form-room at two o'clock, and I shall set you your task. You will remain till five."

" Very well, sir ! " said Erroll quietly.

And he followed the rest out of the Form-room.

" And you're going to let him be detained, you utter rotter ! " Lovell muttered fiercely to Mornington, in the passage.

Mornington did not seem to hear. He walked away with his hands in his pockets, whistling.

He came into dinner later with a smiling face.

Unpopularity is not easy or pleasant to bear, as a rule ; but to judge from Morny's looks, he really appeared to be enjoying it.

After dinner, Jimmy Silver & Co. gave their attention to preparations for the cricket match. The Bagshot cricketers were expected at two o'clock and the game was to begin very soon after.

Kit Erroll stood in the School House doorway, watching the cricketers as they started for Little Side, with a clouded brow. It was not pleasant to give up a cricket match on a sunny afternoon for detention in a dusky old Form-room and grinding Latin. And he knew, too, that his presence was required on the cricket field. But it could not be helped, and he turned away with a sigh.

He was in the Form-room at two punctually, and Mr. Bootles came in a minute later and found him there. With a cold face and freezing voice the Form-master set him his task. Mr. Bootles was very much offended, and he did not conceal that fact. And Erroll, painful as it was to him to fall in the opinion of a master he liked and respected, could not explain. It was for Mornington to explain; and Morny had declined.

"You will remain till five, Erroll!" concluded Mr. Bootles. "I shall expect your task to be completed by that time."

"Very well, sir!"

Mr. Bootles rustled out of the Form-room.

Erroll rose and glanced from the window, which gave a view of a part of the cricket ground. The green field was dotted with white-clad figures, and a crowd of fellows was gathering to watch the game. Bagshot had just arrived, and Jimmy Silver was greeting Pankley and Poole. Erroll gazed at them for a minute or two, and then returned quietly to his desk. As he sat down, he became aware that the Form-room door was half open, and that Mornington was standing there, regarding him with an amused grin.

"Been lookin' at the cricket—like cheery old Moses on the mountain lookin' at the Promised Land!" grinned Mornington. "Feelin' pretty down—what?"

"A little," said Erroll.

"All my fault—what?"

"Yes."

"Why don't you row with me?"

Erroll smiled.

"I don't want to row, Morny. Clear off, there's a good fellow, and let me get to work. I've got a certain amount to grind through."

"Best wishes for a happy afternoon!" grinned Mornington, and he strolled out of the Form-room whistling.

Erroll set patiently to work.

He had always borne with his chum with a patience the other fellows found a little difficult to understand; and perhaps, at this moment, Erroll wondered whether he was a little too patient with Mornington. Friendship, even such deep and sincere friendship as his own, had its limits. Mornington was not likely to keep another friend. But that reflection was enough to determine Erroll to be loyal to his trying chum. With a clouded brow he worked at Latin; but his thoughts were with the fellows on the cricket field.

"Erroll!"

Erroll started to his feet as Mr. Bootles came hastily into the Form-room.

"Yes, sir?"

"You foolish boy!" exclaimed Mr. Bootles, in a moved voice. "Why did you not tell me the facts yesterday? I could not guess that you were shielding another!"

"Oh, sir!" gasped Erroll. "You—you know——"

Mr. Bootles gave him a very kind smile.

"Mornington has just come to my study and confessed," he replied. "It seems that it was Mornington who chalked that disrespectful picture on the door, and you were only trying to save him from his foolishness, when I came in, and supposed—— You should have told me, Erroll!"

"I—I——"

"However, I understand your motives," said Mr Bootles kindly. "You may go, Erroll. Your detention is, of course, cancelled."

"Thank you, sir!" stammered Erroll.

His face was very bright now.

It was not only that he was free to join the cricketers; but his chum had done the right thing; that was what made Erroll's face flush with pleasure.

Mornington followed the Form-master into the room. Erroll's sentence had been transferred to him; he had expected that. He grinned at his chum as Erroll came from his desk.

"Cut off!" he whispered. "They are just goin' to begin!"

"Morny, old chap, I'm awfully glad you——"

"Glad you're goin' to play cricket? Cut off, then!"

"Glad you've done the right thing, Morny. I was wrong to doubt you for a moment."

Morny's face softened.

"I was only keepin' it up to show I didn't care for their silly raggin'. You should have known that——"

"I did know it, Morny——"

"Mornington!" It was Mr. Bootles' voice.

"Yes, sir."

Erroll hurried from the Form-room, with a last grateful glance at his chum. As he went, he heard Mr. Bootles' voice instructing Mornington in the task that was to occupy him till five o'clock. With a light heart, Erroll ran down to the cricket field.

. . . .

Jimmy Silver and Kit Erroll were at the wickets, in Rookwood's second innings, when Mornington strolled down to the cricket field a few minutes after five.

"How's it goin', Newcome?" drawled Morny, joining that youth by the ropes.

Newcome nodded to him. Erroll's presence in the team was a sufficient indication that Morny had done the right thing, and Newcome only wondered why he had not done it earlier.

"We made seventy-five in the first innings, to their eighty. Then they made sixty in their second innings, and we are sixty-two, with three wickets to fall," said Newcome.

"Good egg! We're goin' to win!" said Mornington, cheerfully. "Oh, well hit, Erroll! Well hit, old man!"

And Valentine Mornington joined loudly in the ringing cheer that greeted the winning hit.

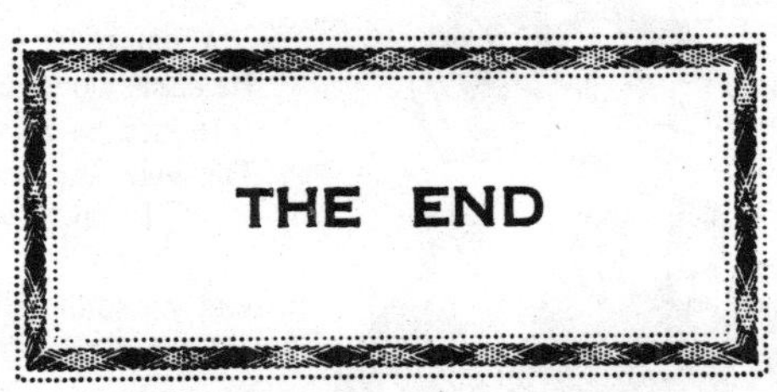

THE CHANT OF A CHEERFUL CHUMP

By TEDDY GRACE,
The Joker of Rookwood.

I WONDER why some fellows think
  A joker hasn't any wits ?
When I put gum in Lovell's ink
  I thought he'd laugh himself to fits ;
Instead of that, he blacked my eye !
    I wonder why !

I wonder why a booby-trap
  Annoys the ass it falls upon ?
The sight is funny for a chap
  Who's standing by and looking on !
I often shake my head and sigh
    And wonder why !

When Tubby ate a doughnut, which
  Had mustard and not jam inside,
His burning features were so rich
  I thought he'd laugh until he cried !
And yet he didn't even try !
    I wonder why !

Old Dalton is a cheerful chap ;
  I thought he'd like my little tricks ;
Yet when a toad jumped in his lap,
  He called me out and gave me six !
Indeed, he smote me hip and thigh !
    I wonder why !

When someone put in Carthew's bed
  A painted rubber rattlesnake,
He came along and punched my head ;
  In fact, he did not seem to take
The joke like a good-humoured guy !
    I wonder why !

And yet some fellows, I agree,
  Are brainless fatheads at the game ;
My study-mates fixed up for me
  A booby-trap, and down it came !
I saw them cackling on the sly—
    I wonder why !

A Thrilling Yarn of Flying Adventure

By CAPTAIN ROBERT HAWKE

THE PRISONER OF DEVIL'S ISLAND

Once he was a famous pilot in Britain's crack fighting squadron—Baldy's Angels. Now, years after the Great War, he is a prisoner in one of the worst penal settlements in the world.

THE FIRST CHAPTER

BLACK PAINT!

UNDER white tropic sunlight the great aircraft-carrier "Kestrel" dropped her bow anchor with a mighty crash and rumble of paying-out chain. Orders were shouted and the bo'sun's pipe shrilled as the men ran to swing out a gangway.

A mile away to port lay the coast of British Guiana, which the "Kestrel" had orders to visit for a day or so during her tour of the British possessions.

Now a smart pinnace came ploughing out, leaving a diamond wake tumbling behind her across the heaving waters. She was brought alongside neatly, and a tall, bespectacled man in a white linen suit clambered up the gangway on to the "Kestrel's" deck.

Squadron-Commander Wagstaff met him at the ladder-head and exchanged greetings. On the after-deck, behind the two, a group of young pilots were entertaining themselves by feats of physical strength. There were shouts of laughter as one of their number, wearing a strained expression and a gold-rimmed monocle, sought to climb, monkey fashion, to the top of a tall signal-mast.

Wagstaff gave a rather irritated glance towards them, for the noise was considerable. But, at the same time, he had to pay attention to the newcomer's words.

"Your arrival is providential—absolutely providential," said the bespectacled gentleman. "As I have already told you, the Government wanted a special survey of this coast, and so they sent me out a pilot with a small, mobile airship. But, unfortunately, the man is down with fever. He is not seriously ill; he will be quite recovered within a week. But this survey is urgent, and must be carried out at once!"

"Quite so, Mr. Tanson," said Wagstaff, looking slightly more irritated as the yells of laughter from the after-deck became still louder. "I take it that you wish me to provide you with an airship pilot who can assist you for a few days? Well, as a matter of fact, I happen to have several men on board who have done airship work."

"Thank you," said Mr. Tanson, in obvious relief. "I had hoped that such might be the case. As Government surveyor, I have carried out this work in many of our possessions, and it is one of my proud boasts that there has never been any delay about my reports."

He smiled rather self-consciously.

"I will not detain your man any longer than I can help," he said. "Indeed, it is quite possible that I may collect enough information in one day's flying to keep me busy in my office for best part of a week. I may be able to release your officer after just that one day."

Wagstaff nodded and turned to lead the surveyor up on the bridge of the great ship. But as he did so the uproar from the after-deck went far beyond the bounds of discipline and good order.

Mr. John Henry Dent—he of the monocle—only reached the top of the flagpost after superhuman efforts and weird and wonderful muscular contortions. Below him, on the deck, half a dozen young pilot officers yelled with mirth, and one especially gave forth a bull-like roar of delight.

Lieutenant A. P. Tarlan, indeed, had a voice in proportion to his size, which was considerable. He was a towering youth of really unusual strength, and, in the queer ways of young men, he was John Henry's most hated rival in all matters that concerned them both.

The warfare between the two was never-ending. It afforded the squadron quite a lot of amusement. Tarlan waved his arms in the air and howled his joy to the high heavens.

"Look at him!" he roared. "Look at the eye-glassed idiot! He can't climb a flagpole without going black in the face! Here, come down, J. H., and I'll show you how it's done!"

Young Mr. Dent came down. He slid to the deck, looking heated and haughty at the same time. Although an athletic youth, he had not Tarlan's enormous strength, and he knew it. He felt, now, that he was going to be "scored over." But suddenly he perceived an object standing near by on the planks, and his eyeglass glittered.

"All right!" he panted. "All right, jolly old Tarzan! You climb the pole. Dash it all, you ought to be able to do it quite naturally! But what I mean, I'll bet *you* can't do it without going black enough!"

Tarlan yelled with laughter again. He jumped at that post and went up, hand over hand, with a strength that certainly no other pilot in the squadron could match. But as he rose higher and higher, shouting down jibes with every foot that he climbed, young Mr. Dent got busy below.

" That's how to climb you glass-eyed tailor's dummy ! " exclaimed Tarlan to John Henry. Then he began to slide down the flagpole again—but not as he intended. As he reached the part John Henry had painted he slid more swiftly, and came down on his face !

He picked up that object which had first taken his attention. It was a large pot of black paint, left under cover of one of the lifeboats by a seaman who had been at work

Young Mr. Dent took the brush and painted that flagpole with swift liberal strokes.

The surrounding pilots suddenly saw the point of the joke and laughed uproariously. Tarlan took about four minutes to reach the flagpole summit —and during those four minutes, John Henry worked industriously

He covered more than four feet of the pole with liberal supplies of the black, shining paint. Then he put down the pot, adjusted his eyeglass happily, and awaited events.

" What-ho, you glass-eyed tailor's dummy ! " howled Tarlan from the summit of the pole. " That's how to climb ! That's how anyone who isn't a narrow-chested, fourpenny rabbit can nip up a pole, without going black in the face. What's your answer to *that ?* "

John Henry clapped applaudingly.

Mr. Tarlan grasped the pole affectionately and slid down.

He slid rather more swiftly when he reached the last six or seven feet ; so swiftly, in fact, that instead of landing on his feet he came down on his face ! He staggered up and looked down at his once-white uniform with an expression of blank, dazed horror.

His legs, knees, chest and arms were shining, dripping black ! There were traces of it on his chin ! Some had streaked his rather sandy hair !

John Henry walked away airily,

and whistled a nonchalant tune. Suddenly, however, his whistle broke off short, as he made a wild plunge forward! His plunge was occasioned by a bull-like roar which punctuated the yells of laughter from the others!

John Henry, in fact, ran like a hare. Young Mr. Tarlan ran, too, scattering black traces over the spotless "Kestrel" decks as he went! The rest of the pilots streamed out behind the chase, almost weeping with delight.

And up on the bridge, the spectacled Mr. Tanson looked distinctly interested—whilst Wagstaff fumed! Wagstaff, in fact, excused himself a second, and went aside to call up a group of duty officers, to whom he gave fiery instructions. The result of those instructions was that the wild chase all over the ship suddenly became interrupted. A couple of grinning duty-officers collared young Mr. Dent and then hauled him, with some difficulty, away to the wardroom.

Three more—armed with protective stretches of canvas—fell upon Mr. Tarlan. They conducted Mr. Tarlan to a bathroom and flung him inside, locking the door. They sent an orderly for a fresh uniform, and they told Mr. Tarlan that when he had once again reverted to the correct colour, as laid down in King's Regulations, for young officers, he was required to interview the commander.

The result was that, within half an hour, two rather sheepish officers faced Wagstaff in the wardroom. A small portion of hard, black paint still adhered to the end of Tarlan's nose—and it appeared to annoy Commander Wagstaff.

Commander Wagstaff, indeed, spoke for ten minutes without repeating himself, or making any great pause for breath. Then he squared his shoulders.

"I repeat, I've had enough of it!" he said. "You two young idiots have got to give up this insane rivalry. You've got to stop larking about like a pair of incorrigible schoolboys. In short," went on Wagstaff, "you've got to go ashore in five minutes' time, and undertake mobile-airship work with the Government Surveyor. And, by gosh, if I hear one word of complaint of any kind when you come back, I'll run you both up for court-martial!"

John Henry groaned, and tried to speak—but Wagstaff gave him no opportunity. The two were dismissed to go and collect their kits. But as they went, John Henry looked so crestfallen that he seemed on the verge of tears.

He hated airships. During the war, he had had one very unpleasant period of work with this type of craft over the North Sea, and he had hoped never to touch one again.

In heartrending tones, he now confided to Tarlan that airships were unsafe; that the smell of gas made you feel dizzy; that their motion in the air was rather like being tossed into a vat of oil when you were feeling bilious; that all government surveyors should be choked at birth; and that, in his opinion, Mr. Tarlan ought to put his head in a bucket three times and only take it out twice!

It was only the whistle of a boat's crew from above that prevented immediate warfare between the two—which was perhaps fortunate for Tarlan, for John Henry was a one-time middle-weight boxing champion of the Flying Corps, and he had no fear of Tarlan's size and strength in any way.

THE SECOND CHAPTER

THE ESCAPED CONVICT !

Two hours later, the rivals were swinging away from the small air-station ashore, in the narrow car of a small airship. John Henry, in command, sat at the controls, whilst Tarlan, for the time being under his orders, attended to minor matters in the stern.

The bespectacled Mr. Tanson sat in the middle, surrounded by cameras, maps, and a weird array of strange-looking instruments. Binoculars were hung round his narrow shoulders, and several pencils on clips decorated his flying-coat pocket, rather like a row of Orders.

At his instructions, John Henry flew the swaying airship far away up and down the coast, and even out to sea about a cluster of small islands. Not, indeed, until the sun began to sink, and evening fast approached, did Mr. Tanson order a return. But then he was looking satisfied.

"This has been excellent," he shouted, above the roar of the engine. "Excellent ! I could not have hoped for better results. Indeed, I think, now, that I shall be able to do without any further flying until my own pilot recovers. Let us now land."

With a sigh of infinite relief, John Henry swung the ship about, and headed towards the ten-mile distant coast, where a faint smudge of smoke showed the position of the "Kestrel" and the town. But as he did so, a tiny object on the sea, far below, caught his eye.

At first, it looked like a lump of wreckage ; but as John Henry swayed down lower, it proved itself to be a boat.

"Golly !" gasped Tarlan. "Look—look—there's a chap in it ! He seems to be dead—he's making no movement !"

Mr. Tanson lifted his binoculars excitedly, and made a clearer report.

"Dear me !" he said. "Dear me ! The poor fellow is a negro ! He's not dead—he moves slightly. But, dear me, he is terribly emaciated ! He appears very ill——"

John Henry swung that airship down to within a few feet of the surface, and throttled back the engine. Running waves now and again slapped against the car—and Mr. Tanson covered his papers excitedly, fearful of their getting wet.

But, slowly, against the prevailing breeze, the airship came up level with the drifting boat, and willing hands reached over to grasp its exhausted occupant.

The negro seemed to be absolutely on the verge of collapse, but he had just enough strength to make the effort that made his transfer possible. Then, gasping and groaning, he collapsed in the bottom of the car, whilst the airship rose slowly again, and got under way.

Tanson and Tarlan bent over him, making him as comfortable as possible, whilst John Henry bent round to watch, as often as he dared take his eyes off the controls.

For some little time the castaway rambled in broken French, but then his eyes seemed to clear, and he spoke fairly good English.

"Don't take me back !" he murmured. "I won't go back ! I rahder die dan see dat Debil's Island agen ! I reck'n I'm dyin' now !"

"Devil's Island !" gasped Tanson. "Why, dear me, that's the French penal settlement. This man must be an escaped convict."

"Devil's Island !" echoed John Henry and Tarlan together.

Both of them had heard, many times, of that terrible French convict-settlement to which long-sentence men are sent as a punishment for their misdeeds. They had heard that Devil's Island is one of the most dreaded institutions in the whole world; that convicts there undergo a regime of hardship only to be equalled by the legends of the middle ages.

They are worked like slaves, and driven to their work in the plantations. They are fed on starvation diet, and are ravaged by fevers. Any convict who manages to escape from Devil's Island is seldom sent back, if he lands in territory owned by any other country. For no other country approves of French ideas of punishment in this way.

John Henry suddenly altered the course of the airship, and made straight for the "Kestrel."

"Dash it all!" he gasped. "I'm not going to take any chances! We'll get this poor beggar on a ship of the British Navy—an' he'll be safe enough there! No beastly French consuls or people will be able to collar him and send him back. By Jove, we can land easily enough on the "Kestrel"—an' they'll take him down to the sick-bay an' look after him. Great snakes—look at his back! Dash it all, he's been flogged like a galley-slave!"

The negro's back was certainly a grim sight—and even the naval surgeon on board the "Kestrel" grimaced over it, when the fellow was handed over to his care after the airship had been moored.

The negro was put in a sick-bay berth, and carefully tended. He was soothed with skilful drugs, and made comfortable. And then, at length, he looked up at Wagstaff and his saviours, who were standing over the bed.

Although very weak, his head seemed to be clearer. Gratitude filled his glazed eyes.

"You English fellers, good fellers!" he said. "All you English good fellers! Me had English pal on Devil's Island—good feller who tol' me he once rode in bird-ships, like you."

"An Englishman on Devil's Island?" gasped Tarlan. "What the dickens was he doing there? D'you mean he was a convict—sent there by the French?"

"Dash it all—a flyin' man?" asked John Henry. "What was his name, my dear old Snowball? What was he there for?"

The negro breathed deeply.

"English feller, name Jameson," he said. "He good to me! He tol' me French debils sent him prison, becos he took photographs near dockyard. He tol' me he didn't mean no harm—but French t'ink him spy! Send him Debil's Island an' not say nothin' to no one! He sick feller, too. He die soon, if he don't get away from dat place!"

"Jameson!"

Two voices rapped that word out—and John Henry and Wagstaff stared at each other incredulously.

Lieutenant William James Jameson had been a member of the old Angels' Squadron, in which they had both served during the days of war. When peace came, "Billjim"—as he was nicknamed—went to the South of France for a holiday. They remembered this fact quite clearly, for "Billjim's" relatives afterwards wrote to both of them.

He had disappeared. Nothing had been heard of him for months, and no inquiries in France could trace his whereabouts at all. He was thought to have been drowned while bathing.

"Billjim!" said John Henry. "Dash it all—why, Wagger, the whole thing fits in ! You know how quiet all matters about spies are kept ? The rotters would send him to jug without savin anythin' to anybody ! Even just after the war everyone was still jumpy about spies ! Dash it all, look here——"

He made a feverish gesture.

" Look here, Wagger," he gasped, " we can't leave him there ! See what a state this poor nig is in ! An' he a French penal settlement ! No—I'll get on to our diplomatic people at once, and have the question raised."

" But," gasped John Henry, " that may take months ! You know how fearfully slow the awful idiots work ! And poor old Billjim's dyin' ! Good heavens——"

" Now, listen ! " snapped Wagstaff. " Get this clearly ! You're going to make no move of your own at all—in

Slowly, against the prevailing breeze, the airship came up level with the drifting boat, and, leaning over, John Henry and Tarlan lifted the exhausted negro into the car.

says Billjim's dyin' ! Dash it all, we must flip over there, an' get him out of that ghastly place ! "

Wagstaff's face had gone white, but he interrupted rather curtly.

" Don't be a fool, John Henry ! " he said. " We couldn't possibly do such a thing. Why, you young idiot, it might create an international quarrel ! We can't have the English Royal Air Force going and rescuing convicts from any way. I order you to put the whole thing out of your mind ! I'm just as keen to get poor Billjim back as you are. But I can't take the risk of raising what might develop into a war between two countries, for the sake of one man ! The whole of Europe is frightened at the moment. There have been rumours of war all over the place ! One ' incident ' like this might cost the lives of thousands of men ! "

He turned away abruptly.

" Get that airship ashore," he said. " And stay ashore until Mr. Tanson releases you to come back here."

Without another word he strode above decks to the wireless-room, where he began dictating messages to a high diplomatic authority in Whitehall.

THE THIRD CHAPTER

ON DEVIL'S ISLAND !

MR. TANSON elected to go ashore in the pinnace. The wind had now freshened considerably, and was blowing half a gale, so Mr. Tanson decided that aerial travel might perhaps be rather more unpleasant than a passage by sea.

It was this fact which gave John Henry furiously to think, as he and Tarlan slipped moorings in the airship, and made heavy going on the way back to the shore.

Tarlan also appeared thoughtful—but John Henry put this down to his inexperience of airships in general, and his undoubted dislike of this one in particular.

They reached the shore safely, and dropped a bow mooring-rope which was caught and fastened to a winch by the landing-crowd on shore

John Henry's mind worked swiftly, and he motioned Tarlan to take control

" Keep her head-on to wind," he said. " She'll yaw about a bit, but keep her as steady as you can, whilst I attend to this head-rope."

John Henry attended to the head-rope He had a good experience of airships and knew all their most unpleasant little ways He knew that if the rope were tautened too much, when a gust struck the vessel in a certain way, things were likely to happen.

The rope, in fact, was more than likely to snap. John Henry worked carefully, keeping his efforts out of sight of those below, who were standing about the winch, winding the vessel down.

The airship, under Tarlan's unskilful control, bucketed wildly. It swayed from side to side—and John Henry saw his chance. He whipped in the slack of that winding rope—and jammed it.

There was a sudden twanging crack—and a wild yell from below !

John Henry rolled on his back in the bows of the car, and Tarlan was nearly unseated at the controls. When they had righted themselves, they looked down in the twilight, to see that the ground had already dropped away a couple of thousand feet ! The winch-men were running about, like frantic ants from an overturned nest.

" Dash it all, we've broken away ! " gasped John Henry—although the large and spreading grin on his face somewhat belied his words of alarm.

" We've broken away, dear old boy ! " he repeated. " We're sausagin' miles away out to sea ! Heaven alone knows where we shall come down ! Dash it all, we might even hit Devil's Island ! "

Whilst he had been speaking, he ripped open one of the canvas water-ballast tanks, and sent a stream of liquid falling down towards the ground and the sea below.

It was seen by the alarmed watchers on the earth. John Henry hoped it would be. It was all part of his little plan !

" Shall we start the engine ? " bawled Tarlan, swaying in his seat, but seeming not unduly alarmed by the whole procedure.

" Not yet," said young Mr. Dent solemnly. " We must wait till we get to a higher altitude, dear old boy. Airships have dangerous ways. Dash it all, if we started the engine now, the people on the "Kestrel" might hear—I mean, the airship might—might get out of control! You don't understand these things!"

Tarlan stared at him, but said nothing. The coastline receded swiftly as that thirty-mile-an-hour wind bore them upon its breast. The airship rose to 10,000 feet, whirling and swaying giddily.

John Henry took control and steadied it skilfully once or twice, at the same time carefully examining the compass, together with a large chart which was amongst the equipment.

At the end of an hour, he announced that it would be safe to start the engine, and once the propeller was working he set a careful course and began to hum to himself a low tune.

The whole thing had gone off exactly as he had wanted it to! No one could say that the airship hadn't broken away by accident. Its engine had not started whilst it was within hearing of the "Kestrel."

John Henry intended to tell Wagstaff, at some future date, that the petrol-tank had been wrenched open with the force of the breakaway—so that the fuel had fallen out, and the engine was useless.

Meanwhile, when the engine had served its purpose, he was actually going to wrench the side of the petrol tank out, as evidence that his story was true!

That was why he had dropped the water-ballast immediately the escape had occurred. He wanted that water to be mistaken for falling petrol!

In all these things, young Mr. Dent was very successful, as events afterwards proved. But now that he had got the airship started, he flew steadily through the night until, far away in the distance, he saw the star-like gleam of a lighthouse illuminating the early greyness of dawn.

John Henry shut off his engine, after carefully gauging the wind. The lighthouse now showed more clearly at the extremity of an island.

Young Mr. Dent manœuvred the airship carefully, so that it was being carried directly towards that island by the prevailing wind. Once again he gave over the controls to Tarlan, and went forward to perform his little efforts on the petrol-tank, which he accomplished quite successfully.

"Now, Tarzan," he breathed as he worked, "there are one or two things I'm goin' to say to you, dash it all, when we've got time for a quiet chat. Meanwhile, I'm going to try to land on that island there. But when we *do* land, we mustn't let 'em know we were able to use our engine at all! We can't have these French fellers gigglin' at the British Royal Air Force. Dash it all, it's not to be borne. I think, by a mistake, I've navigated over Devil's Island, instead of gettin' back to the coast!"

Mr. Tarlan chuckled.

"That's not surprising," he said. "Unless you were blind lucky you couldn't navigate a team of white mice across a suburban back garden! Still, what d'you want me to do with the ship now? Shall I try and steer it?"

John Henry waved him away from the controls and took over. At the same time he tugged on the gas-release valve, so that the airship dropped down almost to water level, and approached the island swiftly.

At his orders, Tarlan threw over two or three more trail-ropes, and, as they approached the coast, young

Mr. Dent drew attention by firing flares, which all airships carry for such purposes.

The French Penal Settlement was just awake. Luckless convicts were being driven out of their hovels, to start their daily terrible labours in the fever-ridden plantations and in the quarries.

The clearing light of dawn showed the airship approaching, and the bang and glare of the flares drew attention to its presence. There were yelled orders, and considerable commotion reigned over the main square of the prison settlement.

Guards organised the convicts swiftly in parties—and as the airship swept low over their heads gangs of men grabbed those trail-ropes and hung on, sliding and kicking in the dust to gain a foothold.

With such a power on the ropes the airship was pulled up within a matter of yards. It was hauled down, pitchingly, as John Henry leant over the side and bawled directions in the best French he could manage.

Finally it was got to ground level. And then, at his advice, some of the gangs were set to work, swiftly filling large sacks with earth and sand, whilst the rest held the airship in place.

Prison officials flocked round John Henry and Tarlan, and, in the manner of their kind, all talked at once and all waved their hands violently.

The governor himself appeared on the scene with a revolver in each hand—having imagined, by the commotion, that there was a mutiny. But directly he announced himself, young Mr. Dent at once became astonishingly polite.

He used his very best French to thank the governor for heroically saving the life of himself and his friend! He said that the airship had broken loose from a British base, and that they had both spent an awful night, fearing that it would drop into the shark-infested seas—which made escape from Devil's Island almost impossible.

The governor was pleased. He hadn't taken the least part in the rescue, but he liked being called a hero. He realised, also, that when these officers were picked up by the British warship which they said would come to look for them, he would be rewarded.

The English might give him a medal! There would, no doubt, be all kinds of pleasant courtesies.

So the governor made much of the visitors. Directly half a dozen enormous sandbags had been filled and attached to the airship's mooring ropes, he invited the pair into breakfast.

He placed his extremely comfortable house at their disposal, and begged them to rest after they had eaten He also sent out wireless calls to the "Kestrel" to notify the British authorities that they were safe

But young Mr. Dent purposely informed the wireless operator of an entirely wrong wavelength He didn't want that message to get to the "Kestrel" too soon!

Nor did he consent to rest. He assured the governor that he and his friend were too overcome with personal relief for sleep to be possible. And he said that, since they had landed in such an unusual place, they would very much like to take advantage of that fact. They would deem it an honour to be shown round the settlement.

The governor agreed readily After breakfast he took the two out and led them, through the growing heat of the blazing tropical sun, into the plantations where the prisoners were at work.

The governor yelled out wildly as the airship suddenly swept into the air above his head. But he little knew that in the sandbag dangling from the car was one of the prisoners of Devil's Island whom John Henry and Tarlan had rescued!

He assured them that each prisoner was a desperate, terrible character, who more than deserved every detail of the punishment he received. French punishments, he said, were designed to fit crimes.

But as John Henry and Tarlan made the rounds of those steaming, humid plantations, they could think of very few crimes which would merit such ghastly punishment as was there shown before their eyes.

All the prisoners seemed in the last stages of emaciation—and all of them showed the vicious marks of the warders' lashes across their bare backs.

Their work was labour of a hardness known in no English prison. Their food was rank and scanty. And the hovels in which they slept were not fit to keep pigs in.

John Henry scanned each strained, sweating face as he passed. His heart fell when he recognised no one—caught no sight of the man he had actually come to find.

But then, when the party reached the quarries, he saw a thin, wasted individual staring at him in utter, blank astonishment.

THE FOURTH CHAPTER

THE RESCUE!

THE man was white, but his skin was burned brown by the beating rays of that brazen sun. He was so thin that his bones seemed merely covered by a skin of parchment. But there was something about his eyes—some vague expression that made John Henry halt suddenly with a gasp.

The governor was walking ahead with Tarlan, and the warders who were scattered about had eyes only for that group just at that special moment.

John Henry made a swift movement. From beneath his tunic he jerked a folded sack which he had managed to pick up and hide during the excitement immediately after the airship's landing.

Furtively he tossed that sack at the man's feet and spoke as loudly as he dared :

" Dear old Billjim ! " he breathed. " Keep your pecker up an' grab that sack ! There are four sacks holdin' the airship down. If I saw *five* of 'em tied to it this evening, just after you go back from your work, the airship might break away ! It might carry that fifth sack along ! D'you understand what I mean, Billjim ? D'you think you can do it ? "

The emaciated man let out a long breath, and then whipped up that sack, tying it round his waist, apron fashion. Many of the other convicts were wearing rags of sacking in this way, so that it would attract little notice.

" I—I understand ! " he gasped. " Great heavens, John Henry, I can hardly believe my eyes ! But I understand. I'll do it, if I get shot in the attempt ! "

John Henry walked on without another word, for at that moment he saw a warder turn. But nothing was observed. Young Mr. Dent caught up with the governor and Tarlan, and so eventually came back to the residency, where a most excellent lunch was served.

After lunch John Henry at last elected to rest, and he and Tarlan were given separate rooms. As evening fell they could hear the unfortunate convicts being herded back to their miserable hovels after that back-breaking day in the heat.

John Henry woke Tarlan and came downstairs in time for the evening meal. At that meal he interested the governor by a long talk on airships and all their ways.

The outcome of this was that John Henry offered to show the governor their especial craft and explain all its various mysteries. The governor was very willing. He provided a few electric torch-lamps, and the three went out, climbing up into the moored ship and spending some time over the various dials, instruments and levers at the control seat.

John Henry's French was not very good on that occasion. He had seen that *five* sacks, in line, were now mooring the ship ! He climbed up last—and gave the end sack a light kick as he did so.

It yielded—not at all in the manner of packed earth or sand !

John Henry finally clambered down and led the governor and Tarlan beneath the ship itself. In the dark he spent some time in explaining details of construction. And, in the dark, he toiled at the knotted ropes which bound the other four sandbags. He got the first and second clear—and above them, the airship pitched alarmingly.

The governor noticed it, and remarked that the wind must be rising—suggested that extra bags should be filled, so that it could be held down more safely.

In the middle of his words John Henry got that fourth rope free—and the governor yelled out wildly as the airship suddenly swept into the air above his head !

It swept up, with one " sandbag " still dangling on the end of a rope.

It shot up into the blackness and swept away over the island, making swiftly for the sea beyond!

The governor yelled orders and warders came running. Lights flashed everywhere. There was a scene of wild confusion.

And, in the middle of it, Tarlan stood swearing vividly. The grinning John Henry heard him, and chuckled outright.

"Dear old boy," he said, "why this heated brow? Does it *matter* that the darned airship's got away again?"

"Of course it matters!" snapped Tarlan sulphurously. "Ever since I caused the darned thing to break away the first time, I've been racking my brains for a way of getting to this island and getting Billjim away! And now the darned thing's gone, and we can do nothing!"

"*You* broke the ship away?" gasped John Henry. "Why, dash it all——"

"Of course I did!" snapped Tarlan. "I kicked the rudder about, whilst we were being hauled down, because I guessed too much strain would break the rope! I thought you'd twigged the idea, too, when you fooled about with the petrol tank, and navigated us here. But now—why, I never even caught sight of Billjim!"

John Henry tottered to his feet.

"But—but, dash it all, you've never met him," he said. "You were never in the old 'Angels' Squadron'!"

"Of course I wasn't!" almost roared Tarlan. "I wasn't old enough to join the Air Force until immediately after the war. But then, Billjim was my instructor at a Home aerodrome, immediately before he went for that holiday in the South of France. Good heavens, don't be such a thickhead!"

John Henry suddenly laughed. He tried to restrain his laughter, but in the prevailing general uproar there was really no need.

"Tarzan," he said; "jolly old Tarzan! Dash it all, I'll ask you one thing. When is a sandbag not a sandbag?"

Tarlan's answer was expressed in no polite terms. He was not at all in the mood for merry jest.

But meanwhile the officials on Devil's Island spent a very trying evening. The governor was wildly angry at the fact that the airship had been tied so insecurely that it broke free. He was also angry at the fact that a prisoner was reported missing.

He ordered the warders out, with guns and rifles, all round the coasts of the island, to catch this convict before he could try to make a raft and get to sea.

He swore violently, and apologised to John Henry and Tarlan with almost tearful emphasis. He said he should never forgive himself for the airship's escape. He said that he felt especially humiliated that a prisoner had made a break for escape whilst such distinguished visitors were there. He said that if he had not been in the car of the airship, a moment before it got away, he would have suspected that the scoundrel had got up in it and made his escape that way. But that, of course, was impossible.

The two agreed that it was impossible. They sympathised with the governor—said that his gallant warders would no doubt round up the fugitive quite soon. And at length they went to bed.

The following morning was made eventful by the arrival of a large seaplane which came to rest just off the island. The governor sent a boat out and the boat brought back Wagstaff—looking as grim as an impending thunderstorm.

Directly he arrived, however, the governor once again plunged into abject apologies for having lost the airship. He told how it had got away —how his fools of men had not moored it securely enough.

He said nothing about an escaped prisoner—not in the least wishing to advertise that fact to a high officer of another country.

Wagstaff's expression cleared, and a grim imp of laughter came into his eyes as he assured the governor that the loss of the airship was a small matter compared with the saving of his two officers' lives.

The two officers stood behind the governor and winked cheerfully.

Young Mr. Dent even went so far as to put out his tongue.

Wagstaff, feeling that he could not keep a straight face much longer, refused the governor's invitation to lunch with polite excuses. And then he took his two subordinates out to that large seaplane, which was immediately started up and flown away.

In the main cabin of the plane, Wagstaff faced them.

"You've disobeyed orders," he said, trying to keep grim. "You've taken an appalling risk of plunging armies into strife. You've—you've——"

"Dash it all, we've done nothin'," said John Henry. "Absolutely nothin', dear old Wagger. We couldn't help landin' there—when the airship's found, you'll see that the petrol tank was busted. We couldn't use our engine. And *we* couldn't help it if jolly old Billjim fixed himself up in a sandbag, and wound one of the mooring ropes round his body, inside it! What I mean, if he floated away like that, we couldn't help it, could we?"

"Good heavens!" gasped Wagstaff, wild relief fighting for pride of place with alarm in his eyes. "Good heavens, d'you mean——"

"I mean," said John Henry cheerfully, "that all's well that jolly well ends well! The governor was on that airship a moment before it broke loose, so he's certain that no convict could have hopped aboard. Now all we've got to do is to scout round, an' find the airship, and pick up dear old Billjim."

Wagstaff drew a deep breath.

"You——" he said. "You——"

He found himself at a loss for words.

Tarlan also seemed at a loss for words.

Five minutes afterwards, however, the small, noisy cabin of that seaplane echoed to a greater noise—that of three voices raised in wild laughter.

Five days afterwards three officers paid a visit to a small hospital in British territory, where an emaciated man was slowly being nursed back to health by the care of doctors and nurses. "Billjim" had made good his escape in the airship after climbing up the mooring-rope to the car, and he had come down safely at the landing-ground on the coast of British Guiana.

The interview between William James Jameson and Wagstaff, John Henry and Tarlan was jubilant, and the conversation ranged about the subject of "getting the sack" from Devil's Island!

THE END

"Stony broke" is a state not uncommon to the cheery chums of St. Jim's, but for once, how to "raise the wind" provides a pretty problem—a problem which, when tackled, leads to more trouble raising than "wind raising"!

THE FIRST CHAPTER

NO LUCK FOR LOWTHER!

"I'VE got it!"

Monty Lowther fairly burst into Study No. 10 in the Shell, with excitement in his face, and gasped out the words.

There were six juniors in the study; and they all stared at Lowther. They had been looking very thoughtful, not to say glum; but as Monty made his breathless announcement their faces brightened up wonderfully.

"You've got it?" exclaimed Tom Merry.

"Yes!"

"Thank goodness!" said Manners, in tones of deep relief.

"Bai Jove, that's wippin' news!" said Arthur Augustus D'Arcy. "Then it will be all wight?"

"Right as rain!" said Monty Lowther cheerily.

Blake and Herries and Dig exchanged glances of satisfaction. The news really was exhilarating.

For quite a long time—it seemed like ages to them—the Terrible Three and Blake & Co. had been in the sad and forlorn state slangily described as "stony."

Study No. 10 in the Shell and Study No. 6 in the Fourth had fallen into the sere and yellow leaf.

The last copper was gone—and the allowances were mortgaged ahead.

One or two remittances that had dropped in had been used to settle up small debts. But the big debt remained—the sum of six pounds, which weighed upon the minds and the spirits of the stony seven.

How the wind was to be raised to square the account was still a deep mystery to Tom Merry & Co., although they had tried many ways and means—from gardening to French translations.

Six of the stony juniors had been holding a consultation on the subject in Tom Merry's study. Their consultations were frequent; indeed, the stony juniors held almost as many conferences as if they had been great statesmen with nothing to do but to exercise their chins.

And then came Monty Lowther, bursting into the study with the news that he had "got it."

No wonder the conference brightened up.

"I weally think this meetin' ought to pass a vote of thanks to Lowthah!" said Arthur Augustus D'Arcy. "It will be no end of a welief to get cleah of that howwid debt."

"Hear, hear!" said Dig.

"And we'll jolly well let it be a warning to us," said Tom Merry. "No more debts for me, after this."

"No fear!" said Blake emphatically.

"Wathah not!" said Arthur Augustus. "I am glad to see that you youngstahs are takin' this lesson to heart——"

"Bow-wow! Lowther, old man," said Tom Merry, "you're a jewel. I was beginning to think that we'd never raise that awful six quid."

"But how have you done it, Lowther?" asked Blake. "Have you had a terrific remittance?"

"Remittance?" said Lowther. "Oh, no!"

"Then how——"

"How did you get it?" asked Herries.

"I was trotting around under the elms, thinking it over, and all of a sudden it came to me!" said Lowther jubilantly.

"Wh-a-a-t?"

"Bai Jove!"

"Are you off your rocker?" roared Blake. "I suppose it couldn't come to you of its own accord, could it?"

"Eh! Of course!" said Monty Lowther, with a stare. "Naturally!"

"It—it came to you of its own accord?" babbled Blake.

"Of course! Suddenly flashed into my mind."

"Flashed into your mind!" shrieked Tom Merry. "How the merry thump could six pounds flash into your mind?"

"He's potty!" said Herries. "Simply potty! I've seen signs of this in Lowther before. The way he makes puns——"

"Six pounds!" said Lowther blankly. "What do you mean? I didn't say I had six pounds, did I?"

The glum expression returned to half a dozen faces. Evidently there had been a misapprehension.

"You burbling ass!" said Blake. "You said you'd got it!"

"Yaas, wathah, Lowthah! You distinctly said you had got it!" exclaimed Arthur Augustus warmly.

"Oh, I meant the idea!"

"The what?"

"The idea—how to raise the wind, you know," said Lowther. "I haven't got the money—I've got the idea."

"Fathead!"

Six voices pronounced that word in tones of utter disgust. The hopes of the stony juniors had been raised, only to be dashed to the ground again. Monty Lowther appeared to think that his idea was practically as good as the money; but it was obvious that the six fellows in the study did not agree with him, not the least little bit.

"Bai Jove! I weally think Lowthah ought to be scwagged!" said Arthur Augustus. "He made us think he had the tin, and it turns out to be only one of his wotten wheezes."

"Collar the silly owl!" growled Herries.

"Here, hold on!" exclaimed Lowther. "You haven't heard the wheeze yet. It's a stunt that will see us through."

"Wats!"

"Rubbish!"

"We don't want to hear it," said Blake morosely. "We know your Shell wheezes. Poof!"

"Look here, you cheeky Fourth-Form ass!"

"Wag him, deah boys!"

"Hold on," said Tom Merry. "Give the silly chump a chance. If his idea's any good, we'll try it. If it isn't, we'll bump him!"

"Yaas, that's fair!"

"It's the stunt of the season," said Monty Lowther impressively. "I wonder I never thought of it before. It came into my head all of a sudden while I was thinking the thing out. We've tried several schemes for raising the wind, but they've come to nothing. Now, this idea is the real article—the real gilt-edged thing. You fellows know how I play the banjo?"

"The—the banjo?"

"Yes. You know how I play it?"

"Like a nigger playing a tom-tom," said Blake. "We know!"

"You silly ass!" roared Lowther. "You know I play it awfully well. And you know how I can make up?"

"Make up?"

"Yes—you've seen me play nigger parts."

"But what the thump has that got to do with it?" demanded Manners.

"Lots! That's the idea! Nigger minstrel, you know—song and dance, and pass round the hat!" said Lowther. "Catch on?"

The assembled juniors simply blinked at Monty Lowther. They could scarcely believe that he was serious.

"Nigger minstrel!" said Blake faintly. "Pass round the hat! Great Christopher Columbus!"

"Bai Jove! I weally feah that Lowthah's bwain is givin' way."

"Well," said Tom Merry, "of all the potty rubbish——"

"Give a chap a chance," said Lowther hotly. "Made up as a nigger minstrel, I'm going to give a performance in the quad——"

"In the quad!" shrieked the juniors.

"That's it! Of course, the fellows won't know it's little me. I shall dawn on them suddenly, you know, made up as Uncle Bones, with banjo complete. I've got the things in the property-box. I shall rig up in the wood-shed after lessons. I give a song and dance in the quad—the fellows crowd round—tumultuous applause—coppers and tanners and bobs rain into the hat—and—and there you are!"

Jack Blake rose to his feet. His expression was grim. He looked round at the conference.

"Lowther made us believe he'd got the quids!" he said. "It turns out to be a stunt—the kind of stunt they'd think of in Colney Hatch on their very bad days. Lowther's asked for it."

"Yaas, wathah!"

"Collar him!"

"But listen——" yelled Lowther, in great wrath and indignation.

But the juniors refused to listen. Apparently they considered that they had heard enough. They collared the unhappy propounder of ripping wheezes, jerked him off his feet, and bumped him on the study carpet. The dust rose from the carpet and a wild yell from Monty Lowther.

"Yoop! You silly asses——"

"Give him anothah!"

Bump!

"Yow-ow! I'll—I'll—— You silly chumps, it's the catch of the season. I'm going ahead, anyhow, and you'll see—— Yarooooooh!"

Bump!

Monty Lowther landed on the carpet for the third time, and then he was left. The meeting broke up, and the hapless Monty was left feeling as if he had broken up, too.

THE SECOND CHAPTER

GOING IT!

Tom Merry and Manners grinned a little when they met their chum in class that afternoon.

Monty Lowther frowned at them.

He was still very much ruffled by the unflattering reception his amazing wheeze had met with. But that unflattering reception had not made any difference to his resolve. He was going ahead just the same, after lessons that day—he was determined on that. If his comrades in misfortune did not choose to back him up, he would "go it" alone.

In the interval between the bumping in the study and afternoon class in the Shell room, Lowther had been busy.

There were signs on his fingers of how he had sorted out his greasepaints and lampblack, and even as he entered the Form-room—in the awe-inspiring presence of Mr. Linton himself—Monty Lowther was humming a coon song that he had been running over to refresh his memory.

When Monty Lowther was "on a stunt" he was often forgetful of time and space and other considerations. He was very unwilling to come into class at all that afternoon; he would have preferred preparing in the study for his great enterprise. Naturally—at least, Lowther would have called it naturally—he could not put this important business out of his head for the sake of such minor considerations as geography and English grammar! What did geography and English grammar matter to a fellow who had the stunt of the term in his active brain, and who was going to save six stony comrades from stoniness in spite of themselves?

Nevertheless, Mr. Linton—quite unaware that more important matters were on hand—persisted in geography and English grammar, in the obstinate and regardless manner common to Form-masters.

When Monty Lowther, absent-mindedly as was natural in the circumstances, told Mr. Linton that America was discovered by Uncle Bones, Mr. Linton stared—and the master of the Shell was still more astonished to hear that Sir Francis Drake was celebrated for playing the banjo.

There was a sound of swishing in the Form-room next; and Monty Lowther, as he rubbed his palms, was brought back to common earth again, as it were, and tried to give up his thoughts to geography.

In English grammar Mr. Linton had another surprise.

The juniors were directed to write each a sentence of his own composition or from memory, and parse it, the papers being handed in to Mr. Linton

More or less melodiously, the nigger minstrel, to the accompaniment of his banjo, began to sing. "Go it Uncle Bones!" exclaimed the juniors, greatly enjoying the situation. But little did most of them realise that the minstrel was Monty Lowther!

afterwards. While they were so engaged, the master of the Shell took a well-earned respite, nodding at his desk in the drowsy summer's afternoon. But he woke up as sharp as a needle when the papers were handed in, and he stared as he looked at Lowther's. Monty had chosen the beautiful sentence :

"Honey, little Honey, you're my
Honey-honey-hoo!
When I strum upon de banjo I'm
a-strummy-umming you!"

"Honey : Proper noun, voc. case, fem. gen., sing. num.

"Little : Adj. of quantity.

"Honey : Prop. noun, voc. case, fem. gen., sing."

Mr. Linton did not trouble to finish reading the parsing exercise. He called Monty Lowther up to his desk.

"Do you call that a sentence suitable for a grammatical exercise, Lowther?" he asked.

"Yes, sir," said Monty.

"Our opinions differ on that point," said Mr. Linton coldly. "It is not a sentence at all, Lowther, but a fragment of imbecility."

"Oh!" said Lowther.

"I fear, Lowther, that you are not thinking of your lessons this afternoon."

"Oh, sir!"

"You will write down another exercise for parsing from my dictation."

"Oh! Yes, sir!"

"Take this sentence; it is from Fielding, and it will be useful to you, Lowther, to study this master of prose; it will help to correct your taste, which I fear is bad. 'An author ought to consider himself, not as a gentleman who gives a private or eleemosynary treat, but rather as one who keeps a public ordinary, at which all persons are welcome for their money.'"

"Oh, my hat!" ejaculated Lowther involuntarily.

"Eh? What did you say, Lowther?"

"N-n-nothing, sir."

"Have you written down that sentence, Lowther?"

"Ye-e-es, sir."

"Very good. You will stay in after lessons, and parse it, and bring me the result to my study before tea-time."

"Oh!"

"You may go to your place, Lowther."

Monty Lowther went to his place, a sadder if not a wiser Shell fellow. For the remainder of the afternoon he tried to keep his thoughts fixed on the pearls of wisdom that fell from Mr. Linton, and to drive away all consideration of his new stunt, and his banjo, and Honey-honey-hoo!

When the class was dismissed, Monty Lowther had to remain in the Form-room to parse that sentence from the master of prose given him by his kind Form-master to improve his taste.

Tom Merry and Manners gave him sympathetic glances as they went out, which was all they could do for him.

They went down to the cricket-ground to put in some practice before tea, expecting Monty Lowther to join them there when his detention task was done.

But Monty Lowther did not appear.

Kildare of the Sixth was putting in some of his valuable time coaching the juniors, so Tom Merry and Manners did not go in search of their chum. They were leaving the cricket-ground more than an hour later, when Baggy Trimble of the Fourth met them, full of excited news.

"Come on, you fellows!" bawled Trimble.

"What's up?"

"He, he, he! There's a nigger minstrel in the quad!" chortled Trimble. "You can hear his giddy old banjo from here! Taggles can't have seen him come in, or he'd have chucked him out. He, he, he!"

Tom Merry jumped.

"A nigger minstrel——"

"In the quad!" yelled Manners.

"Giving a song and dance!" chuckled Trimble. "I say, they'll chuck him out on his neck. Awful cheek, you know——"

Tom and Manners exchanged a glance of dismay, and then they rushed on. Monty Lowther, evidently, was "at it."

He was carrying out his great stunt. Undoubtedly he had "made up" in the wood-shed, as he had planned, as soon as his detention was over—and his chums, occupied at cricket, had been unable to restrain his enthusiasm. The sound of a banjo and a voice greeted the juniors as they ran up, mingled with roars of laughter from a crowd gathering in the quad

"Bai Jove, you fellahs!" exclaimed Arthur Augustus D'Arcy. "It's——"

"Shurrup!" whispered Tom hurriedly.

"Weally, Tom Mewwy——"

"Don't give it away, ass!" muttered Manners.

"I was not goin' to give it away, Mannahs. But weally——"

Blake and Herries and Dig came up, grinning. They could guess who the nigger minstrel was.

But outside the half-dozen juniors, nobody guessed. Certainly Monty Lowther's nearest relation would not have recognised him just then. The crowd was already thick round the performer, and Tom Merry & Co. had to shove a way forward.

Pong, pong ! Tang, tang ! went the banjo.

On the ground stood a large silk hat, ready for contributions. What looked like a Christy minstrel was strumming on the banjo and singing melodiously.

The chums of the School House blinked at him. Was it Monty Lowther, after all ?

The minstrel had a face as black as the ace of spades ; his mouth was widened with chalk until it seemed to extend almost from ear to ear ; his head was covered with black fuzzy hair. His trousers were striped with red on white ; his cutaway coat was sky-blue. His tie was large and flowing, and rivalled in colour the well-known coat of Joseph. If it was Lowther of the Shell, he was marvellously got up.

He was singing, more or less melodiously, the following refrain to the accompaniment of the banjo :

" Honey, little honey, you're my
  honey-honey-hoo !
When I strum upon de banjo I'm
  a-strummy-umming you !
    Oh, my hunky little honey,
    Though my features may be
      funny,
I've a great big heart, my honey, and
  it beats for you-oo-oo ! "

" Ha, ha, ha ! "

" Go it, Uncle Bones," sang out Kangaroo of the Shell.

" Bai Jove ! The awful ass ! "

The minstrel proceeded to his dance, which he performed with some grace. Tom Merry stared towards the façade of the School House, expecting every moment to see a master issue forth to inquire into this extraordinary scene in the quadrangle. The minstrel accompanied his dance with castanets, and the juniors cheered him. It was the first time they had seen such a show in the sacred precincts of the school quadrangle.

" Bai Jove ! Now he's goin' wound with the hat ! " exclaimed Arthur Augustus. " And here comes Wailton."

Mr. Railton issued from the School House as the minstrel ceased his dance, picked up the big silk hat, and walked round the circle holding it out. Quite a shower of coppers fell into the hat, with some sixpences and a shilling or two.

" Better cut off, uncle," whispered Talbot of the Shell, as he dropped a shilling. " There's a beak coming along."

" And here comes Taggles ! " said Gore.

Taggles, the porter, was coming up from the gates, with a stick in his hand, greatly scandalised. Uncle Bones blinked round as Mr. Railton made his way through the throng.

" What does this mean ? " exclaimed the Housemaster sternly.

" Good-afternoon, sah ! " said the minstrel. " You like to see me gib song and dance, massa ? "

Tom Merry almost held his breath.

" Certainly not ! " exclaimed Mr. Railton sternly. " You should not have come in here. Itinerant entertainers are not allowed to enter the school grounds. Taggles, you should not have admitted this man."

" I never did ! " exclaimed Taggles

hotly. "He never come in at the gates, sir! Must 'ave legged it over the wall, sir."

"That is very odd," said Mr. Railton. "However, see him off the premises at once, Taggles."

"You leave 'im to me, sir!" said Taggles, and he dropped a heavy hand on the minstrel's shoulder. "Now then, you vagabond, you come alonger me!"

"I'se comin' when I'se finished takin' de collection, boss," objected the minstrel.

"You're coming now!" grunted Taggles, and he tightened his grip and marched the coloured gentleman away to the gates. And half St. Jim's followed them in a grinning crowd.

THE THIRD CHAPTER

NOT SO BLACK AS PAINTED!

"HOUTSIDE!"

Taggles the porter gave the black gentleman a twirl in the gateway, and sent him into the road spinning like a top.

"Oh, my hat!" ejaculated Uncle Bones.

"Ha, ha, ha!"

"Now, you clear hoff!" said Taggles, pointing an admonitory forefinger at the minstrel. "You 'ook it! You 'ear me?"

The minstrel heard, but, like the dying gladiator of old, he heeded not.

Having reached the middle of the road, opposite the wide gateway, he stopped and put his hat on the ground, and began to strum the banjo again. Taggles stared at him in great wrath.

"Are you a-goin'?" he roared.

Ping! ping! pang! pong! went the banjo.

"You rapscallion, 'ook it!" shouted Taggles.

Pong! pong! pong!

"Let him alone!" chuckled Cardew of the Fourth. "The road's free to him, Taggles!"

"Hear, hear!" chortled Figgins of the New House. "Go it, Uncle Bones!"

"On the ball!" roared Grundy of the Shell.

"Ha, ha, ha!"

There, in full view of the scandalised and outraged Taggles, the black gentleman proceeded to do another dance in sheer defiance. The gateway swarmed with cheering juniors.

Taggles brandished his stick at the coloured gentleman.

"Will you 'ook it?" he roared.

"Go it!" yelled Figgins.

"Play up, darkey!"

"Ha, ha, ha!"

Mr. Railton had gone back to the School House. Taggles was left alone to deal with the strolling performer whose absurd performance was detracting from the scholastic dignity of the ancient foundation of St. Jim's. Taggles brandished his stick in vain.

"He's doin' no harm, old bean," said Cardew. "In fact, he's amusin' us! It's no end amusin' to think that the fellow thinks anybody could want to see a show like that! I'm goin' to give him a half-crown for his nerve!"

"Ha, ha, ha!"

"Go away!" roared Taggles.

"Ha, ha, ha!"

Knox of the Sixth came hurrying down to the gates. The juniors made room for the Sixth-Form prefect to pass.

"Taggles, what the thump do you mean by allowing a rowdy scene like this at the gates!" exclaimed Knox. "Mr. Railton's sent me——"

"He won't go!" gasped Taggles. "I've 'owled at 'im till I'm 'oarse, and he won't go!"

"I'll jolly soon shift him!"

Knox strode out of the gates. He was head and shoulders taller than the minstrel, and it looked like an easy task for him.

" Hook it, uncle ! " shouted Dick Julian.

But Uncle Bones had no time to hook it. Knox fairly rushed him down and seized him by the collar.

" Now, you rascal ! " exclaimed the bully of the Sixth.

" Ow ! Leggo ! "

" Bai Jove ! I wondah Knox doesn't wecognise Lowthah's voice, you know," murmured Arthur Augustus D'Arcy.

" Let him alone, Knox ! " shouted Tom Merry. " He can give a show in the road if he likes."

" I'll show him if he can ! " grinned Knox, all his bullying instincts roused by the fact that the coloured gentleman was evidently not a match for him physically in any way.

And Knox proceeded to shake the unfortunate minstrel till his teeth rattled as loudly as his castanets had done.

" Leggo, you rotter—yow-ow—let go, I tell you ! I'll hack your shins ! " yelled the minstrel.

" By gad ! I—I know that voice ! " stuttered Knox. " Why—what—what—— Great pip ! "

Knox gave a yell of astonishment as the fuzzy wig came off in the tussle, disclosing what was evidently a boy's head, with dark brown hair. The minstrel tore himself away—so forcibly that his coat split down the

" Houtside ! " exclaimed Taggles the porter, whirling the nigger minstrel into the road. " You clear hoff, you rapscallion ! " " Oh, my hat ! " ejaculated Uncle Bones.

back, the collar remaining in Knox's grip. And through the gash in the back of the coat an Eton jacket could be seen.

"My hat!" shouted Figgins. "It's a kid—it's a schoolboy, got up! Who on earth is it?"

"A Grammarian on the jape!" said Levison.

"I know his voice!" said Clive. "I think it's——"

"Lowther!" roared Knox.

"Oh, you rotter!" gasped Lowther.

Knox clutched at him again. He was grinning now. The bully of the Sixth was always glad of a chance to be down on the Terrible Three.

"You won't hook it now!" grinned Knox. "You'll come in with me, my pippin! Precious games for a St. Jim's fellow!"

"Bai Jove! All the fat's in the fiah now, deah boys!"

"Looks like it!" grunted Tom Merry.

In Knox's muscular grip, Monty Lowther was marched in at the gates. Taggles almost fell down with astonishment as he peered into his blackened face and made out Lowther's features.

"Master Lowther!" he stuttered. "Nice goings hon! My word! Ain't you jolly well ashamed of yourself, Master Lowther, got up like this 'ere?"

"Oh, go and eat coke!" snapped Monty.

"Come on!" growled Knox, jerking at the junior's shoulder. "I'll take you to Mr. Railton—just as you are."

"Look here, Knox——"

"This way!" said Knox, in great enjoyment. "We'll see what your Housemaster thinks of this, you rowdy young blackguard!"

"Lowther on the pierrot stunt!" chortled Crooke of the Shell. "Give him a penny, Racke! Here's a ha'-penny for you, Lowther!"

"Ha, ha, ha!"

"Spare a copper for a St. Jim's chap down on his luck!" howled Baggy Trimble. "Give him a penny, somebody! He, he, he!"

Monty Lowther's face was crimson under his dark complexion—though the crimson could not be seen. Tom and Manners gazed at him almost speechlessly. Monty's hare-brained scheme of "raising the wind" for the stony seven did not look like being a success, financial or otherwise. The "stoniness" of the seven was already a standing joke in the Lower School; and Monty's amazing stunt was likely to give it a new advertisement. The whole crowd of juniors yelled with laughter as they followed Knox and his prisoner towards the School House.

Three or four mischievous fellows tossed coppers into the big silk hat which Lowther still held in his hand. He held his wig in the other hand—it was the property of the School House Dramatic Society, and was too valuable to be lost. The aspect of the blackened junior, with a hat in one hand and a fuzzy wig in the other, and Knox's grip on his shoulder, was striking enough, and it made the St. Jim's fellows howl.

"Look here, Knox!" gasped Lowther, as they reached the School House steps. "There's no need to take me in like this——"

"Just where you're mistaken!" chuckled Knox. "You're coming in just exactly like that!"

"You rotter——"

"Knox——" exclaimed Tom Merry.

"Shut up! Get out of the way!"

"Bai Jove! Here's Linton!"

Mr. Linton appeared in the doorway. The master of the Shell stared at Knox, and then at the minstrel.

"Knox! For what reason are you bringing this—this disreputable character into the house?" he exclaimed.

"It's Lowther, sir!"

"Wha-a-a-t!"

"Lowther of your Form, sir!" said Knox. "He's been playing the banjo and begging——"

"I've not been begging!" yelled Monty Lowther furiously. "I've been passing round the hat for a song and dance, and earning the money!"

Mr. Linton fairly gasped.

"Lowther! You—you foolish, disreputable, extraordinary young rascal! How dare you?"

"I'm taking him to the Housemaster, sir," said Knox.

"Quite right. I will accompany you," said Mr. Linton.

Knox marched his prisoner on to the School Housemaster's study, and Mr. Linton brought up the rear with a brow of thunder. It was clear that the master of the Shell did not approve of this method of raising the wind by an impecunious junior. A chuckling crowd was left in the corridor—but Tom Merry and Manners did not chuckle. They were filled with too much alarm for their enterprising chum.

"The uttah ass!" said Arthur Augustus. "Cawwyin' on, you know, aftah I told him the ideah was no good! But it is partly your fault, Blake."

"What?" ejaculated Blake. "How's that, fathead?"

"Yaas, wathah! I was willin' to waise the wind by poppin' my tickah, you know, and if you had not waised objections to——"

"Fathead!"

"Weally, Blake——"

ST. JIM'S JINGLES

GERALD KNOX

(the bully of the Sixth)

A LANKY lout is Gerald Knox,
  A bully overpowering;
Stands nearly six feet in his socks,
  Above the small fry towering.
And woe betide the junior boy
  Who dares to be defiant;
It doesn't pay him to annoy
  This big and burly giant!

I've said sufficient to disclose
  That Knox is not a hero;
For he believes in biffs and blows,
  His patron saint is Nero.
That twisted saying, "Might is right,"
  Is Knox's favourite maxim:
Surely his conscience, in the night,
  Reproaches and attacks him?

He takes no joy in healthy sport,
  Or open-air attractions;
Nor strives to win a good report
  By true and upright actions.
To the "Green Man" by stealth he goes,
  Or else the "Crown and Anchor";
And there his strategy he shows
  At games iike nap and banker.

At periods, in his shady past,
  He's squandered cash on horses,
To find himself in debt at last,
  Then bitter his remorse is.
When Fancy Man or Fairy Elf
  Have failed to win their races,
In Queer Street he has found himself—
  Most undesired of places!

His chum and crony, Gerald Cutts,
  A bird of kindred feather,
With the tall prefect swanks and struts;
  They sally forth together
On many a doubtful escapade
  And shady expedition;
Some day disclosures will be made,
  Then awkward their position!

We do not love you, Gerald Knox,
  Your ways are dark and sinister;
And if this brainy bard could box,
  A thrashing he'd administer!
Towards the ropes he'd make you reel,
  And castigate you fully;
That is the proper way to deal
  With you, you blustering bully!

" Hark ! " chortled Trimble.

From Mr. Railton's study came the sound of a swishing cane, and it was accompanied by a loud howl.

THE FOURTH CHAPTER

NOT A SUCCESS

Mr. Railton looked astonished when his study was invaded by Knox of the Sixth, a nigger minstrel, and the master of the Shell. He was still more astonished when he learned the identity of the nigger minstrel. He gazed at Monty's blackened face as if he could scarcely believe his eyes.

" Lowther ! " he exclaimed. " Is it possible ? "

Uncle Bones stood before his House-master, the picture of dismay. This was not how he had planned his wonderful wheeze to turn out. The amateur minstrel had intended to gather a harvest of coin of the realm for his entertainment, and to retire with the same to a secluded spot—where Uncle Bones would disappear and Lowther of the Shell take his place once more. But the programme had gone awry. Mr. Railton's wrathful and astounded stare made the unhappy minstrel quake.

" Yes, it is Lowther ! " gasped Mr. Linton. " Lowther, of my Form, Mr. Railton. It is incredible—unheard of ! But it is true ! "

" Lowther, what does this mean ? "

" M-m-m-mean, sir ? " stammered Lowther.

" Why are you disguised in this extraordinary manner, with your face blackened ? "

" I—I—I'm a m-m-minstrel, sir ! " groaned Lowther.

" A what ? "

" A nigger minstrel, sir ! " groaned Lowther.

" There is no harm in such an entertainment being given in the proper place, at a proper time, Lowther. But you have appeared in the open quadrangle in this absurd guise——"

" He was collecting money, sir," said Knox.

" Is it possible, Lowther," exclaimed Mr. Linton, " that you have played this astounding prank from so sordid a motive as that of pecuniary gain ? "

" Oh, my hat ! " gasped Lowther involuntarily.

Mr. Linton's way of putting it was most unpleasant.

" Where is the money ? " snapped Mr. Railton.

" In—in—in the hat, sir ! I was passing round the—the hat ! Nigger minstrels always pass round the hat, sir ! " said Lowther feebly.

" Turn it out upon the table."

Clink, clink, clink !

Mr. Railton counted the money. There was quite a stack of coppers, a good many sixpences, and some shillings.

" Dear me ! A total of nineteen shillings and sixpence ! " said Mr. Railton. " Mr. Linton, will you take charge of this sum and place it in the poor-box in the hall ? "

" Certainly ! " said Mr. Linton.

Lowther suppressed a groan. Nineteen-and-six was not the sum he had hoped to raise—and that he might have raised if he had been left alone. But it would have helped the stony seven. Now it was destined to help the poor—certainly a very worthy object, but scarcely comforting to Monty in the circumstances.

" How to deal with this reckless, absurd, extraordinary boy, I hardly know," said Mr. Railton. " I trust that this foolish prank is chiefly due to want of reflection. But you will agree with me, Mr. Linton, that a somewhat exemplary punishment is called for."

" Most decidedly ! " said the master of the Shell, with emphasis.

" If—if you please, sir——" stuttered Lowther.

" What have you to say, Lowther ? "

" There—there was no harm done, sir ! " groaned Lowther. " Nigger minstrel business is a quite respectable way of earning money——"

" I think that will do, Lowther. Mr. Linton, as this absurd boy is in your Form, I will leave him in your hands. There is a cane on my desk. Will you hand the cane to Mr. Linton, Knox ? "

Knox performed that service for Mr. Linton with alacrity and pleasure. The master of the Shell took a business-like grip on the cane. His expression showed that he was not going to risk spoiling Monty Lowther by sparing the rod.

" Hold out your hand, Lowther ! "

Swish !

" Wow ! "

" Silence, boy ! The other hand ! "

Swish ! Mr. Linton put his beef into it.

" Yarooogh ! "

" Lowther ! How dare you utter such objectionable ejaculations in your Housemaster's study ! " exclaimed Mr. Linton angrily. " Hold out your hand again ! "

Swish !

" Woooooop ! "

" I think that will be adequate, Mr. Railton." The Housemaster nodded assent. " Lowther, you may go ! If you should ever play such a prank again——"

Mr. Linton paused, and left the rest to Monty Lowther's imagination.

The hapless minstrel almost limped out of the study, hat and wig in hand, banjo under his arm, and trying to rub his hands in spite of those paraphernalia. A loud chortle greeted him as he emerged into the corridor.

" Here he comes ! " roared Gore. " When did you wash last, Lowther ? "

" He, he, he ! They don't wash in No. 10 ! " chortled Trimble. " What a face ! What a neck ! "

Tom Merry relieved his chum of hat and wig and banjo, and drew him away in time to prevent him from committing assault and battery upon the howling juniors. Study No. 6 followed them upstairs to the Shell passage. They were grinning—they could not help that. Tom and Manners tried hard not to smile.

Monty Lowther glared at them.

" I did my best ! " he growled.

" What a best ! " murmured Blake.

" I raised nineteen and six, anyhow ! " hooted Lowther.

" Bai Jove ! Where is it, deah boy ? "

" Railton's bagged it for the school poor-box."

" Ha, ha, ha ! " roared the Co.

" Is that a laughing matter ? " yelled Lowther angrily.

" Yaas, wathah ! "

" Funniest thing I've ever struck ! " grinned Blake. " This is going to help us out—I don't think ! Don't you fellows fancy it's about time you gave up thinking of wheezes ? Leave it to Study No. 6."

" Oh, go and eat coke ! " growled Lowther.

" Go and get a wash ! " suggested Herries. " You want it ! The fellows are saying that that's your natural complexion, because you never use any soap ! "

" You silly ass ! "

" Ha, ha, ha ! "

" Oh, get out ! " roared Lowther, and he seized the banjo and made a rush at Study No. 6.

Blake & Co. fled, chortling. Lowther gave Tom and Manners a morose stare, and seemed disposed to give them the benefit of the banjo.

"Awfully funny, isn't it?" he snorted.

"Well, now you mention it, it is rather!" assented Manners, with a grin.

"You silly owl!"

"Better go and change, old man," murmured Tom Merry. "Get that jolly old complexion off——"

"Fathead!"

Monty Lowther tramped away to a bathroom, not in a good temper. And Tom Merry and Manners smiled—audibly—when he was gone.

THE FIFTH CHAPTER

A CRISIS!

"GWEAT Scott!"

"Fiver?" asked three voices in eager unison.

"No!"

"Oh, rotten!"

It was a few days after Monty Lowther's heroic—but unsuccessful—attempt to raise the wind. The stony seven were as stony as ever; and Lowther, fertile as he generally was in wheezes, had not propounded any new scheme so far. He appeared a little fed up since the ghastly failure of the minstrel stunt, and, as Jack Blake put it, "since then he had used no other."

On this especial day there was a half-holiday, and the midday post had brought a letter for Arthur Augustus D'Arcy. There was a crest on the envelope, which indicated that it was a letter from home; and Blake and Herries and Digby had gathered eagerly round their noble chum as he opened the letter. For sometimes there was a crisp five-pound note in Lord Eastwood's letters to his second son; and such a remittance, in present circumstances, would have been a terrific windfall.

But in this imperfect universe it is uncommon for things to arrive just when they are wanted. There was no banknote in the letter; there was not even a currency note; but there was evidently news of a much less gratifying nature.

"Oh, come on!" said Blake resignedly. "If there isn't a remittance, no need to read the letter now."

"A chap's pater ought to dub up if he sends a chap a letter," said Digby argumentatively. "I'm really surprised at your pater, Gussy."

"This lettah is wathah important, howevah," said Arthur Augustus. "It nevah wains but it pours, you know. Misfortunes nevah come singly, bai Jove!"

"What's the matter now?" asked Herries.

"The patah is comin' down to St. Jim's to see me."

"No harm in that," said Blake. "Nothing to pull a long face about. He's bound to spend some time with the Head, and he will have a train to catch. Probably won't worry you for more than half an hour."

"Weally, Blake!"

"Perhaps only a quarter of an hour," said Dig encouragingly.

"I twust," said Arthur Augustus, in his most stately way, "that I shall nevah look upon a visit fwom my fathah as a wowwy. You youngstahs are wathah thoughtless."

"Can it!" said Blake.

"But the howwid fact is, deah boys, that Lord Eastwood is comin' down this aftahnoon."

"Oh!"

"He mentions that he is goin' to take the opportunity of havin' a good talk with me."

"Ah!"

"Particularly on account of what

"Hold out your hand, Lowther!" said Mr. Linton, taking a business-like grip on the cane. Swish! "Yar-oooh!" yelled Lowther. His effort to "raise the wind" was having painful results!

he is pleased to wefer to as my extwavagance."

"Hem!"

"He is wathah surpwised at my askin' him to send me a fivah——"

"What rot!"

"When he sent me one only a fortnight ago."

"The one you wasted paying your tailor!" said Herries.

"He thinks it a good ideah to have a little talk with me, and for that weason he suggests havin' tea in the study with me."

"My hat!"

"And he will awwive here at four o'clock——"

"Dear man!"

"And aftah payin' his wespects to the Head, he will come to tea in Studay No. 6."

"I wish now," said Blake reflectively, "that I hadn't chucked away that last sardine. It was getting old. It didn't look nice. But we ought to have something to offer to a belted earl when he comes to tea."

"Weally, you ass!"

"I suppose he won't be thoughtful enough to bring a hamper with him?" suggested Dig.

"It is certainly not pwobable, Dig, that Lord Eastwood will think of bwingin' a hampah in the twain with him."

"And that's one of our hereditary legislators!" said Blake. "Fancy a chap making laws for a nation and not having foresight enough to bring a hamper when he comes to tea in a junior study!"

"I twust you are not alludin' to my patah as a 'chap,' Blake?"

"Bloke, then!" said Blake.

"I stwongly object to my patah bein' chawactewised as a bloke."

"Oh, make it cove, then!" said Blake. "Fancy the old cove——"

"Ha, ha, ha!"

"I wegard your wemarks as unseemly, Blake!" said the swell of St. Jim's severely. "Pway wing off! The question is what is goin' to be done? Studay No. 6 is bound to be hospitable. Besides, aftah givin' me a feahful wiggin' the patah genewally shells out. If we get thwough the tea all wight, and the deah old patah keeps in a good tempah, it is extwemely pwob that the wesult will welieve us of all our financial difficulties. That is what Shakespeare would chawactewise as a 'consummation devoutly to be wished.'"

"Hear, hear!" said Gussy's chums heartily.

"But we have got to play up, somehow," said Arthur Augustus, "and the howwid mystewy is, how are we goin' to stand a weally wippin' tea when we are bwoke to the weawy wide?"

Blake rubbed his nose thoughtfully.

"I give that one up!" he said. "Ask us an easier one."

"Couldn't we take tea in Hall?" said Herries.

"Wathah not! Besides, I should not like him wiggin' me before all the fellahs. There is only one wesource," said Arthur Augustus; "I shall have to pop the tickah."

"Fathead!"

"Weally, you duffahs——"

"If I catch you near a pawnbroker's," said Blake impressively, "I'll give you the licking of your life!"

"Wats!"

"That's barred!" said Digby decidedly. "There would be a row if you were seen going into a pawnshop, you fathead!"

"I shall have to be vewy careful not to be seen, Dig."

"Very likely they wouldn't lend money on a gold watch to a schoolboy!" said Herries. "I believe pawnbrokers are not supposed to deal with minors. Might think you'd pinched it, too."

"Weally, Hewwies——"

"Don't talk rot, Gussy, old chap," said Blake. "We'll think of some way before tea-time. As a last resource, we might raid some grub in the New House."

"I feah, Blake, that there is nothin' for it but poppin' the tickah!" said Arthur Augustus, shaking his head.

"You won't be allowed, old bean!" grinned Blake. "If you haven't sense enough to keep out of trouble, your old pals will manage it for you. I dare say something will turn up by tea-time."

"Wats!"

"Look here, Gussy——"

"Wubbish!"

And Arthur Augustus walked away, in deep thought—evidently thinking out ways and means of "popping" his celebrated gold "ticker." Blake looked for the Terrible Three in the quadrangle.

"Anything turned up?" he asked, when he found them.

Three heads were shaken.

"Lowther had any more brainwaves?" inquired Blake sarcastically.

"Go and eat coke!" grunted Monty.

" Well, Gussy's pater is coming to tea," said Blake. " Just like a thoughtless old nobleman to drop in in a time of famine. You fellows got any suggestions to make ? "

" If you'd backed me up in my nigger -minstrel stunt," began Lowther, " it might have turned out better——"

" My dear man, your wheezes never could turn out anything but rank failures," said Blake kindly. " It was quite benevolent of you to raise nineteen-and-six for the deserving poor ; but it didn't help us much. Feel inclined to sell your camera on this special occasion, Manners ? "

" No ! " answered Manners, with Spartan brevity.

" I'll tell you what——" said Tom Merry thoughtfully.

" Go ahead ! "

" If you succeed in getting a good tea in the study, we'll come ! " said the captain of the Shell. " That's all I can suggest."

" Fathead ! "

Evidently there was nothing doing ; and six members of the stony septette realised that it was very probable that Lord Eastwood's tea in Study No. 6 would be a frugal meal— very frugal. But the seventh and greatest member was thinking the matter out deeply ; and his resolution was fixed to raise the necessary cash by pledging his gold watch to a gentleman whose business it was to give loans on such articles.

THE SIXTH CHAPTER

" POPPING THE TICKER " !

TOM MERRY & Co. were not, during the next hour or two, thinking of their noble and distinguished comrade, the Honourable Arthur Augustus D'Arcy. There was a cricket match going on on Big Side, and Kildare was batting against the New House. Kildare was always worth watching at the wickets, and the juniors gathered to watch him. The great question of raising the wind was left over for the present. In point of fact, there was " nothing doing," and Tom Merry remarked that it was no good worrying about a state of affairs that could not be helped ; and his chums agreed with him. So they watched the senior House match, and in their deep interest in the game they forgot all about Arthur Augustus D'Arcy and his wonderful scheme for easing the financial stringency.

Meanwhile the swell of the Fourth was not losing time. House matches did not appeal to him in the present circumstances.

His noble pater was coming at four o'clock, and there was to be tea in Study No. 6. To own up to the noble earl that he was stony—that there was even nothing for tea—was really impossible. Such a statement would give Lord Eastwood additional grounds for his intended lecture on economy and extravagance. Besides, Gussy wanted to " do " his noble pater well—he wanted the visit to be a success. It was perfectly easy—so long as the ticker was adequately popped ! Upon that course Arthur Augustus was inexorably resolved ; but he would have been glad of some expert advice as to how it was done. After all, it could not be a very difficult matter, Gussy considered. You walked into the pawnbroker's, handed over your watch, stated that you wanted twenty pounds lent on it, and the pawnbroker did the rest. So far as Gussy could see, that was all there was about it.

But it was needful to take care. For most certainly the Head and the Housemaster would have been severely down upon any fellow known to have visited a pawnbroker's in quest of funds. Quite rightly so, Gussy admitted—his own case being a special one, and not coming under ordinary rules!

Then there was the horrid possibility that a pawnbroker might not lend to a schoolboy—might not even do business with minors at all. Arthur Augustus believed that he looked fairly grown-up for his age—he was conscious that he had a stately and impressive manner—but, looking into the glass, he could not consider that he looked twenty-one. This was another difficulty to be overcome.

But troubles were only made to be met and conquered. Arthur Augustus' powerful brain did not fail him.

While the rest of the Co. were watching the cricket on Big Side, Arthur Augustus dropped into Study No 10 in the Shell, where the property box of the Junior Dramatic Society was kept. From that box Gussy abstracted an artificial moustache—a rather large and bushy moustache of a ginger colour. With that handsome adornment on his upper lip, Gussy considered that not only would he pass for over age, but his identity as a St. Jim's fellow would be sufficiently disguised. It would make him safe all round.

With the false moustache in his pocket and a raincoat on his arm Arthur Augustus walked out of the School House and headed for Rylcombe. He had looked out the trains in the time-table. There was no pawnbroker in Rylcombe; and Wayland was too near the school for safety. Gussy had decided on Abbotsford, where he would be unknown. He caught the local train to Abbotsford with ease, and sat down in a state of complete satisfaction with himself and his little scheme.

If his chums missed him, and looked for him now, it would be too late. D'Arcy was quite pleased at having escaped without any trouble or argument. Not that he would have allowed trouble or argument to influence him. He prided himself upon possessing the firmness of a rock when once his noble mind was made up.

He alighted from the train at Abbotsford and looked at his watch. He had half an hour to find a pawnbroker and carry through the transaction before the train left for Rylcombe, which would land him at St. Jim's again in ample time to receive his distinguished visitor at four o'clock. Half an hour, surely, was enough time in which to negotiate a loan upon a gold watch!

The swell of St. Jim's strolled elegantly along the ancient High Street of Abbotsford, looking for three golden balls, the sign of the professional gentleman with whom he desired to deal.

He did not find any such sign in the High Street, though he walked from one end to the other and back again.

A red-faced gentleman, with a straw in his mouth, was supporting a post outside a public-house a little farther on, spitting across the pavement at regular intervals. Somewhat gingerly D'Arcy approached him for information. The red-faced gentleman was more accommodating than Arthur Augustus anticipated.

"Up this 'ere street and first to the left," he said. "You'll see the three pips——"

"The—the what?"

"Three brass balls," said the red-faced gentleman. "Shop at the corner. In at one door and out at the other—wot! Ha, ha! Mind you don't lose the ticket, Charley!"

"Thank you very much!" faltered

Arthur Augustus. And he started up the side street. " Bai Jove ! I wondah why that chap called me Charlay ? He is a vewy obligin' man, but I wish he would not bweathe wum ovah a chap."

A few minutes more, and Arthur Augustus was at the corner shop, which had an entrance on two streets, perhaps for the convenience of customers who did not wish to be observed paying their visits to the establishment. A stout gentleman, with a little bundle in his hand, was strolling past the door with an air of exaggerated carelessness. As he passed it he made a sudden dive and vanished. A swing door closed behind him and he was swallowed up.

As Arthur Augustus lingered and hesitated at the corner, he saw the stout gentleman emerge from the other door and hurry away ; this time without his bundle.

Somewhat gingerly, Arthur Augustus approached the red-faced gentleman. " Can you diwect me to the pawnbwokah's shop ? " he asked. " Up this 'ere side street and first to the left," answered the red-faced man. " But mind you don't lose the ticket, Charley ! "

" This is the place, I pwesume," murmured Arthur Augustus. " It does not seem to take vewy long. Now for it ! "

He stepped into the doorway, felt in his pocket for the ginger moustache, and, after a cautious glance to and fro, fixed it on.

He blinked at his reflection in the shop window, and smiled. Certainly that bushy, ginger moustache made a startling change in his appearance.

Emboldened by the idea that he was no longer recognisable as a St. Jim's fellow, Arthur Augustus pushed open the swing door and entered the stuffy little shop.

In spite of himself the colour deepened in his cheeks as he came up to a counter, where a young man with a well-developed nose and a shiny complexion was examining the interior of a watch. It was a hot afternoon, and doubly hot in the stuffy little shop, and the shiny young man was in his shirtsleeves, the cuffs of which looked somewhat grubby. He looked up at D'Arcy with glistening black eyes, and started a little. Perhaps the ginger moustache had its effect upon him. Certainly it stood out from Gussy's smooth, boyish countenance as boldly and startlingly as a full-grown beard could have done, and equally certain it did not look in the least as if it belonged to the countenance.

" Good-aftahnoon ! " said Arthur Augustus.

" 'Afternoon ! "

The shiny young man's eyes turned to the watch he was examining.

" I am sowwy to intewwupt you," said Arthur Augustus mildly, " but I wish to pop a tickah."

" Eh ? "

" Pway, where do I pop it ? "

" What ? "

" Pop it."

The shiny young man gazed at Arthur Augustus. Then he pointed to the door.

" Stow it ! " he said. " No time for larks ! "

" My deah sir, I am not larkin'. I have come here to pop a tickah, and I should be vewy much obliged if you would tell me where I do it. I undahstand that it has to be popped here."

" Come orf ! " said the shiny young man. " If you want to put a watch in, 'and it over. Time's money ! "

Arthur Augustus detached his beautiful gold watch from the chain, and silently passed it over to the shiny young man. That gentleman stared at it, opened it, and stared inside, and then stared at Gussy with a very peculiar expression on his face. It was a handsome and valuable watch, worth more than twenty-five guineas, which, added to the glaring false moustache, perhaps naturally made the shiny young man suspicious.

" 'Ow much do you want on this ? " he asked guardedly.

" Ten pounds, please."

" I shall 'ave to show it to the guv'nor."

" Vewy good ; but pway lose no time, as I have to weturn by twain to—to where I came fwom, and I have only a few minutes left."

Without replying, the shiny young man disappeared through the doorway at the back. Arthur Augustus heard the sound of a telephone receiver jerked off the hooks, and there was a murmur and a voice. The shiny young man, apparently, was telephoning to his governor.

It was some minutes before he came back into the shop, and he came back without the watch.

" Well," said Arthur Augustus.

" 'Ave to wait a few minutes for the guv'nor," said the shiny young man affably. " Sit down, please."

" I am in wathah a huwwy."

" No doubt—no doubt ! " grinned the shiny young man. " You would be ! But 'old on a few ticks."

Arthur Augustus sat down. He was feeling worried now. Only a few minutes remained to catch the train back to Rylcombe. He was doubtful if it could be done. The next train was in half an hour, which would make him late for his pater. It was a great worry. But, after all, it was useless to go without the loan he had come for. His uneasiness did not escape the notice of the shiny young man, who seemed to be entertained by it. The shop door opened and there was a heavy tread. Arthur Augustus did not glance round. He supposed that it was another customer who had entered. There was an oily chuckle from the shiny young man.

" Good-afternoon, sergeant ! There he is, and 'ere's the watch ! "

THE SEVENTH CHAPTER

AWFUL FOR ARTHUR AUGUSTUS !

A HEAVY hand fell upon the shoulder of the swell of St. Jim's. He gave a convulsive jump.

A portly police-sergeant stood over him.

" So this is the bird ! " said the sergeant.

" That's him ! " chuckled the shiny young man. " False moustache and all ! Swell nob, I reckon. Smart-looking kid for a game like this, sergeant. Know him ? "

" Can't place him for the minute," said the sergeant, staring into Arthur Augustus' bewildered face. " One of the pickpockets that come down for the races, I should say."

Arthur Augustus wondered whether he was dreaming.

" Taking him to the station ? " asked the shiny young man.

" What-ho ! " answered the sergeant. " You come alonger me, young feller ! "

He jerked Arthur Augustus off the chair.

" Gweat Scott ! " gasped the swell of St. Jim's. " Wha-a-at is the mattah ? Pway wemove your hand fwom my shouldah, sir ! "

" So that you can do a guy ! " chuckled the shiny young man. " Ha, ha ! That's good ! "

" I weally do not undahstand you !" said Arthur Augustus, with dignity. " If you are not goin' to make a loan on my watch, pway weturn the watch to me. I shall have to find anothah pawnbrokah's."

" Ha, ha, ha ! " roared the shiny young man.

The burly sergeant grinned.

" Cut it out, and come along ! " he said.

" I fail to undahstand. Where do you wish me to come ? " inquired the amazed swell of St. Jim's.

" Eh ? To the station, of course ! "

" I was about to weturn to the station," said Arthur Augustus. "But, as I weally do not know you, I see no weason why I should go to the station in your company."

" A cool 'and ! " said the shiny young man. " Never 'eard of the stone jug afore, 'ave you ? "

" I have seen a good many stone jugs—at least, earthenware," answered Arthur Augustus. " I do not quite follow what——"

" He, he, he ! " chortled the shiny young man, evidently very much entertained.

" Look 'ere, you come along to the police-station, and not so much gas ! " said the sergeant.

Arthur Augustus gave a jump as if the sergeant had applied an electric wire to him.

" The police-station ! " he stuttered.

" Kim on ! "

" Gweat Scott ! " Again D'Arcy of

the Fourth wondered whether this was some amazing and fearful dream. " Why do you want me to go to the police-station ? Pway explain yourself, my good man ! "

" On 'spicion of stealing that there watch ! " growled the sergeant.

" Bai Jove ! How could a fellah steal his own watch ? "

" P'r'aps it's your own ! " sneered the sergeant. " P'r'aps not ! P'r'aps that isn't a false moustache sticking on your dial."

Gussy's hand went to his ginger moustache, which he had quite forgotten. His face was crimson.

He realised at last that his attempted disguise, and his obvious uneasiness of manner, had impressed the shiny young man with the belief that he was a youthful pickpocket trying to pawn a stolen watch. He realised that the shiny young man had kept him waiting while he telephoned to the police-station for the sergeant. Poor Arthur Augustus' head fairly swam.

" Pway wait a moment ! " he gasped, as soon as he could find his voice. " I assuah you, officah, that it is my watch ! I was goin' to pop my tickah because I wanted to waise the wind, you know."

" P'r'aps ! " said the sergeant.

" I assuah you—— Pway, do I look like a wobbah ? " exclaimed the swell of St. Jim's indignantly. " I assuah you, sergeant, that you are makin' a vewy sewious mistake."

" Does it well, don't he ! " grinned the shiny young man.

But the distress and amazement in Gussy's face had an effect on the police-sergeant. He did not want to make a mistake, and he decided to question this surprising youth before he marched him off to the station.

" Name ? " he jerked out.

" My name is D'Arcy."

" Make it Plantagenet ! " implored the shiny young man, with a chortle of great enjoyment. " Do make it Plantagenet ! "

" Where do you live ? "

D'Arcy hesitated.

" I wathah object to statin' that," he said. " You see, I should get into a wow with my headmastah if it were known that I was poppin' a tickah ! "

" Where do you live ? " snapped the sergeant.

" Is it weally necessawy for me to acquaint you with my place of wesidence ? "

" You'd better ! " said the sergeant grimly.

" St. Jim's ! " said Arthur Augustus reluctantly. " The school, you know, near Wylcombe."

The sergeant eyed him very keenly. The shiny young man, whose knowledge of the world seemed confined chiefly to the seamy side, obviously did not believe a single word of D'Arcy's statements. But the sergeant was a keener man. His grim expression relaxed.

" Why were you wearing a false moustache ? " he demanded.

" I—I did not want to be wecognised goin' into a pop—pawnbwokah's," faltered Arthur Augustus.

" You young idiot ! "

" Bai Jove ! "

" Gammon ! " remarked the shiny young man. " A clear case, I think. Artful—very artful ! "

" I wefuse to be chawactewised as artful ! " exclaimed Arthur Augustus indignantly. " And I ordah you to weturn my watch to me at once ! Undah the circs, I shall not pop it at all."

" I rather think you won't ! " said the sergeant grimly. " Now, young

Gussy gave a convulsive jump as a heavy hand fell on his shoulder. A police-sergeant stood behind him. "So this is the bird?" said the sergeant. "That's him!" replied the pawnbroker. "Gweat Scott!" gasped Arthur Augustus. "Wha-a-at is the mattah?"

man, it's possible you're telling me the truth, and that you're nothing but a silly young idiot, after all. But it's suspicious, very suspicious. You say you're a schoolboy of St. Jim's. Well, in that case, your headmaster will bear you out. As I'm just going off duty I'll take you to the school, and we'll see. I can't let you go unless you prove what you say, and for the present I'll take charge of the watch."

D'Arcy gave a gasp.

"My headmastah will be awf'ly waxy!" he stuttered. "Weally, I would wathah weturn to St. Jim's alone."

"Do you prefer the police-station?"

"Gweat Scott! No."

"Then you had better come with me," said the sergeant. "If you're speaking the truth I don't want to be hard on you. It's thick, but it may be the truth. I'll give you a chance."

"Thank you vewy much!" said Arthur Augustus faintly. "I—I—I shall be vewy, vewy pleased if you will come to the school with me. Oh gad!"

"Come on, then!"

The sergeant nodded to the shiny young man, who shrugged his shoulders and winked his twinkling black eye. Arthur Augustus left the pawnbroker's in the burly officer's company, and walked down the street with him. His face was crimson as many curious glances turned on the pair. The watch, still unpopped, reposed in the sergeant's pocket. But Arthur Augustus was not thinking of "popping" now. Wild horses would not have dragged him into a pawnbroker's again. His ginger moustache was in his pocket now; he was only too glad to get it there. At the railway-station it seemed to Arthur Augustus that all Abbotsford was out that afternoon, and all staring at him. He almost wept with relief when he was seated in a carriage with the sergeant opposite. Even there two or three passengers kept glancing at him and his burly guardian.

At Rylcombe the old porter fairly blinked at the sight of Arthur Augustus in company with a police-sergeant. In the old High Street there were curious stares on all sides. From the very bottom of his heart Arthur Augustus wished that he had never thought of popping his ticker. But who could have foreseen this awful outcome of so apparently simple a proceeding?

But the worst was yet to come.

THE EIGHTH CHAPTER

A SURPRISE FOR HIS LORDSHIP!

"SEEN Gussy?"

Blake jerked at Tom Merry's arm as the captain of the Shell stood on Big Side, watching the cricket.

"No." Tom turned his head. "Isn't he here?"

"The ass seems to have gone out," said Blake, with a worried look. "And his father's come."

"Gone out!" said Manners. "He knew his pater was coming."

Monty Lowther gave a sudden chuckle.

"Has he gone to pop the ticker?"

"I shouldn't be surprised," grunted Blake. "I forgot about him, watching the blessed cricket! We've looked all over the school for him, and he's not to be found. And Lord Eastwood spoke to me before he went in to see the Head; told me to tell Gussy he would come up to the study at half-past four."

"Jolly nearly that now!" said Tom.

"And I can't find him anywhere!" growled Blake. "He must have gone out. I wish I'd put him on a chain, blow him!"

The Terrible Three left Big Side with Blake. The great question of funds was still unsettled—tea in the study for his lordship was as deep a problem as ever. But at least Arthur Augustus ought to have been on the spot to greet his noble pater. As he was absent, it was up to D'Arcy's chums to play up and entertain Lord Eastwood till his hopeful son turned up again.

"He can't be long," said Tom thoughtfully. "He knew his father would be here at four. I suppose he's gone off somewhere and lost a train. He can't have forgotten. Seen anything of him, you fellows?" he added, as Herries and Digby came up in the quad.

"Not a trace of him," said Herries. "Must have gone out of gates while we were watching Kildare."

"Here's the old gent!" murmured Digby.

Lord Eastwood's tall and spare figure appeared in the doorway of the School House. There was a slight frown on his lordship's brow. He had been up to Study No. 6, and, instead of finding there a dutiful and affectionate son, he had found that celebrated apartment vacant. He had come down again, puzzled and a little annoyed. He came out into the quad to meet Tom Merry & Co.

"Where is Arthur?" he asked.

"We—we're just looking for him, sir!" stammered Tom Merry.

"It is very extraordinary! He cannot have gone out, I presume?"

"I—I—I——"

There was a howl in the distance—the howl of Baggy Trimble.

"Oh, my eye! Gussy and a copper! He, he, he!"

Tom Merry & Co. spun round like humming-tops. Trimble's howl was followed by a buzz of voices that grew into a roar. Fellows on all sides were rushing towards the gates.

Tom Merry wondered whether it was a mirage, as he caught sight of Arthur Augustus, with a burly police-sergeant by his side, just within the gates. Taggles had come out of his lodge in amazement, and already thirty or forty fellows had gathered round. There was a sharp exclamation from Lord Eastwood. He had seen his son.

"Upon my word! That is Arthur!" he ejaculated. "What—whatever has happened?"

He strode away towards the gates; and Tom Merry & Co., after exchanging a look of utter, dismal dismay, followed him at a run. What had happened they could not even surmise; but they knew that the unhappy Gussy, somehow or other, had "done it" now!

"Arthur!"

"Oh cwumbs! It's the patah!" groaned Arthur Augustus D'Arcy.

The hapless swell of St. Jim's had hoped that Taggles would identify him to the satisfaction of the sergeant before his father could learn of the awful disaster. But that hope was ill-founded. The tall, spare form of Lord Eastwood towered over the crowd of juniors, who respectfully made way for the peer of the realm.

The sergeant saluted Lord Eastwood respectfully. It was borne in upon his mind now that Arthur Augustus was, in point of fact, owner of the watch he had attempted to "pop," and was nothing worse than, as he would have said, a young idiot!

"What does this mean, Arthur?" asked Lord Eastwood in a deep voice. "Why are you here with this officer?"

"I—I—I——" stuttered Arthur Augustus.

"What has happened, officer?"

"You know this young person, sir?" asked the sergeant.

"He is my son. I am Lord Eastwood," said the old gentleman, with dignity.

"Excuse me, sir—the circumstances were suspicious. This young gentleman was found attempting to pawn a valuable watch——"

"P-p-p-pawn!" faltered his lordship.

"Yes, sir. And as he was disguised with a false moustache, and——"

"What?"

"And seemed very uneasy, the pawnbroker's young man thought it was fishy and telephoned for me," explained the sergeant. "You see, we get a lot of pickpockets come down to Abbotsford for the races, sir."

"P-p-pickpockets!" said his lordship dazedly.

"As he stated that he belonged to this school, I brought him 'ere, sir, instead of taking him to the police-station. Never give the public trouble if we can help it, sir."

Lord Eastwood looked at the honest sergeant and looked at his hopeful son. Arthur Augustus fervently wished that the earth would open and swallow him up. But the earth didn't, and Gussy had to endure that basilisk gaze from his astonished and scandalised parent.

"If you answer for him, sir, and answer for this here watch being his property——" said the sergeant, taking the famous gold ticker from his pocket.

"Certainly!" gasped his lordship. "I gave my son that watch myself on a birthday."

"Very good, sir!"

The sergeant handed the watch to Arthur Augustus. Then he saluted Lord Eastwood again and turned away.

Lord Eastwood made a sign to Arthur Augustus to go in, and the swell of the Fourth limped away with his friends, looking and feeling in the deepest depths of woe and dismay. Lord Eastwood lingered a few moments to speak to the sergeant again in the gateway, and the Abbotsford officer slipped something into his pocket when he finally departed. Then the peer followed his hopeful son across the quad. The crowd of St. Jim's fellows strove hard not to chortle until Gussy's noble parent disappeared into the School House.

Arthur Augustus went up to Study No. 6. His chums went with him—they did not look forward with enjoyment to the coming interview with Gussy's pater—but they felt that they were bound to stand by a comrade in misfortune. So the whole of the stony seven were in the study when Lord Eastwood arrived.

Silence as of the tomb fell upon Study No. 6 as he entered. His face was grim and stern; the juniors hardly dared to look at him. Arthur Augustus was quite limp.

"So," said Lord Eastwood, after a painful silence, which seemed to the juniors to last about a century—"so, on the occasion of my visit to the school, Arthur, I find you attempting to pawn a watch——"

"I—I——"

"And being brought back to the school in custody of a police-officer——"

"Oh deah!"

"Have you any explanation to offer?"

"I—I—I twied to pop the tickah——"

"To—to what?"

"To—to pawn the watch, to—waise the wind—I mean, to waise some money, for—for tea!" babbled Arthur Augustus. "The—the fact is, we—we——we are stonay——"

"You are what?"

"Bwoke!"

"What?"

"I—I mean hard up——"

There was another painful silence. Then Lord Eastwood made Tom Merry & Co. a sign to leave the study. Six dismal juniors filed out, leaving the hapless Gussy alone with his justly-incensed parent. They did not envy Arthur Augustus just then.

They remained in a deeply-troubled group at the end of the passage in dismal silence. What was going to happen they could not tell. Whether his lordship would request the Head to administer a flogging, whether he would take Gussy away from St. Jim's, whether he would administer severe chastisement with his own noble hands, they simply could not guess.

They wondered what was passing in Study No. 6, and they felt deeply for Arthur Augustus. It was nearly half an hour before the study door opened, and Lord Eastwood emerged.

He passed the group of juniors and went down the staircase, evidently departing. There had been no tea in the study, after all. The juniors

"What does this mean, Arthur?" asked Lord Eastwood as the police-sergeant marched Gussy in at the gates. "I—I—I——" stuttered Arthur Augustus. "Excuse me, sir," said the sergeant. "This young gentleman was found attempting to pawn a valuable watch!"

waited till, from the corridor window, they saw Lord Eastwood's tall form crossing the quad towards the gates. Then they hurried along to Study No. 6, eager to hear the worst.

Arthur Augustus looked at them, and nodded. He did not seem so downcast as they had expected.

"Well?" said six voices, at once.

"It was awful, deah boys!"

"What's happened?" exclaimed Tom Merry.

"I have had a feahful lecture!" said Arthur Augustus. "I must say the patah was quite in the wight—I can see that, you know. As a wule, I am not wholly satisfied with the way the patah looks at things, but on the pwesent occasion I must admit that he was wight. His first ideah was to wequest the Head to give me a tewwible floggin'——

"Oh!"

"Then he seemed to think that I had bettah be taken away fwom the school, where I seem to have wathah weckless and thoughtless fwiends——"

"Oh! Oh!"

"Then he gave me a weally impewial jaw. And then," said Arthur Augustus, "I explained the whole mattah."

"Why didn't you explain first, fathead?"

"Weally, deah boy——"

"And then——"

"Then he made me pwomise not to go to a pop-bwokah's again; and I told him steam cwanes and twaction engines would nevah dwag me within sight of a pawnbwokah's, if I could help it! So he gave me a little more jaw, and wang off."

"And that's all?"

"Yaas, wathah!"

"Thank goodness!" said Tom Merry. "You've got off cheap!"

"Yaas. I am only sowwy that, time bein' gone in jawin', the deah old patah was unable to stay to tea," said Arthur Augustus. "He twusts that this will be a lesson to me—as if I needed a lesson, you know! But, now I think of it, I do weally twust that it will be a lesson to you fellahs!"

"Why, you cheeky ass——"

"By the way," added Arthur Augustus innocently, "I forgot to mention one thing—the patah handed me six pounds to square up the money we owe, so that we shall not be in debt."

"Forgot to mention that!" roared Blake. "Oh, you dummy!"

"Weally, Blake——"

"All clear now!" said Dig.

"Yaas, wathah! And he gave me a pound ovah, so we shall be able to have tea in the studay, deah boys——"

"Hurrah!"

Lord Eastwood's visit to St. Jim's had been a success, after all!

. . . . . .

Tom Merry & Co. cleared off their burden of debt within the next five minutes, and within the next ten they were sitting down to a gorgeous spread in Study No. 6. And never was tea in the study so thoroughly enjoyed as it was by the seven chums of St. Jim's—no longer the stony seven.

THE END

Feeding-Time for the Seal

THE animal world is full of good trenchermen, but when it comes to good, honest, stick-out-your elbows-and-get-down-to-it feeding there are very few creatures that can give points to a seal. A New York zoo keeper who tried to find out exactly how much one of his charges could eat had to give up when his supply of sixty pounds of raw fish vanished without seeming to take even the edge off the seal's appetite. On another occasion, a London Zoo seal happened to be "just handy" when a keeper left the supply of fish for the whole fish-eating community of the Zoo unattended. When the keeper returned a few minutes later, there wasn't a single fish-tail left!

But it isn't the amount they eat that makes seals at feeding time a sight which draws crowds to their enclosures at the Zoo. It is the amazingly skilful way they catch fish in mid-air, and the manner in which they dash through the water at terrific speed to get at a distant tit-bit.

Seals are very clever, and can be trained to do the most extraordinary tricks. One circus seal-trainer has taught his pets to walk a tight-rope while balancing big balls on their snouts, to play "God Save the King" by blowing into a series of trumpets tuned to appropriate notes, and to applaud one another's feats in the ring by clapping their fins together.

These circus seals take such an interest in their job that if one of them makes a mistake all the others make reproachful noises, or try to cover up the defect by starting to perform tricks of their own.

Seals are such swift swimmers that they can usually only be captured on land.

"FORGIVE US, GUS!"

By Jack Blake.

(*Of the Fourth Form at St. Jim's.*)

SPEAK, Gussy, speak! Forgive
Your pals, who acted for the best;
For you are always overdressed
And will be while you live!
Did you think it a cheek
For us to take your Sunday hat
And jump on it till it was flat?
Speak, Gussy, speak!

We did not know you would
Turn nasty when we gave away
Your purple socks the other day;
We did it for your good!
It's true we took your clo'
To make a guy for bonfire night,
But we believed it was all right;
We did not know!

You might have guessed that when
We took a dozen pairs of bags
To act as manacles and gags
To bind the New House men,
We did it for the best;
We thought that you would understand
They were the nearest things to hand—
You might have guessed!

We thought it fair to use
That muffler thing you love so well,
For we believed you'd let a pal
Take that to clean his shoes;
For nothing else was there,
Except your fancy summer clothes,
And Dig and Herries collared those—
We thought it fair.

We had to take your suit,
(The one you call a perfect fit),
And let old Towser play with it
To pacify the brute;
We thought for old times' sake
You would be glad to help your friends,
And never miss tne odds and ends
We had to take.

Forgive us, Gus, despite
Your lovely ties! (Alas, no more!)
We used them in a tug-of-war
In dorm the other night;
No longer make a fuss!
Let's have your tact and judgment, pray;
Your fiver, too, that came to-day—
Forgive us, Gus!

The Terror of Devils'

MYSTERIOUS! | **A Thrill-Packed Yarn of Amazing Adventure in the Chinese Interior** | **FASCINATING!**

THRILLING!

THE FIRST CHAPTER

INTO THE UNKNOWN!

MOUNT KULSHAM, they called it on the maps, but to the natives of the desert lands in which it stood its evil reputation had gained it the name of Devils' Mountain.

"And an apt name at that!" thought Alan Steerforth, a good-looking young Englishman, as he stared up at its awe-inspiring heights from the cockpit of his little two-seater aeroplane.

Certainly there was something sinister about the aspect of the great mountain. Silhouetted as it was against the red sky of sunset, it seemed to take on the shape of an incredibly huge primeval monster, and the grotesquely shaped peaks that hid its

MOUNTAIN!

By ROWLAND HOWARD

summit might well have been the palisade surrounding a dwelling-place for demons.

For Alan Steerforth and the party of seven other explorers who were at that moment pitching their tents on the oasis at the foot of the mountain, it was the end of a long journey. Six months had they spent in the mysterious Gobi Desert, unearthing the grisly remains of prehistoric monsters, and one task only remained before they began their long trek through the Chinese interior back to civilisation.

The projected task, which was Steerforth's, took the form of an attempt to fly over the summit of the mountain. It was a task fraught with deadly peril, and a hundred experts had called him mad when he packed up the plane for the journey. But the prospect of probing the mountain's secrets had long fascinated the young explorer, and he felt a thrill run through him at the thought that at dawn on the morrow he would set out on his great quest.

In the quickening dusk he glided

downwards, and in so doing his keen eyes saw in the distance the gleam of fires that told him they were not alone in this remote land. It was with a feeling of slight uneasiness that he climbed out of the cockpit and greeted his comrades.

" And phwat d'ye make av ut, me bhoy ? " asked Mick O'Brien, the big, simple-hearted Irish cameraman of the party who was to go up with Steerforth.

" It's going to be the stiffest job of our lives, Mick—but we'll make it ! " replied the pilot, with a grim smile. " By the way, Doc., I noticed a number of fires about ten miles west of us."

" Luminous phenomena indicative of combustion, eh ? " remarked Dr. Molyneux, the bespectacled leader of the expedition, whose only failing was his inability to use small words where big ones would do. " Your statement, Steerforth, generates apprehensions as to the possibility of our work being subjected to interference from unfriendly natives ! "

" Faith, an' Oi'd rather have throuble wid the natives than the banshees they say haunt that mountain ! " said Mick O'Brien, as he frowned up at the darkening mass of Mount Kulsham. " Glad Oi am, Alan, that we're goin' up in honest daylight, an' gladder still Oi'll be whin it's all over ! "

" Bother your old Irish superstitions ! " laughed Steerforth, as he sat by the fire and started on his rations of bully beef and biscuits. " Air-pockets and currents will be our enemies to-morrow—not mountain banshees ! "

" What's that ? " asked Ralph Shaw, a young scientist of the expedition.

They listened in wonderment to the noise that had suddenly begun to echo down from the heights of Devils' Mountain. It was a noise such as none of them had ever heard before —a hideous chattering and wailing that seemed to shake the starlit sky. Brave though they all were, not a man among the explorers could repress a shudder as that terrifying din filled the air.

" For the love av Pete, phwat is ut ? " asked Mick O'Brien hoarsely.

Dr. Molyneux was peering upwards through his big horn-rimmed spectacles.

" My personal impression is of inordinate dissonance emanating from a considerable altitude ! " he said, in quick tones that betrayed keen inward excitement. " Is it, I wonder, the voice of the ' spirits ' by which the credulous natives of these parts believe the mountain to be inhabited ? "

" Arrah ! We moight have known no good would have come av spendin' a noight under a mountain av divils ! " cried Mick O'Brien. " Faith, an' Oi'd sooner spend a noight in the haunted room av the ould castle at——"

" Look ! " yelled Ralph Shaw, and there was terror in his voice.

The whole party jumped to their feet, staring at the sky. They saw them simultaneously—two nameless black shapes that were descending at frightful speed right on to the camp.

A shriek arose from the native porters behind them, while the Britishers stood petrified with horror. A roaring tempest seemed to strike the camp. Something huge and horrible came—passed—and was gone.

The nerve-shattering din died away and the explorers woke out of their momentary stupor. From the shadows beyond the camp fire's glow came a rush of feet as the native porters poured in, wailing hysterically.

" Look ! " yelled Ralph Shaw, and there was terror in his voice. The whole party jumped to their feet, staring at the sky. Two nameless black shapes were descending at frightful speed right on to the camp !

" They got one of the men ! " said Alan Steerforth huskily. " I saw them snatch him up like a bird snatches a grub ! It was ghastly ! "

Dr. Molyneux faced the yelling natives, his arms gesturing fiercely for silence.

" Silence, if you value your skins ! " he shouted furiously, in the native dialect. " Who is missing ? "

The trembling lips of the head man framed some half-inarticulate words and Dr. Molyneux listened attentively. When the man had finished, he shouted another stern order for silence, then rejoined the Britishers, his face grim and set.

" You were right, Steerforth," he said, in the stress of the moment omitting even to employ his usual elaborate phraseology. " In fact, it's even worse than you thought. Whatever those—those things were, they carried off two living creatures of our party—a man and a mule. The men think they were devils."

" And who'd be bold enough to say they were far wrong, begob ? " ejaculated Mick O'Brien. " Ye're not suggestin' they were man-eatin' birds, Doc ? "

" There was no time to see what they were—but they were horrible beyond words ! " said Ralph Shaw, with a shudder. " What can we do ? "

Before Dr. Molyneux had time to reply, the problem was solved for them. During the hubbub of the native porters, a party of horsemen had been approaching the camp from the bush, and now, in a sudden and momentary lull, the thudding of hoofs could be heard. Instinctively, the Britishers turned in the direction from which the sound was coming, and their eyes saw the flickering of lights near at hand.

" Mongols from the camp that I saw ! " said Alan Steerforth, between his teeth. " They may be friendly—but I doubt it ! "

" Your guns—quick ! " snapped Dr. Molyneux. " But utilise them only in the ultimate extremity ; we cannot afford to make enemies unnecessarily here ! "

The explorers ran for their rifles ; but they scarcely had time to secure them before the invading Mongols were upon them. The lights from their flaming torches and from the camp fire of the explorers shone on faces that were wild and ferocious and eyes that gleamed with a fanatical light.

" Halt ! " shouted Dr. Molyneux, as the porters scattered wildly before the newcomers. But a guttural order from the leader of the Mongols drowned the rest of his words. A score of wild-eyed men reined in their mounts and leaped to the ground, swords drawn as they rushed into the fray.

" Let 'em have it ! " yelled Alan Steerforth, and his own gun roared out, winging one of the raiders as he dismounted. But the defenders' preparations were too late. The time for shooting had gone and already they were using their guns as clubs. The din of a furious hand-to-hand battle filled the camp.

It was a sharp and merciless fight while it lasted, and a dozen of the enemy were lying about disabled before the finish. But the odds were too great against the defenders and the end was inevitable. Soon the Mongols had closed in on them, and at last, by sheer weight of numbers, had overwhelmed them and forced them into submission.

" And phwat's goin' to be the end av us now, bhoys ? " demanded Mick O'Brien, from the arms of three ugly Mongols.

" Speculation is inopportune since the facts are easily ascertainable ! " panted Dr. Molyneux, regaining his gift for polysyllabic expression now that the fight was over. " Possibly the gentleman who is about to address me may bring enlightenment ! "

The leader of the raiding band had approached the explorer and saluted him. Now, he began to rattle off a fire of remarks which were almost completely unintelligible to most of the captives. Dr. Molyneux listened in silence. When the Mongol's rapid fire of speech had ended, he looked round at the rest.

" Tell us the woirst, Doc ! " urged Mick O'Brien.

" My news is of a lugubrious character, I fear ! " said Dr. Molyneux. " These Mongols, who have been living on this oasis for some time, are in a state of terror from the mountain ' devils ' and are looking for some means of appeasing their wrath. They have made us prisoners with the idea of leaving us on the mountain side to be carried away by the ' devils,' hoping thereby to propitiate them and escape further visitations ! "

" Then it's certain death for us ! " remarked Shaw grimly. " It means either that we starve slowly or else ——"

He did not finish the sentence, but they knew what he meant. It was starvation or else a sudden swoop from those nameless horrors of the night which, but a few minutes before, had spirited away man and beast to take them to a fate which none could bear to contemplate !

" Shure, an' it's meself that would rather they murthered us in cold blood than lave us at the mercy av those craithures ! " muttered Mick O'Brien, whose superstitious fear of the mountain " devils " was only one degree less than that of the Mongols themselves. " Phwat are we goin' to do, Doc ? "

" I can tell you ! " shouted Alan Steerforth, as the leader of the captive explorers hesitated. " Doc, I've got an idea—the greatest idea you ever heard ! Tell them that at dawn to-morrow we'll hunt out the mountain ' devils ' in their lair and destroy them ! See if they'll fall for that ! "

Dr. Molyneux's eyes widened in the flickering reflection of the camp fire flames.

" You are indicating that if they'll permit you to carry out your flight to the summit, you can make them believe you've put an end to those creatures ? But I'm afraid, Steerforth, that unless you can actually accomplish it——"

" Well, why not ? " retorted the young pilot, eagerly. " We're scientists, and this is a scientist's job ! Let me go up and find out what they are and where they are ; then we can put our heads together and find a way of dealing with them and so help these afflicted natives and at the same time save ourselves ! "

There was a murmur from the captured explorers. Dr. Molyneux's eyes gleamed with a sudden hope.

" Steerforth, my boy, your suggestion shows most commendable mental initiative ! " he said. " If only I can convince them that we can deal with these 'devils'——"

He broke off and started speaking rapidly to the Mongol leader in his native tongue. The Mongols listened, indifferently at first, then with growing interest till they almost hung on the white man's words.

A torrent of argument followed Dr. Molyneux's speech. Opinions were evidently sharply divided. At length, the Mongol leader held up his hand for silence and, when the noise had died down, addressed Dr. Molyneux again.

The face of the white leader was still tense when he turned back to his comrades, but his eyes were shining behind his big glasses.

" We've got a respite," he said. " They have never seen or heard of an aeroplane, but I've told them we have a magic dragon that carries us into the air and they've agreed to release two of our party at dawn to-morrow to go and fight the ' devils.' But if the two fail——"

" Phwat then, Doc ? "

" The rest of us die ! " said Dr. Molyneux soberly. " Heaven knows, Steerforth, how it lies in your power to destroy an army of ' devils ' possessed of the power of our late visitors. But it's a respite."

" And while there's life there's hope ! " said Steerforth, joyously. " It's a trip into the Unknown, Doc. But it gives us a chance and that's all we can ask ! "

THE SECOND CHAPTER

THE FLYING FURIES !

At dawn on the following morning, after an hour of feverish activity, Alan Steerforth and Mick O'Brien climbed into the little aeroplane in which all hopes were centred. Heavy leather suits, electrically heated, protected their bodies against the intense cold they would encounter in the upper regions and oxygen masks hung round their necks, ready for use in the rarefied air into which they would fly.

While a crowd of Mongols stood away at a respectful distance, Dr. Molyneux, temporarily released for the purpose, gave the propeller a twist. The engine roared out an almost immediate response. A few seconds later the plane took off and, amid a howl of amazement from the natives and from the Britishers a cheer that gave expression to a desperate hope, roared away over the little camp to the forbidding mass of the mountain of mystery.

Upwards, ever upwards! Below, the panorama of sandy plain and stony foothills moved steadily away as they soared skyward. The camp, with its seething crowd gazing up at the diminishing speck in the sky, became a mere dot on an infinity of landscape.

"Everything O.K., Mick?" asked Alan Steerforth, through the mouthpiece of the telephone that connected him with his passenger.

"Not a throuble in the wor-rld if it weren't for the bhoys bein' in the camp an' meself flyin' to meet the banshees on this divil-ridden mountain!" answered Mick, who, despite the heavy odds that existed against the resultant negatives ever seeing the inside of a developing-room, was busily preparing his movie camera for use. "Alan Steerforth, me bhoy, would ye be thinkin' we can race 'em if we meet any av the evil craithures?"

"I'm thinking nothing about it till we meet them," was Alan Steerforth's cheery reply. "Get busy with your camera and forget the blessed banshees!"

Soon, they had donned their masks and turned on the life-giving oxygen. The altimeter was creeping steadily up—10,000 feet, 15,000 feet and then 20,000 feet were registered by its quivering needle and still it moved forward.

Emerging out of a bank of light cloud at 20,000 feet, they came into a region of crystal-clear air and saw, for the first time, the desolate grandeur of the great mountain's upper heights. A wilderness of ice and snow stretched away from them into the distant haze, while immense peaks of bare grey rock towered above them, it seemed, to the very sky.

Mick O'Brien soon had his movie camera going, pausing only at intervals to take still shots with the ordinary cameras that were also in his outfit.

An amazing phenomenon came into view as they rounded one of the great peaks. Right down the mountain-side a huge cloud of powdery snow was rising upwards from a gorge that extended down as far as the eye could see. In the bright sunshine it looked like a gigantic white serpent writhing down to the foothills.

"And phwat d'ye make av that?" asked Mick, through the telephone.

"It's a vast air-current blowing up from some natural funnel in the mountain!" came the pilot's reply. "Get all the pictures you can of it, for it knocks spots off Niagara Falls from this position!"

"Shure, an' it's meself that belaves the whole place is haunted!" muttered Mick, as he bent over his camera once more.

Still they climbed, till at last they were at the crest of the mountain. Then, as they peered down, they saw the summit below them—and with it a sight that froze the blood in their veins! For in the huge, shadowy, boulder-strewn hollow that formed the top of the mountain, reclining in a sleep which changed to wakefulness as the roar of the plane disturbed them, were scores of black creatures of stupendous size and nightmarish hideousness.

" Merciful heavens! The banshees! " Mick O'Brien's husky voice breathed through the telephone.

he had gazed was one that would have inspired fear in any human being. The loathsome creatures that littered the summit of Devils' Mountain were fully thirty feet in length. Their necks were long and sinuous and their bodies fat and ungainly, with two stumps of legs just sufficiently long to enable them to waddle

" Let 'em have it! " yelled Alan Steerforth as a score of wild-eyed Mongols rushed to the attack. His own gun roared out, winging one of the raiders as he dismounted. Then the din of a furious hand-to-hand battle filled the camp.

" Not banshees, but animals! " yelled back Steerforth. " Animals such as no living man has ever seen! Keep your camera going, Mick, and for heaven's sake don't lose your head! "

The hands of the young pilot were shaking as they moved over the controls, for the sight on which

about on land. But it was the wings and head that brought the feeling of revulsion to the airmen. The wings, fleshy, furry, bat-like members, had an enormous spread. The head, immense in size and snake-like in appearance, was crowned with a row of waving air-suckers—by which alone the hideous creatures could have survived at this height—over gaping jaws that revealed double rows of serrated teeth.

With a roar that awoke the echoes of the foul place the aeroplane skimmed across the sleeping-den of the monsters. Then, as the creatures bestirred themselves, arose a sound that drowned the engine and filled the air with its deafening discord. It was that weird wailing and chattering that had echoed down from the mountain-top the night before. The next instant a dozen of the monsters were moving over the ground with the slow, sticky movement of giant sloths, and a moment later their huge wings were spreading and they were soaring up at the intruder.

The airmen realised at once that, lethargic and ponderous as the great creatures might be on land, they were like flying furies in the air. They shot upwards like shells from a battery of guns.

Alan Steerforth wheeled in a desperate attempt to turn back on his course. He had known from the previous night's experience that they could swoop at tremendous speed, but he had not reckoned on their being able to reproduce that speed in soaring. Unfortunately, however, they seemed almost capable of that incredible achievement. Too late the young pilot repented of his daring in flying over them.

A host of fleeting black shadows suddenly blotted out the sunshine that bathed the mountain-top. Something huge and terrifying flew straight at the nose of the aeroplane and a shattering blow shook her from tip to tail. A strangled animal wail rang out.

The black shadow fell away and a grinding sound told of damage to the plane. With a sickening sense of horror Alan and Mick suddenly realised that the wounded monster had torn away both propeller and engine with one blow of its mighty wing.

From a gaping hole in the cockpit they stared with fascinated eyes at the dread vale below them. Only the high wind and strong currents of the mountain-top prevented them dropping like a stone. As it was, they were drifting downwards at quite an uncomfortable speed, with the black forms of their hideous hosts whirling furiously around them as they descended.

Crash!

They landed at last, with a shattering impact that almost knocked them senseless. Where they were, for a moment they had no idea. They only knew that they were lying in the wreckage of the cockpit and that a black cloud of flying furies was rushing downwards to destroy them.

THE THIRD CHAPTER

THE SNOW SERPENT!

It was a desperate moment; but in such moments the human instinct for self-preservation finds ways of escape where none seem to exist. That was what happened on this occasion. In the moment when their fate seemed sealed and their brains had become numbed with the realisation of the horror that threatened them, the wrecked airmen found themselves leaping out of the cockpit and diving into a little alcove formed by an overhanging crag.

The swooping monsters thudded to the ground with a screaming and chattering that awoke hideous echoes in the cup-shaped mountain-top. But for the moment their intended human prey had eluded them, for the opening to the alcove was far too small for their gigantic bodies.

Crouched against the rock-face in their little hiding-place, Alan and Mick looked at each other. Had their faces been visible, they would have been seen to be strained with intense anxiety, but as they were concealed by their oxygen masks and goggles, they registered their feelings with expressive gestures instead.

Their plight hardly bore contemplating. They had a reserve oxygen supply strapped to their backs and the batteries that heated their clothing were intact ; but it would be only a matter of hours before oxygen and heat both gave out—and when that happened, death, within a few minutes, was certain.

Even if the supplies of oxygen and heat had been greater, escape seemed impossible, for in the open they could hardly hope to elude the horde of monsters that menaced them, and in any case knew that a descent on foot of the colossal ice-bound mountain, with its great precipices and sheer walls of rock, was out of the question.

The telephone apparatus having been destroyed, the stranded airmen had recourse to pencil and paper. Alan wrote : " Are your heat and gas coming through all right ? Mine O.K."

" Me too," wrote back Mick. " But I can't see how we'll get out of this mess at all. Got any hunches ? "

" The plane's in order but for the engine." This from Alan.

Mick responded with : " For the love of Mike what's the use of it to us if the engine's missing ? "

Alan wrote back : " I had gliding in mind, but it wants a lot of thinking about. It's the problem of getting away from these creatures. Let's think it over."

They did so. The result in Mick's case was evidently not encouraging, for after an interval of a quarter of an hour he took up his pencil again and wrote : " Sure, and it does seem tough, everything ending like this entirely. I wouldn't mind for myself so much, but it's worrying to know that when we don't return the rest will pay for it."

" Stop croaking," was Alan's reply. " There's still a chance. Taking bearings, I see we've landed not far above that snow spout—the thing we saw writhing down into the plain like a white serpent. If we could hang on to the cockpit and go over the top in the plane, that air current might give us a fairly easy glide most of the way down, and I should be able to manage her the rest of the way."

" Sounds like suicide to me, but anything's better than just dying here," wrote Mick. " I'm with you, boy ; but don't forget the plane's a lot heavier than the average glider."

" The engine's the heaviest part, and that's gone," Alan scribbled. " Of course, I realise that she's not a glider and the odds are that we shall crash. But there is the chance that the air current extends far enough down to keep her buoyant to the bottom. Is there any hope of getting away while the beasts are sleeping ? Daytime seems resting time for them and we may be able to slip away quietly without arousing them."

Sure enough the black monsters of the mountain-top began to lumber off soon after and in a short period all had gone. Hope rose high in the breasts of the airmen.

But that hope was speedily extinguished at their first attempt to move from the alcove. Ere they had taken half-a-dozen steps, there was a stirring in the shadows of the cupped mountain-top, and from all directions the weird monsters of Devils' Mountain were advancing upon them, grotesque and ridiculous in their awkward gait, but terrifying in their size and strength. Frantically, the two Britishers raced back to the alcove and sought again the welcome shelter of its rocky walls.

They eyed each other through their heated goggles with eyes that had a hunted look in them. Slothful as the monsters might appear on land, it was evident that they had the instincts of wolves on the track of prey—that their watch for the human beings who had fallen into their lair would not relax for an instant. Even the remote chance of escape that lay in a wild leap into the air over the mountain-side in the engineless plane seemed denied them.

The two explorers were in an agony of mind. Staunch and unselfish both, their thoughts in this dark hour turned to their comrades, prisoners in the hands of fanatical devil-worshippers and doomed to die now that they could not help them.

They crouched back against the rock, desperately racking their brains for a solution to the problem. But the hours went quickly and ideas came all too slowly.

The sun was low in the west, and a drowsiness that betokened the petering out of their oxygen supply was beginning to creep over them when at last inspiration came to Alan Steerforth. He had been looking across the dip at the trail of petrol that had leaked over the ice-bound rock when the engine fell and rolled down into a cavity on lower ground. Suddenly he threw out his arms in a frenzy of excitement. Mick roused himself to read the message he started writing immediately afterwards.

" Have you got a match or lighter ? " was the message.

Mick's answer was to produce a box of safety matches from an outside pocket. His colleague took it and scribbled a second message.

" There's a trail of petrol starting outside which ends up at the engine. Expect tank has leaked dry by now, but the fumes inside it should make it as good as a bomb, and it's resting in a hollow which may add to the effect. We'll fire it, hoping to scatter them, then push off in the plane. Agreed ? "

For answer, Mick put his arms round his comrade's shoulders and hugged him.

Both knew that it would be only a matter of minutes now before the oxygen gave out and they fell into a sleep from which there would be no awakening, and both preferred a last desperate fight to such a tame and ignoble surrender to fate.

Throwing off, with a mighty effort, the drowsiness which was rapidly dimming their senses, they prepared for their bid for freedom. For the hundredth time since their landing, they measured with their eyes the distance separating them from the plane, which was sheltered behind a huge crag almost on the edge of the mountain. Alan scribbled out detailed instructions as to the exact position his colleague was to take up in the cockpit ; then they stood ready.

Alan struck the match and sent it skimming across to the glistening spot where the petrol trail began.

The flash back was instantaneous. An ear-splitting roar shook the mountain-top, and a sheet of flame blazed over the home of the mountain monsters. It was as though the mountain had suddenly become a raging volcano. The hollow into

Suddenly an ear-splitting roar shook the mountain-top, and a sheet of flame blazed over the home of the mountain monsters. Then, before the awe-struck eyes of the Britishers, great cracks appeared, and the denizens of Devils' Mountain disappeared into unknown depths.

which the engine had rolled had, in fact, been accumulating petrol fumes and become a live "bomb" of enormous explosive power.

Jagged pieces of rock flew into the air in a shower as the two Britishers picked themselves up and raced madly to the plane which, in its protected position, had missed the force of the explosion completely. Then, at the very moment when they stood alongside the cockpit, ready to push her off and take the great leap, came the amazing aftermath.

Their awe-struck eyes were suddenly made aware that great cracks and fissures were appearing in the hollow mountain-top, and that the army of black monsters, stunned into helplessness by the violence of the explosion, were sliding down into depths which the eye could not penetrate. Alan Steerforth's amazingly successful "bomb" had dealt the defective surface of the mountain-top a blow that had caved it in! The nesting-place of the foul denizens of Devils' Mountain had been shifted hundreds of feet lower into the centre of the mountain and changed simultaneously into a tomb, for not one of them was fated to survive the fearful drop!

With the feeling that the whole world was crumbling away under their feet, Alan and Mick pushed off, climbing into the wrecked cockpit as the engineless plane slid down the ice-bound mountain-side towards the writhing " serpent " of powdery snow on which their forlorn hope of surviving depended.

Faster and faster they descended the slippery slope till the white trail of the air funnel seemed to be rushing to meet them. Mick crouched behind, while Alan sat in front, his eyes glued ahead of him and his hand on the control-stick. It looked as though no power could possibly be strong enough to get them into the air ; but as they neared the snow-serpent and Alan moved the stick, they felt themselves leave the mountain-side and begin to ride over the terrific current that swept upwards from the gap.

Tossed and buffeted about like a cork on a stormy sea, the little plane swept earthwards down the trail of spouting snow It was a weird and terrifying experience, to be riding through a blinding spray of snow twenty thousand feet above the earth, with the knowledge that nothing but air currents could save them from a drop to death when the snow trail ended ; but Alan Steerforth, in the remains of the pilot's seat, was as coldly efficient as he would have been with the engine roaring out its cheering music.

With amazing suddenness the snow spray ended. Alan took a split second to glance over the side and he could have shouted with joy at the discovery that they were gliding with surprising evenness over the foothills below the mountain. The plane had, in point of fact, been catapulted off the current with such force as to send her on a glide of several miles towards the plains beyond the mountain.

The young pilot glanced down again and saw in the distance the ant-like figures of human beings and the gleam of a camp-fire. Taking full advantage of the power with which the last kick of the great air current had endowed his engineless plane, he slanted her tail and guided her towards the fire, and with a slowness that was a sheer delight the earth came nearer and nearer, the ant-like figures became recognisable human beings, and the little plane at last came to rest within a hundred yards of the spot from which she had started twelve hours before.

The conquerors of Devils' Mountain heard the hysterical cries of the Mongols and the wild cheering of their fellow-explorers, and knew that victory had been won. Then everything went dark. The inevitable reaction had set in and both had fainted.

. . . .

One night without molestation from the monsters of the mountain was sufficient to convince the Mongols that the white men and their " dragon" had slain the " devils " that had so long menaced their lives, and they were happy to release their captives on the following day.

" Well, it is an incredible narrative we have to relate," remarked Dr. Molyneux, as they started their long journey back across the desert. "How unfortunate that we did not manage to secure a single specimen of those engrossingly interesting prehistoric survivals before they were engulfed in the mountain ! I am somewhat apprehensive that the world will be incredulous and suggest that we merely witnessed an example of the visual phenomenon known as the mirage ! "

" Then the wor-rld can see that same mirage for itself, Doc., an' it'll be all aloive an' kickin' ! " chuckled Mick O'Brien. " For if that fillum Oi took from the plane doesn't bate anythin' Hollywood iver thought av, then Oi'm a Dutchman ! "

THE END

GETTING OVER GUSSY!

By TOM MERRY
(Junior Captain of St. Jim's)

When Gussy's on his dignity he's an awkward customer to deal with—as this humorous story of the chums of St. Jim's fully proves!

THE FIRST CHAPTER
THE HIGH HORSE!

"FIVE quid!"

"Eh?"

"Five quid—or, to be strictly correct, a crisp, rustling fiver!" grinned Jack Blake of the Fourth at St. Jim's. "Gussy's just received it!"

"Oh, good!" said Herries and Digby together.

It was a Wednesday afternoon in early December, and a grey mist had blotted out football. Herries and Digby had been rather disconsolate as they gazed out into the murky quad., but they brightened up considerably as Blake burst into Study No. 6 with his cheery announcement.

"Couldn't have happened better," remarked Blake. "We're all stony, and I was almost reconciled to rooting about the House for the afternoon. Now we can go out."

"Good egg! What about Wayland, the pictures and tea out afterwards?" asked Digby.

"Just about meets the bill!" nodded Herries. "Where's Gus, Blake?"

"Up in the dorm., trying on a batch of new ties. We'll soon yank him out of it," said the leader of the Fourth. "Ready, you men?"

"Ready, aye, ready!"

"Kim on, then!"

The trio quitted the study and went upstairs, in great spirits. The prospect of a trip to the talkies, with tea out afterwards, put a fresh complexion on the gloomy day.

Arthur Augustus D'Arcy was alone in the Fourth dormitory when they tramped in. He did not look up. He was surveying, with a thoughtful frown, an array of brand-new ties spread out before him on his bed. Ties, like all other articles of personal adornment, were a source of unfailing interest to the swell of the Fourth. He looked, on this occasion, as if he could quite happily have spent the remainder of the afternoon concentrating on them.

"Hurry up, Gus!" Blake said briskly. "No time for rooting about. There's a train to catch, you know."

Arthur Augustus turned round with a start and looked at Blake in some surprise through his celebrated monocle.

"Bai Jove! How did you know I was catchin' a twain, deah boy?"

"We've just arranged it!" grinned Blake. "Put on your coat and bonnet, old bean, and don't forget to bring the oof. We'll tell you the programme as we walk down to the station."

"Weally, Blake, you appeah to be takin' wathah a lot on yourself. As it happens, I am goin' to Wayland an' I shall natuwally be pleased to have you all with me, but——"

"If you don't stop wagging that chin of yours, we'll miss the train," said Blake. "Put on a collar and one of those dazzling things you've got set out on the bed and trot along with us—pronto!"

The swell of the Fourth eyed his leader coldly.

"Weally, Blake, if you are in such a huwwy as that, pewwaps you'd bettah go without me. I find it wathah difficult to choose a tie to weah this afternoon, an' I uttahly wefuse to be huwwied in my choice!"

"And we utterly refuse to hang about the dorm. for the rest of the day while you choose a blessed tie!" retorted Blake cheerily. "This'll do! Where's your collar?"

Arthur Augustus glared.

"If you imagine, you wottah, that you're goin' to fix my collah an' tie for me—yawooooop! Hewwies, you wottah! Dig., you wank outsidah——"

"Sorry, old bean, but there's really no time to argue about it!" said Digby, as he helped Herries to hold the swell of the Fourth while Blake got to work with the collar and tie. "Manage, Blake?"

"Easily!" grinned Blake. "Just a little slip-knot like this and now jerk it tight—so! You look great, Gus—just as though you'd stepped out of a giddy Christmas cracker! Take his arms, you fellows—we'll have to rush if we're to catch that train at Rylcombe!"

Blake bundled the remainder of D'Arcy's dazzling ties into the locker by the bed, and Herries and Digby rushed their noble chum to the door. Arthur Augustus uttered a wild yell.

"Welease me, you wuffians! I wefuse to come to Wayland dwessed like a twamp! I wefuse to weah this collah an' tie. I wefuse——"

"Rush him through the House before someone stops us and makes a kidnapping affair out of it!" gasped Blake. "Be a sport and can it, Gus. You're coming to Wayland with us, whether you like it or not, so it makes no difference!"

"I uttahly wefuse——"

And Arthur Augustus kept on refusing all the way down the stairs, across the quad., and half-way to Rylcombe—though his refusals had no other effect than slightly to delay their journey to the station.

At the half-way mark his verbal remonstrances petered out and the swell of the Fourth lapsed into a frigid silence, which his three chums endured with stolid fortitude. Arthur Augustus frequently rode the high horse; but his elevated periods were usually of short duration, and once they got him into the pictures, they knew he would soon come round.

Blake & Co. were not, however, destined to get the swell of the Fourth into the pictures on this occasion. As they came in sight of Rylcombe Station, he broke away from Herries and Digby and made a sudden dash.

Blake gave a shout, as he spotted the train through the mist.

"After him! Train's just starting—he wants to leave us behind!"

"Gus, you fathead——" howled Digby.

But Arthur Augustus was sprinting towards the station like a champion on the cinder track. The rest of the Co. raced after him. But Arthur Augustus, who was one of the best sprinters in the Fourth, simply streaked away from them, rushed through the barrier, and was just in time to board the last carriage on the train.

And Blake and Herries and Digby were left to gaze after the disappearing local with feelings that were too deep for words.

THE SECOND CHAPTER

BLAKE'S WASTED BRAINWAVE

"YOUR fault!"

"You mean your fault!"

"If you hadn't let go of him——"

"You mean if you'd hung on to him——"

"Chuck it, you idiots!" snorted Blake. "I've heard that record all the time we've been tramping here and I'm tired of it. Here we are in Wayland now, and there's no sense in talking about what happened at Rylcombe. Problem is, what to do now we've arrived?"

"Find Gussy!" suggested Digby.

"Fat lot of good it'll be when we do find him!" growled Herries. "You know what Gus is when he feels like it. Ten to one he won't even look at us for the rest of the afternoon; and how we're going to get him to take us to the talkies in that case——"

"Here's Kerr!" interrupted Digby. "Let's ask him. Hold on, Kerr. Seen Gussy?"

Kerr of the New House, who had just come out of an outfitter's shop, carrying a parcel, stopped and nodded.

"Yes, he's in that shop. I've been in buying the clobber I wear in our new crook play. Gussy's in the collar and tie department talking colour schemes——"

"And I've got the very idea which will put things right!" broke in Blake, excitedly. "Don't you take the part of a burglar in that play, Kerr?"

Kerr stared.

"Right on the wicket; but what——"

"Come into this doorway, all of you, and I'll explain," said Blake. "Hurry, he might come out any moment."

"What's the big idea?" asked the surprised Kerr, as he followed the School House juniors into the doorway of an untenanted shop.

"The idea's just this," said Blake, after he had briefly explained the position: "Gussy's bound to ride the high horse with us for a bit yet and we don't stand an earthly of going to the pictures on his invitation unless something extraordinary happens. But something extraordinary can happen!"

"By which you mean——"

"Gussy can be attacked by a desperate crook," was Blake's surprising answer. "His pals—Herries, Digby and I—can rescue him. If that extraordinary event happens, mere common decency will compel Gus to hold us to his breast and call us his long-lost brothers!"

"I suppose it will," said Kerr, in astonishment. "But if Gussy is attacked by a desperate crook in Wayland this afternoon, it will be more than extraordinary—it will be miraculous!"

"Not now that you've turned up!" grinned Blake. "Especially as you've turned up conveniently supplied with a crook's clobber!"

"Eh?"

"Oh, my giddy aunt!" gasped Digby. "You—you mean we can frame the whole thing? Kerr can rig up as a footpad and we can do the rescue stuff!"

"Just that!"

"M-m-m-my hat!"

Kerr and Herries and Digby looked at Blake and looked at each other. Then they grinned. Finally, they roared. Blake glanced through the mist towards the outfitter's with rather an anxious eye.

"No time for cackling," he said. "Are you game, Kerr?"

"I'll do it," grinned Kerr. "No time to do it as I'd like to do it, of course, but I've got a cap I can pull over my eyes and a muffler I can wrap round my neck——"

"Hurry!" said Blake.

Kerr slipped off the string that bound his parcel and rummaged among the contents.

In a matter of seconds, an artistically adjusted cap and a woollen muffler, combined with a change of facial expression such as only a skilled actor of Kerr's ability could have managed, transformed the New House junior into a creditable imitation of a crook.

The juniors saw Arthur Augustus step from the shop into the misty street, as Kerr completed his handiwork.

"Now!" said Blake.

Kerr, leaving the remains of his parcel in the doorway, ran after D'Arcy's retreating figure. The watching juniors saw him reach the swell of the Fourth, then fling his arms round D'Arcy's neck.

"Money or your life!" they heard Kerr growl. "Come on, young shaver, part up!"

There was a gasp from Arthur Augustus, then a yell.

"Help! Wescue! I'm being wobbed!"

Blake and Co. wasted no time; it would hardly have done to attract a crowd before they gave Kerr a chance to get away. Jumping out of the doorway, they scudded along the misty pavement.

"It's Gussy, you men!" Blake yelled, for D'Arcy's benefit. "He's being attacked by a robber. Rescue!"

"What-ho!" chortled Herries and Digby.

Blake & Co. fairly swooped down on the supposed footpad and made a remarkably realistic attack on him—so realistic, in fact, that Kerr had to utilise none of his theatrical ability in emitting a yell of pain and collapsing in disorder on the pavement.

"Oh, cwikey! Lucky you turned up!" gasped Arthur Augustus; then, as Kerr jumped to his feet: "Gwab him, deah boys! Don't let the wottah escape!"

"Look out—he's armed!" Blake shouted, thereby causing the enthusiastic swell of the Fourth to lose his enthusiasm and jump back rather hurriedly.

Kerr took advantage of the respite to dodge back into the doorway in which he had deposited his purchases. Having retrieved the parcel, he rushed off and was quickly swallowed up in the mist.

Arthur Augustus mopped his perspiring brow and adjusted his eyeglass.

"Bai Jove! He'll nevah be caught in this w'etched mist!" he remarked. "Wathah a pitay!"

"Can't be helped!" said Blake, philosophically. "Are you all right, Gus?"

"You're coming to Wayland with us, Gus," gasped Blake, "whether you like it or not!" "I uttahly wefuse——" began Arthur Augustus. But his chums promptly grasped him and rushed him across the quad.

"Yaas, wathah! Thanks vewy much for your pwompt assistance, deah boys!"

"Oh, it was nothing," said Blake airily, closing that eye which was beyond D'Arcy's range of vision. "We only did what anyone else would have done in the circs."

"Just that!" said Herries.

"A mere trifle!" grinned Digby. "Don't mention it, old bean!"

Arthur Augustus beamed at his three chums.

"Nevahtheless, it was vewy sportay of you, aftah our little diffewance of opinion earliah on. I'm weally sowwy now, deah boys, that I wushed away as I did. But all's well that ends well, an' this little incident has at least bwought us togethah again. Now if there's anythin' I can do to make amends——"

Blake smiled.

"Well, strangely enough, Gus, there is. You may remember that we're all broke to the wide?"

"Bai Jove!"

"Whether you do or not, we are, anyway. And if there's one thing more than anything else you can do for us this afternoon, it's stand treat for the lot of us at the pictures and perhaps take us out to tea after. That'll just about make it quits, I fancy!"

"What-ho!" grinned Herries and Digby.

"Bai Jove!"

"Well! Anything wrong with the wheeze?" asked Blake.

The swell of the Fourth gazed at his colleagues in dismay.

" Nothin' whatevah, deah boy. I think it's a weally wippin' ideah ; but—— "

" Then the ' buts ' don't arise ! " said Blake, cheerfully. " We'll toddle along to the cinema right away."

" Bai Jove ! I'd love to, deah boy ; but, as it happens, it's quite imposs. ! "

" How's that, then ? "

" You see, deah boys," explained Arthur Augustus, " I've just been in to pay for that batch of new neckties I had delivahed to-day an' the bill came to pwactically a fivah. As I say, I'd simplay love to take you all to the pictuahs. But I can't—I haven't got the monay ! "

Blake and Herries and Digby blinked at their noble chum. Then they blinked at each other. Their thoughts were of all the trouble they had taken—their trip to Wayland, their amazing little scheme to rescue Arthur Augustus from the clutches of a footpad conveniently provided by themselves.

Suddenly, with one accord, Blake, Herries and Digby made a rush.

" What the mewwy dickens—whoop ! Yawoooop ! Yooooop ! " howled Arthur Augustus D'Arcy, as he felt himself seized and raised and bumped and finally rolled into the muddy gutter.

" There ! That's relieved our feelings ! " panted Blake. " Now, chaps, we'll foot it back to St. Jim's ! "

And Blake and Herries and Digby walked away. And Arthur Augustus D'Arcy was left reclining in the mud, on his face an expression of which speechless indignation and inexpressible astonishment were just about equally balanced !

THE END

RADIO ST. JIM'S !

Monty Lowther Calling:

HELLO, everybody ! Hiking through long grass irritates me, complains Crooke. He sounds nettled ! Like the Irish business man who put up a notice in his office, reading : " Persons having no business in this office will please get through with it as soon as possible ! " As another Irishman said : " The time has come when we must strip to the waist and roll up our shirt-sleeves ! " The warder confronted the " old lag " in gaol. " You're to be discharged to-morrow ! " he announced. " Lor' ! Wot 'ave I done now ? " demanded the prisoner indignantly. Mr. Selby, the master of the Third, went down to the seaside from Saturday to Monday. He returned very sunburned about the head—as Wally D'Arcy said, sunburned on his " weak end " ! Two sailors were shipwrecked on a South Sea island. " Don't be nervous ! " said the first, looking at the dancing cannibals. " They're only singing welcome ! " " Welcome be blowed ! " returned his companion. " They're singing grace ! " Blake told Cutts of the Fifth, whose hair is very wavy, that he ought to go to sea. " Why ? " asked Cutts. " A life on the permanent wave ! " answered Blake—and ran for dear life ! Wally D'Arcy stopped Kildare in the lane the other day. " You know Knox's neck ? " asked Wally casually. " Yes. Why ? " asked Kildare. " Well, he's fallen into Farmer Blunt's pond up to it ! " responded Wally calmly. George Gore is still tinkering with his home-made radio set. In our opinion the best thing he could get on it would be whatever it would fetch at the pawnbroker's !—We're telling you !

The GREYFRIARS TREASURE!

(The treasure consists of the rich monastic appointments and possessions buried by the old Grey Friars at the time of the Reformation. It will be worth a fabulous sum of money if it is ever found—if! Some Greyfriars celebrities tell you what they would do with the money if they ever had the luck to find it.)

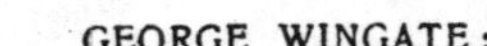

GEORGE WINGATE:
A fortune, they say, brings no pleasure,
But only a packet of worry;
So, if I discovered the treasure,
I'd lose it again in a hurry.

HARRY WHARTON:
I'm afraid I can't do as I'm bidden
And say what's requested of me;
But if you know where the stuff's hidden,
Just tell me—and then you will see.

FISHER T. FISH:
I guess if I went
And cinched the whole store,
I'd count every cent,
And wish there were more.

WILLIAM GEORGE BUNTER:
Wot? If I fownd the Greyfriars stuff,
You arsk me wot I'd do?
My reeders kno me well enuff
To kno my amser, too.

HORACE JAMES COKER:
Well, first I woold go
And buy up the skool,
And whop every fag in the place;
I'd boss the whole show
Currajeous and cool,
And kick Wingate out in dissgrace.

PAUL PROUT:
I should, of course, relinquish my employment,
And spend some happy, profitable years
Among my former haunts, and find enjoyment
In spreading death in buffaloes and bears.
Such is, I may explain, my fond intention
When I retire from the scholastic state.
I do not think you've ever heard me mention
That once, out hunting bears, in '98——
(Yes, yes; we've heard that one before.—Ed.)

LORD MAULEVERER (yawning):
Ya-aw! I don't care a fig for it,
You see!
Some other chap can dig for it;
Not me!

GOSLING:
If I found the "rhino"
(Which I ain't!),
I'd fall upon the lino
In a faint.

The LAST LAUGH!

A Christmas Play in Verse for Amateur Actors

By the GREYFRIARS RHYMESTER

SCENE:

(*Study No. 7 in the Remove Passage.* PETER TODD *is whistling* " *Good King Wenceslas* " *and staring at a pile of school books on the table.*)

TODD (*jubilantly*):
No more prep at all this year,
No more pain and sorrow;
Good old Christmastime is here
And we break up to-morrow!
That's something worth a song—about,
So——(*sings*):
Good King Wenceslas looked out
(*He picks up a book and shies it across the study.*)
That's for Virgil—serve him right!
(*Picks up another.*)
Euclid! Ugh! (*Shies it.*) Get out of sight! (*Picks up another.*)
Dr. Arnold's Latin Prose!
Lot of piffle. (*Shies it.*) There it goes! (*Picks up another.*)
Galt's Advanced Arithmetic——
The look of it makes me feel sick!
(*He hurls it towards the door just as* BOB CHERRY *comes in. The book crashes on his waistcoat.*)

CHERRY (*roaring*):
Ow! Wha-at was that, you lunatic?

TODD (*grinning*):
Oh, Galt's Advanced Arithmetic.

CHARACTERS.

Harry Wharton	**Captain of the Remove**
Bob Cherry	**Of the Remove**
Johnny Bull	
Frank Nugent	
Peter Todd	
Billy Bunter	**The Fat Boy of Greyfriars**
William Gosling	**The School Porter**

(NOTE.—*This play may be performed by readers of the* HOLIDAY ANNUAL *without fee or licence on condition that the words* " *By permission of the Editor of the* HOLIDAY ANNUAL " *appear on every programme.*)

It seems to have advanced too
quick !

CHERRY :
You burbling, babbling bander-
snatch !
You ought to be in Colney Hatch !
Now listen ! This is Christmas-
tide,
And we've a gift for you outside.
We've got it waiting for you, Toddy,
With kind regards from every-
body
In the Remove ! You needn't grin !
(*Calls off stage.*)
All right, you fellows ! Bring it in !

(WHARTON, NUGENT *and* BULL *enter, leading in* BILLY BUNTER *by the nose.* BUNTER'S *hands are tied together behind him and he is gagged with an old duster. Round his neck is hung, by string, a large piece of cardboard bearing the words in black ink,* "*WHO WANTS BUNTER?*")

TODD (*jumping*) :
Ye gods ! It's Bunter ! Oh, my
hat !
But why's he gagged and bound
like that ?

WHARTON :
He's trying to get, as you may bet,
An invite for the Vac.,
He won't take, "No !" for answer,
so
We've kindly brought him back !

NUGENT :
He's tried to dodge in Wharton
Lodge,
We said, "It can't be done !"
He rolled on then to Mauly's den
And set him on the run !

CHERRY :
And then he thought Brown might
be caught
To spend the Christmas with ;
But Browny rose and pulled his
nose,
So he tried Vernon-Smith.

BULL :
But Smithy's boot helped him to
scoot,
And Hazel made a fuss
When he blew in, so with a grin
He wandered back to us.

WHARTON :
We didn't wait to hear him state
The nature of his biz.,
We simply bagged him and we
gagged
The Porpoise—here he is !

TODD (*laughing*) :
Ha, ha ! So that's the trouble is it ?
Thuswise the gagging stunts !
Well, who wants Bunter for a visit ?
Don't all speak at once !

(TODD *unties and ungags* BUNTER, *and the fat junior gives an indignant roar.*)

BUNTER :
Beasts ! Rotters ! Villains ! Yah !
You rotters !——

ALL (*laughing*) :
Ha, ha, ha !

BUNTER (*wrenching off his label*) :
There's nothing at all to cackle at !
I won't go with you now—that's
flat !
To treat a chap this way, you beast,
Who comes to ask you to a feast !

ALL (*staggered*) :
You what ? Great Scott !
Don't talk such rot !

BUNTER :
I came to ask you to a feed !
You collared me with such a speed
I couldn't say a word of it——

WHARTON (*grinning*) :
That famous feed ! We've heard
of it !

BULL :
We've often heard him tell of it,
But never got a smell of it !

CHERRY :
You've chosen the wrong day for it
If you want us to pay for it.
(*All laugh.*)

BUNTER (*yelling*) :
I tell you there'll be tons to eat ;
I'm standing you a Christmas treat !

TODD :
Where's the grub, you fat defrauder ?
Coming with your postal-order ?

BUNTER (*with dignity*) :
That's quite all right ! You'll see it soon !
My hamper comes this afternoon ;
Sausages, sardines and salmon,
Cake and chocolate and——

ALL (*grinning*) :
Gammon !

BUNTER :
I wrote last Saturday, you see,
To my maternal grandpa,
And asked him if he'd send to me
This Christmas-time a hamper.
My granddad is a ripping sort ;
He lives with us at Bunter's Court.

Peter Todd : Galt's Advanced Arithmetic. The look of it makes me feel sick ! (He hurls the book towards the door and it crashes on Bob Cherry's waistcoat just as he is entering the room.)
Cherry : Ow ! Wha-at was that, you lunatic ?

WHARTON :
My dear old Porpoise, that's all bosh !
You know by now that yarn won't wash !

BUNTER :
I tell you it's the truth, you beast !

WHARTON :
All right ! If you produce this feast—
Enough for four or five, at least—
Then I'll put paid to all your worry
And ask you to my place in Surrey,
Where you can gorge and eat your fill
And guzzle till you're taken ill ;
But should it turn out otherwise
And your spread *not* materialise,
You'll give your word that you'll abstain
From ever asking me again.

NUGENT (*grinning*) :
Hear, hear ! Now that's a bargain, Billy !

BULL (*grunting*) :
But he won't keep his promise, will he ?

BUNTER :
I say, old fellow, I agree !
The spread is bound to come, you see !

CHERRY (*grimly*) :
He thinks we're spoofing him, perhaps ;
We'll keep him up to it, you chaps !

NUGENT :
Yes ; if this yarn about the feed
Is just another dodge,
You give your word you will not plead
To come to Wharton Lodge ?

BULL :
If he mentions it, we'll bump him !

TODD :
Poor old Bunter ! This will stump him !

BUNTER :
Yes, I agree ! I'm not afraid !

The hamper's bound to come, old sport!
But if it should have been delayed—

WHARTON:
Then you'll go home to Bunter Court!
(*All chuckle.*)

BUNTER:
All right! With you I'll spend Christmas like a bird!

WHARTON:
Right-ho, my podgy friend;
And mind you keep your word.

BULL:
Well, wheres the feed? I'm hungry as a hunter!
(*A tap on the door and* GOSLING *enters, bowed down under the weight of a large hamper on his shoulders. He is grunting and gasping as he comes in.*)

Todd (as Wharton, Nugent and Bull enter, leading Bunter by the nose): Ye gods! It's Bunter! Oh, my hat! But why's he gagged and bound like that? Wharton: He's been trying to get, as you may bet, an invite for the vac. He won't take "No!" for an answer, so we've kindly brought him back!

GOSLING:
'Scuse me! (*Puff.*) This 'ere's for Master Bunter!
(*With frightful exertion, he lowers it gently to the floor and stands mopping his brow. The juniors dumbfounded.*)

CHERRY:
Well, my only summer bonnet!
This fairly puts a stopper on it!

TODD:
I can't believe my eyes—I can't!
I can't speak! I've gone dumb!

BULL:
My only sainted maiden aunt!
It's actually come!

GOSLING (*panting hard,—and with a curious grin on his face*):
My word! That's 'eavy for a bloke!
My bloomin' shoulder's nearly broke!

BUNTER (*beaming*):
He, he! This takes you down a peg!
He, he! You thought you'd pull my leg!
But there's the hamper, hard and fast,
And he laughs longest who laughs last!
He, he, he!

Bull : Well, where's the feed ? I'm hungry as a hunter ! (Gosling enters the room, bowed down under the weight of a large hamper.) Gosling : 'Scuse me ! This 'ere's for Master Bunter !

WHARTON (*ruefully*) :
We were wrong ; that's very clear !
We can't dispute this evidence.

GOSLING :
What I ses, gents, is this 'ere,
That 'amper's mortal 'eavy, gents !

BUNTER (*feeling in his pockets*) :
I'm out of change ; this is a fix !
Say, Wharton, lend me two-and-six!

WHARTON (*producing some money*) :
One-and-six ! That's all I've got !
(*Gives it to* BUNTER, *who gives it to* GOSLING.)

BUNTER :
Thanks ! Here, Gossy ! Take the lot !

GOSLING (*with a lurking grin*) :
Master Bunter, you're a toff !
If I'd a 'at, I'd take it off !

WHARTON :
Why do you keep grinning like a cat ?

GOSLING :
Oh, nothing, sir—there's nothing to grin at !
(GOSLING *shuffles out, grinning.*)

NUGENT :
Oh, dear ! This is a nasty smack !
We're booked with Bunter for the Vac.

WHARTON :
Yes, it appears
That we must keep our vow.

TODD (*rather entertained*) :
If you have tears,
Prepare to shed them now.
(BUNTER *begins to lay a cloth on the table.*)

BUNTER :
I say, you chaps, you must admit
You've fairly put your foot in it !
I'm coming with you—he, he, he !
We'll talk it over during tea.
I say, that is a ripping hamper.
Don't you fellows try to tamper
With it—bring it over here ;
I'll unpack it now—and cheer !
You lift it, Cherry, and you, Harry—it
Needs the two of you to carry it.
(CHERRY *and* WHARTON *seize the hamper and with a mighty effort, heave it into the air. As, however, the hamper appears to contain nothing more solid than fresh air, they shoot backwards on to the floor, with the hamper on top of them. Two wild yells ascend. The others stare blankly.*)

TODD :
Why, what the dickens made you fall ?

CHERRY (*roaring*) :
The hamper's no dashed weight at all !

WHARTON :
There's nothing in it, I should say. Great pip !
Old Gossy spoofed us, just to get a tip !
That's why he was grinning !—Eighteenpence !

(JOHNNY BULL, *with one hand, raises the hamper above his head.*)

BULL (sarcastically) :
What I ses is this, it's 'eavy, gents !
(*Drops it down.*)

BUNTER (*blankly*) :
Here ! Wh-what is this, you men ?
If there's nothing in it, then
What does it mean ? Look here, I say—
Wh-what is—Here, geddout the way !
(*He wrenches it open, and looks inside.*)
Empty ! (*Roars.*) Rotters ! Villains ! Cads !
This hamper isn't my granddad's,
This is a joke between you lot——

NUGENT :
No ; honour bright, old bean, it's not !

TODD :
Once more the thing is very plain :
It's Bunter Court for Bill again !
That hamper—that's an ancient dodge ;
A feed's required for Wharton Lodge !

BUNTER :
You rotters planned this some time past !

CHERRY :
Oh, he laughs longest who laughs last !
But we've not done it ; you know better——
(BUNTER *suddenly dives into the hamper and brings out an envelope.*)

BUNTER :
Why, what's this ? Oh, it's a letter !
(*He opens it and reads it out.*)
"Dear William,—Just a wish I send :
A Merry Christmas may you spend !
You ask me for a hamper, and
Although I do not understand
The reason why you should require it,
I send it since you so desire it.
I meant to send a silver pencil,
And not this basketwork utensil,
But you shall have it, as you'd rather,
From your affectionate—
Grandfather."
(*There is an astonished pause.*)

CHERRY (*roaring*) :
Oh, crikey ! I shall burst in half a minute !
He didn't know you wanted something in it !

WHARTON (*wiping his eyes*) :
Poor old grandpa, he would never spot it !
You asked him for a hamper——

BULL :
And you've got it !
(*All shriek.*)

BUNTER (*gasping*) :
Oh, crumbs ! Oh, lor' ! Oh, crikey !
My sainted sister Psyche !
(HARRY WHARTON & CO., *roaring, stagger out of the room.*)

TODD (grinning) :
You made a bargain and you meant it !

Bunter (feeling in his pockets): I'm out of change : this is a fix ! Say, Wharton, lend me two-and-six !

Now it's too late—you can't repent it !
No more cadging after Wharton ;
If you do, I'll try to shorten
Your fat nose, my podgy barrel !

BUNTER :
Oh, really, Toddy ; don't let's quarrel !
As I can't go with Wharton—well,
I'm sticking to my dear old pal !
All right, old chap, I'll come with you !

TODD :
My dear old bloated buzzard—do !
I'm quite prepared to make you welcome ;
And if you want to come, you *shall* come.

BUNTER :
My dear old fellow, like a bird !
Your place is not much class, I've heard ;
Your pa's a poor solicitor—
He'll like me for a visitor !

TODD :
Now make your mind up whether
We shall stick together !

BUNTER :
I have, old fellow ! There's my hand !

TODD :
Now that's a bargain ! Understand?
(*They shake hands*. TODD *goes over to the door*.)
There's one thing I forgot to say :
That both my parents are away ;
They sail to-day for Mandalay
From good old Liverpool !
My Christmas won't be very gay ;
No home, no fun, no feast, no play !
For they will pay for me to stay
This Christmas at the school !

BUNTER (*furiously*) :
You spoofing rotter ! Yah !
You bony freak !

TODD :
Ta-ta !
I'll go and get some tuck for tea ;
Those chaps shall have their feed with me.
At spoofing, Bunter, you're outclassed—
He laughs longest who laughs last !
(*Exit* TODD.)
(BUNTER *remains deep in thought, and then suddenly cackles*.)

BUNTER :
He, he ! So this is spoof ! My hat !
Well, two of us can play at that !
(*Enter* WHARTON, *grinning*.)

WHARTON :
Hallo, old nut ! Got over it !
I want my duster——
(*He picks up* BUNTER's *late gag*.)

BUNTER :
Wait a bit !
About the holidays, old scout !
I'd like to ask you——

WHARTON :
Cut that out !
You promised me you wouldn't speak
Of that again, you podgy freak !

BUNTER :
Well, I'm not going to, you beast !
Or, not about myself, at least !
I want to say that poor old Toddy
Is not booked up with anybody
For the Vac. His parents aren't
At home, and poor old Toddy can't
Fix up for Christmas anywhere.
He's staying here ! At Greyfriars ! There !
I'd ask him home to Bunter Court,
But——

WHARTON (*grinning*) :
When the holidays begin
You always have the brokers in.
I know ! But is this really so,
That Toddy has nowhere to go ?

BUNTER :
Yes ! Honour bright, it's really true !
Why don't you ask him home with you ?

WHARTON:
I will, by Jove, with pleasure!
Old Barrel, you're a treasure!
But, dash it, this is very strange—
You're being decent for a change!

BUNTER:
Oh, really, Wharton——
(TODD *enters with some food and ginger pop, followed by* CHERRY, NUGENT *and* BULL)

TODD:
Follow me!
There's eggs and sausages for tea!

NUGENT:
This seems to be the sort of spread
That makes a fellow feel well fed.

BULL:
These sausages and apple pies
Beat Bunter's banquets hollow!

CHERRY:
We'll swallow them, but Bunter's lies
We simply cannot swallow!

WHARTON (*awkwardly*):
Listen, Todd! We'll be delighted
If your Christmas you will spend
At Wharton Lodge, and you're invited
To the party as my friend.
We're one short, anyhow, by chance,
So you can't leave us in the stewpot!
For Inky has gone out to France
To join his uncle, Ram-Jam-Gluepot!

TODD (*drily*):
You've heard I'm booked for Greyfriars, what?
Thanks all the same, I'd rather not!

CHERRY (*encouragingly*):
Come on, old bean! Join in the fun!

TODD:
No, thanks! Let's get these sosses done!

BULL:
Pig-headed ass! You cannot shake him!

Cherry and Wharton seize the hamper and with a mighty effort, heave it into the air. As the hamper, however, appears to contain nothing more solid than air, they shoot backwards on to the floor.

BUNTER (*cackling*):
I say, you fellows, you can make him!

NUGENT (*blankly*):
Can we? How, you bloated freak?

BUNTER:
He, he! Do let a fellow speak!
The silly ass and I just now
Between us made a solemn vow
That we would stick together through
This Christmas Vac. All you need do
Is ask *me* to come home with you,
And Toddy's bound to join up, too.

TODD (*roaring*):
You spoofing, cunning owl! My hat!

BUNTER:
You spoofed me first; it's tit for tat!

CHERRY:
Wharton would take Toddy home
If Todd would only let him;
But if we ask the Owl to come,

Why, then we're *bound* to get him.

TODD:

Hold on! I'll spoil the rascal's game!

I'll come, and never mind the weather!

BUNTER (*cackling*):

But I'll go with you just the same,

For we agreed to *stick together*.

WHARTON (*laughing*):

That's so! He's caught you on the hop!

But still, you've got to come, old top!

If you are feeling rather loath

To join me—well, I ask you both!

And as we're bound to get our Billy,

You'll have to join us, willy-nilly!

TODD (*with a grin*):

Oh, I'll come! Many thanks, old top!

We'll drink a toast of ginger-pop.

(TODD *pours ginger-pop into glasses and hands them round.*)

BULL:

Now Bunter's planted on us fast!

BUNTER:

He laughs longest——

ALL (*grinning*):

Who Laughs Last!

(*They raise their brimming glasses.*)

WHARTON:

We'll drink a toast, you fellows!

And wish you all good cheer!

A Very Happy Christmas——

ALL (*heartily*):

And a Bright New Year!

CURTAIN

MAKE-UP HINTS

Gosling should really have a bald head, but those who cannot afford to hire a wig (and home-made wigs are never satisfactory) should give him grey hair by sprinkling starch on the actor's hair and rubbing it well in. It is easily brushed out afterwards. His uniform can easily be made from an old overcoat and pair of long trousers. Get your mother or sister to sew gold braid round the lapels and down the leg of the trousers. This braid is very cheap. Grey side-whiskers made out of crêpe hair add to the effect. You may buy this at many hairdressers' at a charge of threepence a foot, and two inches will be ample!

A Reminder:

Harry Wharton & Co. appear every week in The MAGNET, on sale Saturdays, price 2d. Tom Merry & Co. appear every week in The GEM, on sale Wednesdays, price 2d. Also, Harry Wharton & Co., Tom Merry & Co., and Jimmy Silver & Co., of Rookwood, appear in The SCHOOLBOYS' OWN LIBRARY, on sale the First Thursday of Every Month, price 4d. per volume.

INDEX

INDEX—(*continued*)

 The Amalgamated Press, Ltd., The Fleetway House, Farringdon Street, London, E.C.4.